Helpless

By Dou

© 2020 Douglas M. Kent
All Rights Reserved

No part of this book may be reproduced, or stored in a retrieval system, or transmitted in any form or by any means, electronic, mechanical, photocopying, recording, or otherwise, without express written permission of the publisher and Douglas Kent.

While this is a work of non-fiction, I realize that my personal recollections and memories (and Mara's) could easily differ with those of others who were directly or indirectly involved in our lives. With the exception of her abuser, I consider everyone else to be decent and caring human beings who were doing the best they could, in whatever ways they knew how. I've changed names and other details where possible. While I believe this book to be accurate, it's still told through personal perception.

First Printing

Table of Contents

Prelude 1
Chapter 1 - The Night We Met 5
Chapter 2 - When She Told Me 12
Chapter 3 – Early Days 16
Chapter 5 - Baby 33
Chapter 6 - One Step Forward, Two Steps Back 39
Chapter 7 - An Open Letter to Bart and Cheryl 45
Chapter 8 - When You Play Monopoly, Never Trust the Banker 53
Chapter 9 – Why Did I Stay? 59
Chapter 10 - Moving Out 65
Chapter 11 - An Artistic Interlude 74
Chapter 12 - Can't Win for Losing 82
Chapter 13 - Sick 91
Chapter 14 - Rahway 101
Chapter 15 - And the Hits Just Keep on Coming 113
Chapter 16 - Breakdown 119
Chapter 17 - It's a Madhouse! 127
Chapter 18 - Blame, Denials, and Recriminations 135
Chapter 19 - Running Through a Minefield 143
Chapter 20 - Hurry Up and Wait 150
Chapter 21 - Here Comes the Bride 158
Chapter 22 - Maybe Things Will Go Better at Your Next Wedding 173
Chapter 23 - The Honeymoon- Part I 185
Chapter 24 – The Honeymoon – Part II 189
Chapter 25 - Life Goes On, and On, and On 193
Chapter 26 - I Don't Need Anyone Except You 203
Chapter 27 - Spiraling Down 209
Chapter 28 - A Moment of Levity 216
Chapter 29 - When is Rock Bottom? 223
Chapter 30 - Everything is Bigger in Texas 234
Chapter 31 - A Period of Adjustment 253
Chapter 32 - Is there a Doctor in the House? 259
Chapter 33 - The Days Go Slow, but the Weeks Add Up Quickly 267

Chapter 34 – Circular Patterns 272
Chapter 35 - The Knife 282
Chapter 36 - The More Things Change... 286
Chapter 37 - Both Shoes Drop 299
Chapter 38 - Merry Christmas 312
Chapter 39 - I Quit 321
Chapter 40 - Back to New Jersey 329
Chapter 41 - Tying Up Loose Ends 333
Chapter 42 - At Least Things Can't Get Worse 344
Chapter 43 - Bits and Pieces 352
Chapter 44 - Slipping Away 359
Chapter 45 - Return to Sender 365
Epilogue 386

Dedication

This book is dedicated to anyone who faces the darkness and finds the strength and courage to climb back out into the light.

Acknowledgements

There's no such thing as a book put together by one person. I wrote this book, and lived it, but I certainly could never have finished it without help and encouragement from many corners.

First of all, I need to thank Shawn Burkett of Concept Media (www.conceptmediallc.com) for his selfless assistance in designing the book cover. The drawing is an actual portrait of Mara as a young child which I decided long ago would be the main cover image for this book, if I ever got around to writing it. Shawn volunteered to take that drawing and build a beautiful cover around it, despite my abominable visual skills. I think he did an admirable job.

I also want to thank my friends and family who read various drafts of this book and offered general and sometimes very specific ideas, edits, and corrections. In particular I should mention W. Andrew York, Heath Davis-Gardner, Dana Dickerson, Barbara Kent, and Taylor Holmes. I fear I am leaving a name or two out, in which case please forgive me. I truly appreciate the time and effort all of you put in to helping me tell this tale.

Finally, I want to thank anyone who read my first memoir "It's Their House; I'm Just a Guest." Despite the flaws in that book which I am all too aware of, I was unexpectedly overwhelmed by the number of people who had kinds words to say about it. Thank you all, and I hope you find this book to be a step forward in my journey as a writer.

While this is a work of non-fiction, I realize that my personal recollections and memories (and Mara's) could easily differ with those of others who were directly or indirectly involved in our lives. With the exception of her abuser, I consider everyone else to be decent and caring human beings who were doing the best they could, in whatever ways they knew how. I've changed names and other details where possible. While I believe this book to be accurate, it's still told through personal perception.

Prelude

Her name was Mara, but her Hebrew name was Miriam or Miryam, written מִרְיָם. The very first day I met her, and for some time afterwards, she wore a thin gold chain around her neck with that Hebrew script as the charm in the middle. I had no idea what the letters on her chain meant, but eventually I asked her, and that's what she told me.

I'd never met anyone with the name Mara, but she always told me that she loved the way I said it. Part of the reason was that I pronounced it correctly (with no forethought on my part); she hated it when people pronounced it differently. Sometimes she would correct them, but usually she would just stew or sulk. I'm sure the other part of why she liked to hear me say it had to do with how much I loved her, but she never specified. For Mara, it had a calming effect on her. On some of her worst days - in agonizing pain from Crohn's disease, in a state of mental collapse, or unable to stand any light or sound from another crippling migraine headache – she'd ask me to stroke her hair and whisper it to her slowly. Whether it made her feel much better, at least it gave me something to do so I didn't feel so useless.

From what I've learned over the years, Jews do not always make a direct connection between their Hebrew name and their Anglicized name. In the Old Testament, Miryam was the sister of Moses. She saved his life by hiding him in a basket by the river's edge, obscured by the bushes, until Pharaoh's daughter found him there. In later years, she was punished by God, either for speaking out against a woman Moses was to marry, or for questioning Moses' exclusive religious authority (versions differ). Regardless, God inflicts *tzaraat* upon her, which is loosely translated as any of a number of skin-based afflictions from scaling to leprosy to cancer. Moses prays for her forgiveness and, after she suffers for seven days, she recovers.

Mara also appears in the Bible. Naomi, the mother-in-law of Ruth, in grief over the deaths of her husband and sons, takes the name Mara herself as a representation of that unhappiness.

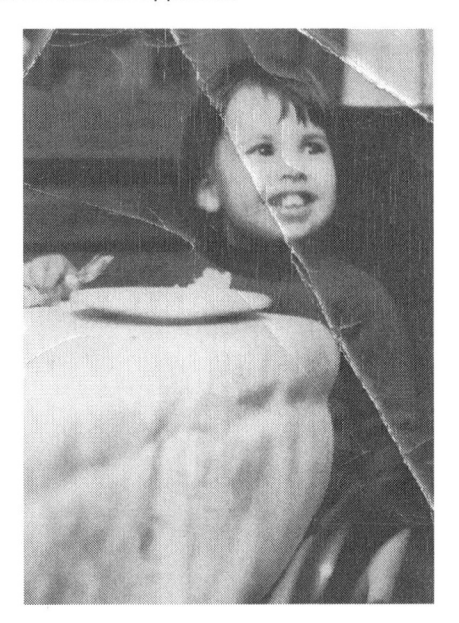

Coincidence or not, the names are commonly translated in modern times to mean bitter or embittered, among other things. Her naming was rather prophetic, considering how her life went. If I had to choose, despite the fact that she never used the name Miriam, that is the one which in hindsight best represents her. She would cry over the innocent and helpless (especially animals), and try to save them, as Miryam saved her brother. And during the portions of her life when she believed in God, in the depths of her deepest and darkest fits of crying and sobbing and helplessness over her life and suffering, she would ask me why God had chosen her for such misery. What had she done to deserve it? Why had God chosen to punish her, so relentlessly and constantly?

I don't believe Mara was singled out in that way. Her life was a serious of unfortunate circumstances, bad luck, poor choices, and the effects of human actions. It was not a supreme being who took a promising life and twisted it until it could never be straight again. There was enough damage from people in her life – deliberate and not – to chip away at her physical, mental, and emotional strength until nothing was left.

I carry a tremendous amount of guilt in my heart from the years we spent together. No matter what others tell me, I believe I deserve at least *some* of that guilt. But only those who unfairly want to wash the blood from their own hands point their fingers at me as the cause for Mara's life. It could be that they simply don't understand how she became who she was, but I'm too cynical to accept that notion as the full explanation. Place blame on me all you want, those of you who stood by and did nothing to help (or worse); you know who you are. Deep in your heart of hearts, you know what sins you hide, and nothing you say or do can change that. You haven't convinced me otherwise, and I do not think you've convinced yourselves either.

Sadly, no amount of prayers would save Mara from her fate. By the time I met her, she was already in pieces, despite the fact that neither of us understood that or the consequences. Perhaps if we had, things would have turned out differently. One of the thousands of regrets and what-if's I carry in my heart. Regrets that serve no real purpose now but to allow me to punish myself. But I can't seem to let them go, or I don't want to. Someone should pay for the sins of her world, and in this case, I haven't been able to find any other volunteers.

At least this book will give me the opportunity to tell her story. Maybe that will help in some way; help me accept what was and what is…or help someone else. If nothing else, the truth she always wanted others to know, and to understand, will have been presented.

Chapter 1 - The Night We Met

I didn't have many close friends in High School. I was casual friends with a lot of people, and friendly with nearly everyone, but I never fit in with a specific clique. I crossed over too many genres, and while that was inclusive in some ways, it also left me out in the cold when it came to group events. I was smart, but I wasn't an academic. I was considered a bit of a druggie, but by High School I'd already done my experimentation. I loved sports but I didn't play them. I was in Band but I didn't take it seriously despite having a talent for reading and understanding the music. We didn't have money; I had no fashion sense; our family shared my Mom's station wagon. Aside from my buddy Fritz who worked at the newspaper store with me, most of the time my only social interaction was in school itself. When the final bell rang, I was out on my own.

One of the benefits of my High School was off-campus privileges. If you did not have a class, you were permitted to leave school grounds. This, combined with some matching free periods, led to one small social circle I managed to penetrate: a group of us would walk down the street to get breakfast once a week at the Bagel Chateau. It wasn't a large crowd, but it had a cross-section of people who fit together elsewhere but didn't necessarily spend a lot of time together. It was through this breakfast group that I found myself invited to a party at Trip's house that weekend. I'd known Trip through Band and some classes since Middle School, and he was a regular with the Chateau crowd. It was going to be a small party, with only about ten people. Nothing out of hand. We'd hang out, play some cards, drink beer, and play quarters. Aside from one girl I knew, Kara, it was mostly going to be guys.

But then Trip mentioned that at the party I'd get a chance to meet Oscar's girlfriend Mara. I didn't even know Oscar **had** a girlfriend, and said so. "Oh yeah," Trip said. "She's buying the beer. She's a senior."

Oscar seemed like an unlikely candidate to have a girlfriend in the senior class. For one thing, he was nerdy (this was back in the day when being a nerd wasn't cool…more bad timing on my part. I was born 15 years too early). He wore frumpy clothes (but I suppose looked better assembled than I ever did), had acne (again, not as bad as mine), and in general had a quiet and boring personality. Oscar had started an investment club called the "Gnomes of Zurich" with some other fellows. They planned to pool money together to invest in stocks using specific grading rules and strategies. I'd gone to a meeting or two when it first formed, but lost interest since the most I'd ever come up with was $20. These guys were from wealthier families and were talking hundreds of dollars each. That club was the only place I knew him from. I knew his older sister better; she was a senior herself but somehow, we wound up in one or two classes together (maybe it was Spanish class).

I admit I was curious to find out what this mystery woman looked like. If she was hooked up with Oscar, she couldn't be **that** cute. Between that and just being included in something for a change, I was certainly looking forward to Trip's little party.

The big night arrived, and as usual I had no means of transportation. So, I walked to Trip's house, which took a good thirty minutes or more. I actually didn't mind walking, especially at night. The side streets were generally empty and quiet, and I enjoyed the midnight blue sky and the leaves crunching under my feet as I made my way there. I hadn't been to his house before, so I wasn't 100% certain I found the proper house. But it matched the address I had written down, so I walked up to the front door and rang the doorbell.

There was just one problem: nobody answered. I tried again, and then walked quietly around the house, peering in windows. I didn't see a living soul. Did I have the wrong house after all? Or could I have somehow completely misunderstood what night the party was?

As I rounded the house and approached the front again, my worries quickly faded. Two cars had pulled up to the front of the house, with people piling out of them. Apparently, everybody had left to do a quick beer run, and my timing was simply as bad as usual.

I followed along inside and down to the basement, where the party was going to be held. There I said hello to everyone that I knew, which was every person except one striking girl. I knew that had to be Mara, and I was shocked.

I couldn't believe I hadn't noticed her in the High School building before. We must have had schedules that kept us separated, because I was certain I would have remembered passing her in the hall. She had loosely curled wavy dark hair, dark brown eyes with a sparkle of mischief, and a devilish crooked pirate smile. A little below average height, Mara was a sculpture of voluptuous curves instead of the typical suburban pseudo-skinny types that populated most of the classrooms. She was wearing a simple red and white striped short dress with a blue cloth belt, blue tights, and red suede ankle boots.

She was **beautiful**, and for some reason she was dating *Oscar*. It was just further evidence that I had no idea how the social circles in this town worked. I tried not to gawk, smiled at her, and busied myself with helping set things up for a game of quarters.

For those who aren't familiar with the game (or the version we were playing), quarters is a fairly simple drinking game. The players sit around a table (in this case a low coffee table). A glass is placed on the table. Players take turns throwing a quarter at the table, with the goal being for it to bounce once and then land in the glass. If you miss, your turn is over and the next person goes. But if you make it, you choose any other player and that person must take a drink. Then you continue to take your turn until you miss.

The game started out slowly with a lot more conversation than actual bouncing of the quarter. We were all bullshitting about music, movies, television, teachers; the usual stuff. Everybody had an open beer and we were sipping at the bottles as we talked and laughed. If we had to "take a drink" for the game, it was generally agreed that was a *large* swig of beer from your bottle. It was fun, and we were all relaxed and enjoying ourselves.

When it was my turn to throw, I managed to make a few shots before missing. Me being me, I chose Mara to be the one who had to take a drink. Teasing is a way I show interest or affection, so I suppose it was only natural. Mara took it in good nature and warned me that she would seek her revenge when it came to her turn.

In the meantime, Oscar was becoming a thorn in her side. I don't know if he was trying to show off, or to mark his territory, or what…but he would not leave Mara alone. He was constantly asking for a kiss or trying to hold her hand. When she got tired of that and tried to focus on the game, Oscar announced to the group that Mara was wearing Garfield the Cat underwear. It became an obsession with him, and every time there was the slightest lull in conversation Oscar would encourage Mara to show all of us her underwear. For her part, Mara didn't seem to have any interest in doing so, and the more he mentioned it the testier she became. Pretty soon she was ignoring Oscar altogether.

Oscar was also hopeless art the game. He would tell Mara he was going to get her drunk, but I don't think he made a successful shot all night. Instead he sat and sulked and sipped his beer; he wasn't able to force Mara to drink, and nobody was choosing him as the victim when they made a shot. On the other hand, Mara started off pretty badly, but the more beer she drank the better her aim seemed to get. As promised, every time she'd make a shot, she'd tell me to drink. We were building a decent rivalry, which was fun for us, amusing for the rest of the party… and depressing for Oscar.

After a while, a few of the guests had to leave. Trip offered to drive a couple of them home. A few others went along for the ride to keep Trip company on the way back. Mara stayed saying she'd had too much to drink to drive safely. The next thing I realized, there were only two of us left at the house: me, and Mara.

Exactly what happened while everyone was gone remains a bit hazy. We talked a bit. Mara stumbled and spilled some beer on my shirt, which she jokingly licked off; it sounds sexual but it wasn't, it was funny. We walked around the house and found ourselves in the master bedroom. She sat on the edge of the bed and we talked and laughed. We were stupid drunk.

Then Mara started complaining about how irritated Oscar had made her, and what a whiny pain in the ass he could be at times. Suddenly she stopped and moved to one of the bedroom windows. "Oh fuck, they're home. Hide!" She raced into the master bathroom and stepped inside the bathtub, urgently motioning for me to follow. I stepped in and she closed the glass shower door. And we stood there, hiding and suppressing laughs, for absolutely no reason.

After a few minutes, we could hear footsteps coming up the stairs. They wandered around, and then approached the bathroom. A dark shadow entered the room and stretched out towards the shower door. It slowly opened...and there stood Oscar. He didn't even look at me. He just stared at Mara with a mad expression, turned, and walked out of the room. Mara muttered "oh for fuck's sake, what a baby" and went after him.

I don't believe Oscar ever asked me about why we were hiding in the shower. Either Mara's explanation was sufficient (whatever explanation she gave him) or he simply didn't care to know. But it was a surreal couple of minutes. A lot of drama, a complete lack of sense or meaning, and a hazy dream-like state. That would not be the last time I experienced those sensations with Mara.

The party was winding down. Trip was pretty adamant that the only two beds anyone could use were his (which he was going to sleep in) and one other. I could have walked home, but instead I asked to spend the night in a rocking chair in the upstairs hall. It wasn't comfortable, but I'd had enough to drink that I would be able to fall asleep. Besides, it was only for four or five hours, since we all had to be out first thing in the morning.

As I sat there thinking about the episode in the shower, I started to laugh. I thought I was laughing silently, but apparently it was out loud, because soon Mara came out in the hall to find out what I was laughing at. I grinned and refused to tell her. "It's a secret," I said. "Maybe I'll tell you one day. Ask me at school sometime." I figured that was an easy way to make sure I saw her again.

"Fine, I will" she said. "I'm going to hold you to that. Or else next time I spill beer on you, I'm going to leave it there." She quickly returned to the bedroom where she and Oscar were sleeping, and I closed my eyes. It had been an enjoyable evening. As time would eventually reveal, it was also the most impactful night of the first stage of my adult life.

Chapter 2 - When She Told Me

One of the most formidable obstacles for me when I am writing about the past (or simply thinking about the past) is putting me in the same position I was then. It is too easy to take my current self and drop that level of experience, that mindset, that knowledge into past events. This helps explain why I have such trouble forgiving myself for things that – at the time – were the best decisions I knew to make. It takes a lot of focus and a lot of consideration to adjust for what I didn't know back then, what I hadn't learned, and what wasn't common knowledge.

I remember when Mara first told me she had been sexually abused by her paternal grandfather. It was New Year's Eve, or more correctly it was in the early morning hours of New Year's Day, only a month or so after we'd started going out. I'd been invited to spend the evening with her family and their friends in a celebration, and despite my misgivings it turned out to be a pretty good time. There was champagne punch, which was weaker than the alcohol I was used to consuming at age 15 but still enjoyable. There were party games, including "pass the orange" which I'd first seen in Charade; that's still one of my favorite movies. There was a game of Trivial Pursuit where our team won, in part because Mara's father thought James Bond preferred his martini's stirred and not shaken. There was also a game of Password which Mara and I won outright. We did get a lot of funny looks and some half-joking accusations of cheating when I said "Florida" and she knew to respond "ashtray" but it made sense to us and that was all that mattered.

I walked home from the party, and called Mara a little after settling in as she had asked me to. We laughed about some of the evening's excitement on the phone, and then she told me she had something she needed to tell me. "I was molested by my grandfather, from when I was an infant until at least when I was twelve years old." And I told her I was sorry. That was it.

It is difficult for people to understand that neither of us knew anything about the long-term effects of sexual abuse back then. Society seems to choose one secret issue at a time and expose it to the masses through movies, news specials, Judy Blume books and after school specials. Alcoholism was already a known commodity by then. When we were just reaching puberty, drugs were getting their day; movies like "Not My Kid" focused on the problems with pills, marijuana and harder stuff. And eating disorders were only beginning to make the rounds. We'd just learned the difference between anorexia and bulimia, and a few of the supposed reasons behind them. But sexual abuse, which today is talked about like it happens all the time (and it does), that was still a dirty little secret. Nobody talked about, nobody admitted it, and most of all nobody I knew understood the long-term effects. So, when Mara told me, for her it was more about sharing a shameful secret that she might worry would make me see her as gross or disgusting. And for me it was just an explanation that fit into some of her family dynamics. But for both of us, the fact that she had been sexually abused – even for so many years – was almost the same as her telling me about a car accident she had been in. It was something bad that happened. There was no real significance in the present, except that she didn't want to be around her grandfather.

I know it isn't my fault, and I know we were both ignorant of the truth, but it took many years to forgive myself for how wrong we were about the impact it would have – and already was having - on her life.

So much of the problem was just bad timing, and unfortunate circumstances. Mara was my first girlfriend, my High School sweetheart. She was the first person I had sex with, and the first woman I fell in love with. I had no basis of comparison to see how odd some of her behavior really was. It wasn't like I could compare Mara to my mother. At that age I didn't know the specifics of an alcoholic schizophrenic, but I knew enough to realize my mother was a mess. I didn't have a "normal" female role model to use as a guide. As time passed and Mara grew depressed, acted crazy, slept with anybody who showed an interest in her, had blackouts where she couldn't remember anything, or seemed to become an entirely different person for hours at a time I just thought that's how most women were. Or at least that's how Mara was, and so I'd have to accept her that way. It wasn't a question of why she did what she did. That was just her.

'arly Days

The relationship between Mara and me started out as simply friends. Once we'd met at the party, we started saying hello in the school hallways or talking a bit here and there. She was still "dating" Oscar, but it seemed he had suddenly fallen out of favor. I'd casually mentioned meeting Mara to Oscar's sister in Spanish class, and that had led to the unintentional grounding of Oscar from doing anything after school for a few weeks; he had lied to his parents about where he'd been, and his sister took the opportunity to turn him in. Mara wasn't mad at me for this. In fact, she seemed rather pleased. It was almost as if she saw doing things with Oscar as a chore or an obligation. Or maybe she just lost interest after his behavior at the party.

I was very interested in Mara, but I had no idea how to go about pursuing a relationship with her. She was older than me, very beautiful, and in my mind completely out of my league. Then again, any girl was out of my league as far as I was concerned. I daydreamed about girlfriends, but I couldn't realistically imagine any of the girls I knew in school having the slightest bit of interest in me. It seemed as improbable as meeting a favorite television star and having them star dating me; utterly unattainable. The one time I had invited a school crush of mine to a small party at my house, the moment she had realized I was interested in her she feigned illness and went home. I didn't think I would ever be known for my prowess at attracting women.

As Mara had a car, I did manage to convince her to give me a ride home one day after school. We sat in the car outside my house and talked a bit, and then I got up the courage to ask for a kiss. She turned me down, but not in a way that hurt my feelings. Maybe I expected a no, or maybe it was that the way she turned me down implied it wasn't a final no, just a no for that moment. As the years went on, I always took that initial "No" as a positive, and a sign she actually liked me at a level deeper than other men. Her inability to turn back or reject the advances of men that I would discover later made It seem special somehow.

A week or so later, Mara asked if I'd be interested in spending the weekend at her house. Her parents would be out of town, and she didn't want to be stuck there by herself.

"My sister is gonna have one of her motorcycle buddies over, so she said I could have someone stay over too, as long as I kept my mouth shut to our parents. I thought we could hang out and stuff."

I was completely surprised by the invitation, but quick to accept. "Do you want me to bring anything? I can try to get some liquor?"

"No," she said. "If you want to bring a few records we can listen to those. My parents will probably rent a movie or two before they go, to give me and my sister something to do and keep us out of trouble."

We made plans for me to walk to her house Friday evening. "I don't want to come pick you up," Mara said, "because I bet my Mom told our neighbors to keep an eye out for when I come and go. They're nosy jerks."

"Oh," Mara added, "There's no funny business this weekend. Okay?"

That was fine with me. I just wanted to hang out with her and have a good time. I was expecting anything.

As usual, at my house very little explanation was required. I told my Mom that I'd be spending the weekend at a friend's house but that I might come by after work Saturday or Sunday morning. I had a job assembling

Sunday newspapers at 5am both days at the local news shop. Getting up that early on the weekend was a real beating and the work was tedious and repetitive, but the pay was decent and we always seemed to have a few laughs there. My Mom didn't ask any questions; if I hadn't bothered to tell her I doubt she would have noticed my absence. With six children living in the house, all fending for ourselves much of the time, it was hard to keep track of who was where.

As it turned out, "funny business" was basically all Mara had in mind, which completely surprised me. I'd never even kissed a girl in a truly romantic way before that night, but by the time we fell asleep early Saturday morning I'd done a lot more than that, and Mara had relieved me of my virginity (willingly, of course). Her sexuality had completely overwhelmed me. But we also spent time lying in her bed with the warm glow of the stereo light illuminating the room slightly, listening to music and talking endlessly.

We spent Saturday watching a few movies and listening to music, and grabbed some dinner. We sat around for a while drinking coffee and talking with Mara's sister and her motorcycle friend, who clearly were spending their time doing much the same as we had been. Later, Mara filled me in on her sister's involvement with one of the larger bike gangs, and how her parents hated that. Neither of them had personalities that made me want to get to know them especially well, but they both seemed friendly enough and there was the mutual "let's all mind our own business and have a fun weekend" comradery.

I needed to be at work at 5am on Sunday morning, and I was happy to walk. But Mara insisted on driving me, which saved me thirty minutes and some cold temperatures. She pulled out of the driveway with her headlights off to try and keep the neighbors unaware, and dropped me off up the street from work, at the local train station. Better safe than sorry, I suppose. We decided just to end the weekend there, so I brought my clothes and records with me so I could walk home from work and get some more sleep. It had been the most exciting weekend of my life, and without realizing it was even a possibility, we went from friends to lovers, boyfriend and girlfriend in the space of 36 hours.

Mara called me Sunday night and let me know her parents were back, and they were **not** happy. They knew there had been guests over, probably more than one. And the evasive answers Mara and her sister had given were enough to confirm the obvious suspicions that it had been males rather than females.

"I'm sorry you drove me to work, I knew it was a bad idea," I told her.

"Yeah," she said. "The neighbors reported on that, the jerks. A car pulling out before five in the morning set off alarms in the nosy brains. But that's not what got us caught."

"No?" I asked. "What was it?"

"It was my sister and her stupid friend. They used almost every towel in the damn house. I don't know how many showers they took but it was a lot."

Mara was "banned" from seeing me for a few days, and then her parents asked Mara to bring me over for dinner. They never asked me any questions about what went on that weekend, but I could see they were not impressed with Mara's new boyfriend. I heard Mara's mother hiss at her later that evening "He's not even Jewish, is he?"

I suppose all in all they hoped I was a phase, and they set down some simple ground rules which I said I would follow. If I came over to the house with Mara, we could only be in the family room unless one of her parents was home. If we went upstairs to her bedroom the door had to remain open, and I was told there was one more rule.

"If you're in the bedroom," her Dad told me, "You have to keep one foot on the floor at all times."

Later Mara and I went upstairs to talk and listen to the radio before I went home. As instructed, we had the door to Mara's room open. I was standing at the stereo changing stations while Mara playfully danced around the room. Her Dad came up to check on us, and seemed unconcerned by our behavior. Mara stepped backward and sort of jumped onto her bed, and there was a loud cracking noise. She screamed and jumped up again.

Mara's Dad got an angry look and raced over. Apparently, Mara's bed was some kind of antique, and she'd cracked one of the old wooden side rails. I was told "Doug, it's best that you leave now" and off I went. Later that night I called Mara and she explained her Dad was pissed off, but that he did see the humor in being a witness to how it happened, as given the lack of honesty he felt his daughters had been providing recently there was no way he would have swallowed a story of Mara just bouncing onto the edge of the bed as the explanation for how it cracked. He repaired it the next day with a metal bracket for reinforcement, and no major damage was done.

A few days later at school, Oscar heard rumors of Mara and I being overly friendly in the hallways and decided to confront her about it. She didn't say anything about the weekend I spent there, but she did admit that I'd been over a few nights ago.

"And what went on?" Oscar demanded, in what I was told was a very uncharacteristically possessive tone.

"Well, to be honest," Mara told him, "we broke the bed. I guess this means you and I are officially over."

Oscar never said a word to me about any of it. In fact, I can't be certain if we ever spoke again. I just remember in a class a few days later our mutual friend Alan said something about how "I hope my friend Oscar feels better soon, because Doug stole his girlfriend."

I may have been an accessory to theft, I admit, but this hadn't been my plan. I wasn't involved in any of the decision making, as far as I could tell.

Usually I'd go over to Mara's house after school a few days a week, and we'd watch the later soap operas she was into while we snacked on pretzels or popcorn. We'd sneak some kisses and other things when we could, but we were more careful after the "weekend" incident. When Mara wanted to get especially amorous, we would do that in her car, or on rare occasion at my house.

One day Mara decided that she wanted to go over to my house instead of hers. She told her Mom in advance, and assured her that yes, my mother would be home. When we got there after school, sure enough, my Mom was home and confirmed she'd be staying home for the rest of the day.

We went upstairs to watch Mara's soap operas. In my mother's bedroom there was a small TV on a wheeled stand, so we moved that into my bedroom so we could relax in there and watch in privacy. We weren't doing anything sexual, not even kissing…just watching her dopey shows.

About halfway through the first soap opera, I sat up and listened. I could swear I could hear someone calling Mara's name. I turned the volume down.

"Do you hear that?" I asked.

"What, I don't hear anything" Mara said.

And then it was slightly louder. "Mara? Mara?"

I jumped up. "What the fuck is that?"

We walked out of my room, and standing there in the hallway was Mara's mother. She had a very angry look on her face. "You lied to me!"

"What are you talking about?" I asked. "We're just watching soap operas. My mother is downstairs."

Only she wasn't. My mother had disappeared in her station wagon. Mara's mother had looked us up in the phone book and driven over to check on Mara, and "caught" us.

"You come with me young lady!" she barked, and Mara just shrugged her shoulders and followed her out. Later, my mother returned from her "emergency" trip to pick up more beer for herself. She offered to call Mara's mother and explain, but I didn't see the point. Her parents would get over it, and it wasn't as if she caught us having sex.

A few days later my oldest brother Paul asked me about what had happened that day. I didn't really know how he knew anything about it until he revealed that he was lying on his bed in the next room, completely naked, when he heard this strange voice calling through the house. He was debating storming out of his room to confront whoever it was and ask them what the fuck they thought they were doing uninvited in our house. Paul being Paul, he would have gone ahead and done that naked, more for shock value than anything else.

I've always kind of regretted that he didn't.

Still, things have a way of evening out. Mara may have gotten in trouble that day for something that wasn't out fault, but there were other times she skated by. One night we went to see a movie, and then decided to park in an empty parking lot to make out for a while. It was about 9:30pm, and Mara was supposed to be home by 11:00. Things got pretty heated in the car, with the windows completely fogged up. After a while, we took a break and Mara asked me what time it was.

I looked over at the clock in her car. "It's, uh...ten to one."

We both nearly popped up in the air. Ten to one? Holy crap! Mara started warming up the car while I ran around wiping all the windows down so she could see. My house was in the opposite direction, so I didn't even let her think about driving me home. I just put my coat on and started jogging in the cold, while she raced off to what was likely the guillotine.

I waited until a decent hour the next morning and gave her a call. Mara said nothing had happened; her parents were asleep when she got home, and they never realized how late she had been. She had gone quietly upstairs and went to bed. Considering that we had been unintentionally burned by my mother's desperate need for beer a few weeks earlier, it only seemed fair.

For years and years later, if Mara or I asked the other one what time it was, there was a decent chance the first response we'd get was "ten to one."

Chapter 4 - College

There had never been a question about whether or not Mara was going to college when she graduated. That was a done deal. The only questions were: where was she going to attend, and would we be continuing our relationship after she left?

The former was decided rather quickly. She visited a few campuses (I think among them were Brown and Ohio State) and she soon settled on the University of Maryland. There was no specific reason she chose there besides the fact that she was accepted, and that they had a well-regarded Chemical Engineering program (which was what she planned to study). In retrospect, I think a smaller campus might have suited her better, but I didn't know anything about colleges at the time. I doubt she would have taken advice from me on the matter anyway.

Late in the school year it also became clear Mara wanted to continue an exclusive relationship with me after she went to college. Her plan was to see me as much as she could over the summer while she lived with her parents at their lake house. Then I'd visit her on campus a couple of times each year, and of course see her when she came home for Christmas or Spring Break. And in a few years, I'd choose a college somewhere between New Jersey and where she was (if not the University of Maryland specifically) so we could see each other quite often. I wasn't sure if that kind of plan was going to work in the long run, but for the time being I didn't see a reason to argue. It wasn't as if I had been dating anyone before I met Mara, so if she wanted to continue as a couple there was no harm in giving it a try.

Summer passed rather quickly. I worked weekends at the newspaper store and spent a few nights up at the lake house with her family. Other than that, we occupied ourselves writing letters back and forth (since intrastate phone calls were very expensive at that time). Mara was very excited about getting away from her family and having the independence of a college student, as most kids are. I was a bit surprised at how torn up she was about having to leave me behind. There was one afternoon at the lake she dragged me into the middle of the woods and made us swear to each other that we'd stay together while she was gone. She demanded that we each prick our fingers and then drip blood onto this huge, long, boulder-sized rock we had walked to. Then she mixed the drops of blood together, and afterwards we had sex. It wasn't supposed to have any actual power; it was just meant to symbolize our commitment to that promise.

I think that may have been the last time I saw Mara before she left for Maryland, although there may have been one brief goodbye at her house while she packed up. Her parents drove her down there, and I went about getting ready for my Junior year in High School. Life – and the usual crap – had to go on whether Mara was still local, or hundreds of miles away.

It didn't take long for our plan of speaking on the phone once a week (or less) to turn into something much more frequent. Part of the problem was Mara simply missed me too much. She had her classes, and her friends, and her roommate in the dorm. All of those things kept her busy. But her ability to focus and concentrate was somewhat poor. The classes were difficult and she didn't think she was doing very well. The photos she sent me of her and her new friends – both male and female – always showed her with a big smile (and a streak of bright pink hair she had dyed into her normally dark locks). But she wasn't happy. She was miserable.

Her unhappiness didn't just stem from problems with her classes. Finally, on her own, she was experiencing more and more trouble with her sexual issues. At this stage we didn't know they were in any way connected to the sexual abuse she had suffered for years as a child, but most of these sexual problems were connected, and at least subconsciously, she must have known because it made them that much more painful to deal with.

The main issue Mara seemed to have was twofold. First, the only way she really knew how to show she fond of a man was to have sex with them (or sexually gratify them). And second, it was next to impossible for her to say no to a sexual advance of any nature. Not only couldn't she say no, but she would initially feel the only way to experience positive thoughts about herself would be to acquiesce. Unfortunately, within a few hours she would hate herself for what she had done, both because she had betrayed my trust and because she could not stand the terrible reputation she was inevitably earning for herself.

Unbeknownst to Mara, I had a lot better idea about what she was doing – and had done in the past – than she thought I did. I knew for a fact that she had cheated on me at least three times in the eight months we had been together before she left for college, so I only assumed she would do so while she was at college. They always seemed to be one-night stands (so to speak), and I knew she genuinely loved me. So, forgiveness wasn't the hardest thing in the world. Besides, she was a beautiful college woman, while I was a gangly, skinny, geeky, acne-covered High School kid. She was the first woman I'd had sex with. I couldn't be expected to compete with more experienced partners might be able to do. And then there was the rationalization that for all I knew I'd be willing to cheat on her if I had the chance. It just happened that I couldn't imagine anyone having that kind of interest in me.

It did hurt me sometimes, especially on the one or two occasions she felt the need to confess her infidelity and ask for forgiveness. Her behavior at those moments was a little strange. She was unable to use the phrase "I'm sorry" so she'd twist words in pretzel shapes if necessary to get her point across. For whatever reason she simply couldn't say "I'm sorry." I was also surprised that my reaction - expressing disappointment and being upset without actually getting angry – seemed to be the worst possible choice for Mara. It would drive her nuts. "Get mad at me, yell at me, hit me, something!" she would plead. But that wasn't my instinct, and it wasn't what I needed to do. I actually felt guilty about that later on, because I realize now she might not have beat herself up as badly about her transgressions if I had given her the angry, screaming reaction she was looking for.

Regardless, her occasional exploit was becoming more frequent on this huge campus, which served to make her feel worse about herself and to fear a bad reputation. It wasn't a good situation to be in. And Mara felt very alone in such a huge place. She had never liked the city; living close to New York City meant nothing to her, as she preferred the quiet and relative safety of the suburbs. The University of Maryland College Park campus had over 25,000 students, and I could certainly understand the discomfort of being in such a huge crowd but feeling alone at the same time. Mara was starting to realize this hadn't been the greatest college choice for her.

I went down to visit her once, skipping one day of school on the process to make it a long weekend. She was ecstatic to see me, running at me like I had just come home from a war zone. Her friends did their best to make me feel comfortable – even the ones who had slept with her behind my back – but of course I felt like more of an outsider than Mara did. These folks were three years older than me and looked like they belonged on a college campus. I looked like I should be a freshman in High School, at least as far as I could tell.

Soon after my visit, Mara started to get sick. At first it was dizziness. Nausea followed. She thought it was the flu or something, but she never felt achy. She started missing classes, staying in bed, feeling too bad to walk across campus. She would call me on the phone, crying, and as usual I was helpless to do anything about it. I didn't know what was wrong, and while the thought of an STD creeped into my mind, I didn't say anything about it. All I could suggest was that she go to the college health clinic.

Mara went, but they didn't find anything wrong. I think they even ran blood tests, which showed nothing. They gave her a prescription for a mild anti-nausea drug, but that did nothing to improve the symptoms. All it did was make her tired enough to fall asleep now and then, which was a blessing in itself because with the room spinning all the time she was in real torment. She even confided to me that she had started to see some blackish vaginal discharge. I had no idea what that meant, but I knew it couldn't be good.

As usual, Mara didn't get the kind of support or help she was looking for from her parents. Her father had no suggestions, even being a doctor. Her mother, on the other hand, was much more concerned about how badly she was slipping in her classes than anything to do with her physical or mental health. Her suggestion was that she "push herself" to get to class. To me that sounded about as useful as telling a suicidal person to "cheer up."

And suicidal wasn't that far from the truth at this point. The dizziness and nausea were awful, but the lack of sleep was driving Mara absolutely nuts. A second visit to the clinic brought no help. Thanksgiving was coming up and Mara was far too sick to travel back home, nor did she want to.

As it happened, Mara had become good friends with a girl named Donna who I met when I was visiting. They had really hit it off well and had been discussing being roommates in the dorm. Donna's parents lived fairly close to the university, but she lived in the dorm because she wanted to be on her own and feel more a part of the campus community. It was Donna who suggested Mara come spend Thanksgiving at her place. At least she wouldn't be alone in the dorms, and if she wasn't up to socializing, she could stay in the spare bedroom and rest.

Arriving at Donna's house, Mara was introduced to her parents. While apologizing for her disheveled appearance and less than pleasant demeanor, it was revealed that Donna's father was a doctor himself. He listened to Mara's symptoms, and left the room to get his bag. When he returned, he pulled out his otoscope and peered into Mara's left ear, and then her right one. He shook his head as he reminded Donna why he had warned her in the past about relying on the medical clinic for any advice. "They're just there to hand out rubbers, if you're sick go see a real doctor."

Then he turned to Mara. "You, sweetie, have an ear infection and a good deal of fluid in your inner ear. That is the source of all your trouble, and it pisses me off that it hasn't been taken care of much earlier than this." He explained to her how important the inner ear is to balance and stability in the human body. In effect, Mara had been walking around with severe motion sickness for close to ten days (and an infection to boot) because the equilibrium of her body was in constant turmoil while the fluid in her inner ear sloshed around.

He went out for a while and returned home with some prescriptions for Mara, including antibiotics and a prescription-strength antihistamine to begin the drying out process. "Unfortunately, the best cure for this is going to be time, now that you'll be getting some treatment," he explained to her. "There's no way to remove the fluid quickly. The medication will help you feel better, and so will this." He handed her a bottle of Bonine. That was the best immediate treatment for the symptoms: motion sickness pills.

By early the next week Mara was able to get back to class and begin to catch up. Her professors were mostly understanding, especially as she wasn't fully recovered and probably looked pale and sick. But it really made no difference. Mara had pretty much decided she didn't like going to school on such a huge campus. And she was determined to leave when her first semester was over and go to school somewhere close to home.

During Christmas break she broke the news to her parents. I wasn't present during those conversations, but Mara recounted them for me in great detail. From her point of view, her parents ignored or waved away all of her reasons for wanting to make this switch (emotional, psychological, cost, and everything else). Instead, they listed a litany of reasons why they were against the idea, some of which were actual reasons and some of which were just emotional statements. They included:

- How could you do this to us?
- Why do you want to throw your future away?

- Do you want to be known as a quitter?
- Do you know how this will look to everyone?
- What are we supposed to tell our friends?
- After all we've sacrificed, this is how you repay us?
- Why don't you just tough it out?
- Did Doug put you up to this?
- Are you determined to be a disappointment?

There were more, but I am sure you get the idea. Mara dropping out of college and continuing her education locally was an embarrassment for them, one they didn't want to have to explain to their friends and neighbors. Mara was hurt by their reaction, but it was exactly as I had expected.

There wasn't a lot they could do about it, and when they realized there was no talking Mara out of this decision, they made sure she had plans on where she'd be going to school and what course plan she was going to follow. The nearby county college had a Chemical Engineering program, and she anticipated joining that program and following the same career path she originally envisioned. Her parents seemed to be living under the illusion that if she enrolled there, she might decide to transfer back to Maryland (or elsewhere) after a semester or two.

I should point out that while I found their lack of empathy cold, Mara's parents' attitude toward the importance of going to a "big name" college was not unique. The town's entire school system seemed to revolve around making it into an Ivy League school or some other prestigious program. I remember hearing classmates discussing what college they were going to attend when we were still in Junior High School. It was completely foreign to me, but I would smile and nod as if I had some kind of master plan or family pedigree I was supposed to follow.

Either way, the decision was made. Mara would leave school and enroll at the county college. She'd live with her parents and her younger brother (and older sister, when she made a reappearance from her time on the road with motorcycle gangs and whatever else she was doing).

I don't believe Mara would have survived another semester at the University of Maryland. But I also recognize now that this wasn't a singular stumble. It was the beginning of an accelerating decline.

Chapter 5 - Baby

The period when Mara started attending county college became the strangest of my life up to that point. I had a feeling when she couldn't even begin the Chemical Engineering program without a problem that the whole thing was destined to fall apart in short order.

Mara was actually very excited about starting classes again, and on her first day she went out to the campus with a very positive attitude. By the time she came by my house late in the afternoon, the enthusiasm was gone. She had waited outside the lab with her new classmates where they were supposed to meet for the entire morning, but nobody ever came to let them in the classroom. While they waited, they all talked and joked and got to know each other; it was a group of six women and two men. After lunch, the group went down to the admissions office to try and figure out why their professor hadn't shown up.

Unfortunately, after some additional confusion and phone calls, the woman at the admissions office was able to tell them the reason: the program had been cancelled at that campus because not enough people had signed up for it. So, Mara went home and told her mother, and then came over to vent to me. Nothing ever seemed to go easily for her, and I had to agree with her for the most part.

The next day she made phone calls and was able to find the same program offered at a different county college. It was further away but the drive would be tolerable. Still, Mara was already feeling negative about it. "By the time I register and start classes, I'll be three days behind." I tried to comfort her and reassure her that she wouldn't have missed too much in those three days, and some of what she missed would be stuff she learned during her semester at Maryland.

"It isn't just that," she explained. "I got along so well with those people at the first college. We had fun that day. When I get to this new program I'll be the outsider, the one who is joining in after everybody else has already made their new friends and settled into a routine. I'll feel all alone." As much as I tried to convince Mara that she'd be fine, I knew deep down that considering all the problems she had been having in the last year, that kind of late start was bound to affect her much more than it would some other people. It was an obstacle she was going to have to fight to get over.

Still, Mara had no choice, and she bit the bullet and started her new classes. I could tell it was stressful for her, and she never talked about anybody she had made friends with or even had an interesting conversation with. And the classes were giving her a great deal of trouble.

Physics, in particular, was something Mara couldn't get her head around. I didn't know much about the subject, but I did my best to read along in her textbook and explain the concepts to her in various ways when she was stuck. But her patience was razor thin. I can remember two occasions of sitting on my living room couch trying to fight our way through an assignment, where Mara became so frustrated, she threw the book all the way across the room. Another time she ripped a handful of pages out and crumpled them up. I'm not exactly the most patient person to begin with, and because of that I can be a less efficient teacher than others, but I was grinding my teeth and biting my tongue, refusing to speak up or let her frustration get the better of me. She had to get through this material and pass the class. There was simply no other option.

During this period Mara was spending nearly all her free time at my house, unless her parents had demanded she attend some kind of family function. She would come by after class and leave when it was time for me to go to sleep. We'd sometimes take a nap together or fall asleep for a while watching TV or listening to music. And this is when things got completely screwed up.

One early evening, as I woke up from a nap, Mara was lying in my bed in the fetal position, sucking her thumb. I asked her what she was doing, but she wouldn't respond. When I tried pulling her thumb out of her mouth she yelped and stuck it right back in. I couldn't get anything out of her. Then she started to drift off to sleep again, and when I gave her some time and tried to wake her again, she finally spoke.

"I'm not Mara. I'm Baby." I was going to laugh out loud, but I realized this wasn't some practical joke. She was really having some kind of mental episode where she was identifying as an infant. She didn't want to do anything or say anything; just lay there and suck her thumb. She wouldn't respond to any name except for Baby. And to that, her responses were simple and childish, but obviously she had an adult command of the English language.

I'm not sure if I believe in multiple personalities. I grew up reading "Sybil" and watching the movie, so I was familiar with the subject, but it all seemed very fake to me. This, on the other hand, seemed all too real, but not an actual second personality. It was more like some kind of psychotic episode. And it freaked me the fuck out.

The next day I tried to explain to Mara what I had witnessed. At first, she thought I was making it up. Baby made an appearance a couple more times, in much the same way. Mara would sometimes ask if Baby had shown up, and I'd tell her about the last time I'd seen "her," but I didn't mention it otherwise. The whole thing was making me nuts. As I said, Baby may have acted like a child, sucked her thumb, and preferred the fetal position, but her knowledge of the English language and conversational skills were obviously at an adult level.

I don't think Mara believed that I was being completely truthful about Baby until one weekday evening. We were watching TV on the couch and suddenly Baby appeared again. This time I was irritated because we had just been discussing Mara needing to study for her classes about fifteen minutes earlier, and whether this was on purpose or just a function of her mental issues I was pretty certain her convenient timing was a way to avoid doing the schoolwork. We got into a bit of an argument, or at least that's how I would describe it. I'd tell Mara or Baby or whomever I was talking to that she needed to cut this shit out and get going on her homework, and Baby would whine and squirm around and was becoming visibly upset. Finally, she screamed, grabbed her purse, and ran out of the house. I heard Mara's car start and the tires squeal, and she roared off.

In my mind, Mara was simply pissed off, nothing more. I knew she'd call or come by later on after she had calmed down. When she did call, it was the next morning as I got ready for school, around 6am. And Mara was furious. But not just furious…she also sounded terrified.

"Don't you EVER do that to me again!" she yelled. I tried to get her to calm down and explain what had happened. As near as I could tell, Mara had found herself sitting in her car on a quiet street near midnight, a good four hours after she had left my house. She drove around for two hours trying to figure out where she was and how to get home, but the more she drove the worse the neighborhood got, so she pulled into a church parking lot that had a few vans in it (so she felt safer) and went to sleep for a few hours.

Mara had no memory of leaving my house or driving away, nor of driving. Her first conscious memory was finding herself in an unknown location. Again, I don't believe in multiple personalities, but I do believe this episode – and the entire Baby persona – were a result of stress and long-standing mental issues Mara had suffered from. At this point neither of us understood how deeply sexual abuse had scarred her psyche, but obviously in retrospect that was a large contributing factor.

Yet despite all that, her panic was real. She had been truly terrified to have no memory of how she got to the middle of nowhere. Around 5am she had woken up in the church parking lot and found a well-lit gas station to get directions back to friendly territory. As it turned out, she had driven all the way out to the edges of East Orange. I don't know anything about that area today, but back then there were a number of high-crime parts of East Orange where a confused woman like her could have been in serious danger. Then again, I wonder how much danger she had been in (and everyone else on the road) while she drove around under the guise of Baby.

Mara made me promise to never allow her to leave my presence when she was acting like Baby again, even if it required physically restraining her. Perhaps her own fear was a deterrent because Baby only showed up one or two more times after that night. I was thankful for that, because I was scared of how much worse things might get. There was only so deeply she could travel in the Twilight Zone before Mara would need to be hospitalized.

Things hadn't reached that point yet, at least as far as Mara and her family were concerned. Those days were still a few years off. But as things stood, I couldn't help but envy my preppy classmates who were busy talking about college and what kind of car their parents were getting them for their 16th birthday. Everybody has stress, and everybody has troubles making it through their teen years in some form, but I felt utterly alone. I was dealing with crap I couldn't even begin to describe to anyone that I knew. How would I explain Baby, or the things to come, to someone whose biggest worry was doing well on the SAT's?

Chapter 6 - One Step Forward, Two Steps Back

For a few weeks after the Baby fiasco, Mara seemed to settle back into a routine and even seemed more upbeat. Her stress level appeared lower and she didn't have daily stories about struggles with her classes. She even gave me a gift that she was very proud of: a small Canon automatic camera which would let me take a lot more photos of us and our time together. She had a tiny old-style camera with the flash wand for the flash cubes, but this camera had a build in flash and automatically rewound the film when you for to the end of a roll. It was a pretty big deal, even if it wasn't outrageously expensive. It was the kind of thing I would never have thought to buy for myself.

It was a relief to see Mara in a better mood. She even told me about how she'd gotten an A- on her latest Physics quiz. If she was able to grasp that class and do well, I knew she wasn't going to have any real difficulty with her other classes, at least not this semester. The Chemical Engineering program was a multi-year schedule so I expected things to get a lot more difficult for her in future semesters, but this was the first time in a long time that Mara was exhibiting signs of confidence. Maybe the rest of the program wouldn't be that difficult for her after all.

As it turned out, she had no trouble with the rest of the program.

That's because she hadn't been going to class for nearly a month. Mara revealed the truth one day when I was a little late coming home from school and she was already at my house waiting for me. I knew that given her schedule there was no way she should have been done before I was. Had she skipped a class? And why wasn't she spending much time on her homework? I didn't want to see her get lazy and start to struggle again.

When I asked her about it, Mara matter-of-factly told me that she hadn't been near the campus in almost a month. I could feel a huge lump form in my stomach as she talked about it. She hated her classes, she couldn't understand them, and she had no friends there. So instead she had been spending her days at the mall walking around, or in her room at her parent's house if she knew they weren't going to be there. She would watch television, play with Sampson (the family dog), walk around one of the area malls, and then come by my house when she ran out of things to do.

It wasn't that I felt Mara needed a college education to work and have a productive life. It was more that her cycle of not finishing things was getting worse. Not to mention, she was going to need to tell her parents about this. Whether she was fully honest or not, she was going to have to let them know she was dropping out of school entirely and had no intention of going back.

That conversation went about as you would expect. Her parents were horrified (although she didn't tell them about not going to class for a month). There was a lot of anger, some yelling, and some threats about living on the street and having to panhandle to survive. But what could her parents do? Mara wasn't going back. She was firm in that position no matter what kind of pressure or lever they tried. Of course, already having failed every class she was enrolled in was a secret that helped Mara not be swayed by their pleading and shouting.

By the time the stamping and slammed doors had ended, things calmed down a bit and the three of them were able to have a semi-civil conversation about the future. Mara would be allowed to continue living at home as long as she had a full-time job or, at worst, two part time jobs. There were the expected comments about *maybe* Mara would decide to take some classes and eventually go back to school...*maybe* she would want a better future for herself...*maybe* she would feel a responsibility to try since her parents had paid for her college up to this point.

Her parents tried inserting some house rules about a curfew and about how much time she was going to be allowed to spend with me. Somehow, I was the root source of the problem in their minds. I don't know why they imagined a scrawny teenager three years their daughter's junior was some kind of Svengali dedicated to ruining their daughter's life. Maybe they didn't completely believe that, but it was always more convenient to blame me than to look in the mirror and wonder what they might have gotten wrong. It always is.

Mara held a variety of retail or low-level bank jobs in the coming months, and while there were some major issues (as I discuss later in this book) in general Mara was doing okay. She stayed gainfully employed and tried to keep out of her parents' way, but she hated living at home. In one breath she would complain about how her parents wanted her to eat meals with them and occasionally participate in family activities, and In the next Mara would complain about how living there felt like she was nothing but a boarder. Either way she hated it, and the stress between herself and her parents grew.

Finally, one day Mara announced to her parents (and later to me) that she had decided to take a job as an au pair for a couple with a newborn in a neighboring town. It seemed like the perfect solution to her: a full-time job, a room of her own, and the ability to go back to her parents' house on weekends if she felt like it. It was a nice neighborhood, a big house, and she'd get away from the stress of her family. Her overall goal was to keep the job until I graduated High School, and then we'd get an apartment together while I went to work.

The shift from my going to college to my going to work immediately after graduation was slow but steady, starting with when Mara dropped out of the University of Maryland. From then on, her stories about me going to school close by changed to my skipping college altogether. As usual, I just sort of went along for the ride. On the basis of my PSAT scores as a Junior I knew I was accepted at Rutgers University if I chose to go to school. All I had to do from that point forward was pass my classes and graduate.

But a few obstacles remained even if I wanted to choose that path. First of all, I had no idea how I would pay for school. I don't remember how it worked in the 80's, but I seem to recall loans and financial aid were a lot harder to get back then. Or perhaps I just didn't investigate very far. I knew my Dad made too much money for me to qualify for any aid because they made no allowances for having six kids and things like that. One of my older brothers was going to go to Rutgers, and it was in New Jersey and residents paid a much lower tuition than non-residents. My father had been able to foot most of the cost of that, but I felt asking him to do the same for me would be a heavy burden.

The other problem was one of direction. I had no idea what I wanted to do, or what I wanted to be. And my creativity in that kind of thought seemed to be nonexistent. I understood I was intelligent, and I had things I was more interested in than other things (music, history, movies, computers – which had just hit the first PC stage) but how did those interests translate into a career? My classmates had their whole lives pre-planned (although whether by choice or coercion I have no idea). I was a steady underachiever; I did only what I needed to do in order to get by, and I did well on tests for reasons I didn't quite understand. I wasn't confident about anything in myself. The general push of support back then was always "you can be anything you want to be." I didn't get much of that to begin with, but when I did that was useless. What I really needed, but never got and never knew to ask for, was a lot less of "you can do anything you want" and a lot more of "have you ever considered you might be good at or like doing *this*?"

At the end of my Junior year my Dad hooked me up with a summer job for a friend of his in Manhattan. He taught me a lot about financial markets, the psychology of trading, technical analysis, and things like that. I also spent weeks building a BASIC program which would test two market theories he had. He liked my work and the results, and how quickly I grasped concepts, and told me if I wanted to try working for him after graduation a job offer was on the table. The work was interesting, but more importantly it was a way of earning money and affording an apartment with Mara. From the moment she heard about the offer, the full court press was on. We were moving in together, and I was going to work. That solution seemed easier than trying to figure out how to pay for college...not to mention how I would see Mara or help her through her weakening mental state if I went. So, the subject was closed.

But in the meantime, Mara was desperate to get out of her parents' house and away from the arguments and stress. I don't think the actual job really mattered. She would have taken a job as a test subject for CIA torture devices if that was the first thing she came across that would give her somewhere to stay until we could move in together. Instead, she stumbled across this job as an au pair in the paper (which is a fancy name for a live-in babysitter). Once she'd latched onto that idea, and the job opening, nothing else mattered.

Mara was very skilled at putting on faces, and job interviews is one area where that ability proved highly valuable. It took only one long meeting with the parents to convince them she was the perfect candidate for the job. As far as they were concerned, Mara was kind, compassionate, dependable, solid, reliable, and mentally sound. They offered her the position and she quickly accepted.

I had grave reservations, but Mara dismissed any suggestion she reconsider. Her parents were more concerned about this being a job that had no future and would do nothing to help build a true career, and those were legitimate points too. No matter, Mara's mind was set. It was the answer to all her immediate problems. She'd get space from her parents, earn some money, and still be able to see me on nights and weekends. All she had to do was watch over a baby, feed it, change it, and keep it safe. How hard could that be?

If nothing else, this experience was about to teach me that loving Mara was a full-time job. If I was going to help her find her way and discover happiness and fulfillment in life, I was going to need to make that my primary objective, above all others. I could either accept that responsibility or run. I never considered the latter, even though it may have been the much better choice both in the short and the long run. I didn't know it, but my life was now as pre-planned as everyone else's, by my own choices.

Chapter 7 - An Open Letter to Bart and Cheryl

This chapter is an "open letter" I wrote years ago as an essay, directed to the couple that had hired Mara as an au pair. It was never sent to them or printed anywhere they would have seen it, but was instead just meant to tell the story of what happened and how I felt about it after many years had passed.

During the never-ending process of cleaning out my storage unit, I have come across quite a few photographs that I never knew existed, or that I had forgotten about. Some were of my mother and her parents; I'd never seen her as an infant or her father as anything but an old man. I don't even remember her mother, who died when I was two or three years old. So those were interesting to look at, as were some very old photos of the ancestors of my maternal grandfather, which is a side of the family I had not been able to learn anything about back when I found myself interested in my family history.

As you might expect, I also found photos from my own childhood, some of which I'd seen before. My siblings, my parents...places I don't recognize, friends I barely remember. And there were photos I took myself, mostly from when I was a teenager, almost exclusively of Mara...Mara, my first girlfriend, who would become my first wife.

And, I found two photos of your little girl.

To be honest, I can't be 100% certain anymore if she was a girl. You know how babies are...the defining characteristics are often difficult to see until they're a bit older. But I think she was. I can't remember her name though.

The photos are rather generic; one is of her lying on the bed, and in the other she is playing with the coiled cord of a pair of stereo headphones. I'm not a big fan of babies, but she's cute in the photos, and that's how I remember her. She was cute; a bit of a crier, but still cute.

I have a better memory of the two of you than your child. Cheryl: your hair an orange/red, always tense and rigid. Even your smile was nervous in its own way. I remember you telling me what a difficult pregnancy it had been; you'd nearly lost her, and I can't be certain if there had been a miscarriage earlier or not. But you had struggled and fought to make it work, and it had. Your baby was healthy and safe.

And Bart; thick coke-bottle glasses, short but unkempt hair, goatee trimmed to a medium length. I believe you were a professor of sorts, at one of the New York schools. We bumped into each other on Broadway one afternoon, as I was walking back to the World Trade Center to catch the tube to Hoboken. You made a semi-snide comment about my briefcase, as if I was playing at being an adult. I shrugged it off and smiled, but inside I remember that it bothered me. I may have only been 16 years old, but I was working full time in the city that summer, at a job which I'd continue at when I graduated.

To you I was a gawky teenager with acne and a girlfriend too good looking for me. To your wife I was a horny male who might break your household rule of no sex in the house one day when you weren't home. You were both right, in your own way. But I was much more too.

I was the one who saved your child's life.

Your house was a nice size, maybe a bit large. Semi-sterile, but as your daughter grew it would be a nice place for her to grow up. It was nestled on one of the quiet side streets in Westfield, with a few beautiful trees to drop colorful leaves in the fall. It was the sort of house I hoped to live in someday if I stayed in the area, with beautiful hardwood floors and a long staircase leading to the second story. That's where your bedroom was, and Mara's room. No, wait...her room might have been on a third floor, with only a storage room on the other side of the hallway. It's hard to remember, but that might be right.

I'm not sure why you hired Mara as your live-in au pair, except she seemed to have an amazing knack when it came to interviews. In the coming years she would be hired for nearly any job she interviewed for, including some she was woefully unqualified for. I suppose she simply knew how to fake her way through it, hiding the truth and showing the world what it wanted to see. She'd learned that skill well during her years as an abuse victim. I remember one time she was hired as a bookkeeper for a small firm. Her first morning at work they showed her around the office, gave her master keys to just about everything in the place, and left her alone in her room to start working. She had absolutely no idea how to do any of the work she'd been hired to do. So, she made herself look busy until lunch, then left and never went back. She wouldn't even answer or return their phone calls, where they begged her to return the keys so they wouldn't have to change all the locks.

That was a few years after she worked for you. Mara had dropped out of college and worked a few jobs, as a bank teller and a clerk at a pharmacy. But she wanted to get out of her house and away from her parents. Her mental state was worsening, and she felt that working for you - which included a place to live - was just what she needed. I had strong doubts, but as usual she wouldn't listen to me. All I could do was be supportive.

She started the job in August, while I was still working full-time. But when I helped her move some possessions into her room that Sunday before she started, I remember you giving Mara "the lecture." Cheryl was going back to work and was terribly anxious about it. Not anxious about the job itself, but anxious about leaving her baby in the care of someone else. And Mara had to be serious about this job. She was young by your standards, so you were nervous about the possibility of being forced to find a replacement if Mara suddenly changed her mind and decided she didn't want to work there any longer. You needed Mara to commit to at least a year...if after nine months or so she'd tired of the job, that would give you time during the following summer to find somebody new. But the difficult pregnancy had kept Cheryl out of work much longer than expected before the actual birth, so she couldn't afford to miss any more time. This arrangement **had** to work out.

At first, everything seemed fine. Mara had Sundays off, so I'd see her then, and then when school started, I would spend every lunch break or free period in the phone booth on the second floor, talking to her and listening to her. The baby wasn't much of a problem; Cheryl was. She was so nervous about everything; Mara was not allowed to leave the house at all, not even to take the child in a walk in a stroller. After a few weeks Mara was starting to feel quite claustrophobic. Cheryl was also very precise about how she wanted things done; there were quite a few testy conversations with Mara about things she'd supposedly done wrong. Still, she was away from her parents, which is what she wanted.

After six weeks or so, you loosened up a bit and Mara was allowed to take the baby out of the house for short trips. This helped take some of the tension out of the air, but not a substantial amount. Then Mara got sick. I am sure you remember; she was sitting in the living room watching Fraggle Rock with your baby (that show seemed to hypnotize her) when she got a sudden pain in her abdomen. Mara stood up, took two steps, fell to the floor, and immediately vomited and defecated all over your imported rug.

You could have been a bit more understanding about it. What person would do that on purpose? Mara's father promised to pay to have the rug cleaned or replaced if necessary. Being a doctor, he was able to prescribe her some medication, and in a few days, Mara was fine. But you mentioned that rug at every opportunity. I hope you weren't as critical of your daughter as she grew.

And I still remember the big day: the day Mara and I stood in front of you and she gave you one week's notice. She told you that we'd discussed it and this job simply wasn't for her, and that she couldn't even give you a full two weeks. How angry the two of you were; this was a major inconvenience in your life. Now you'd have to find someone else, quickly, or Cheryl might miss time at work again. You had such a look of disdain and disrespect in your eyes. Here were two young adults, only one of whom was out of school, and they clearly had no appreciation for what they were putting you through. Did Mara even **understand** the meaning of the word commitment? Obviously not. She had agreed to keep this job for at least nine months, and it hadn't even been a **month**!

I don't know what you did after that. I imagine you griped and bitched and moaned about the situation to every friend and colleague you had. "Kids today…no morals, no ethics, no idea what it means to make a promise and stick to it. Try to give a young adult a break, and they spit in your face." That sort of thing.

I don't blame you for feeling that way. I might have been the same. Or, maybe instead of getting completely pissed off and throwing a fit, I might have wondered – or asked – if there was more to the story. **Why** wasn't this job for Mara? Why couldn't she give more than one week's notice? What was so important that she get out of taking care of your daughter so quickly?

You didn't ask any of those questions…unless you asked them amongst yourselves. But the attitude both of you carried before and during the time I knew you, the superior and smug looks on your faces all the time, suggest to me you never did consider any other explanation.

So, this letter is to give you the reason. The **true** reason.

One day between classes I called Mara from the usual payphone. When she answered, I could tell she had been crying, and I could hear your daughter crying as well, in the background. I asked Mara what was wrong. Was she sick again?

"I can't take it any more Doug. She won't stop crying. I've tried everything. It is making me crazy, like I want to kill myself."

I tried to calm Mara down, and to take some deep breaths. Go to another room, get away from the baby. I didn't want her doing something stupid and hurting herself. But Mara just laughed...a crazed laugh.

"I know what to do. I am going to put a pillow over her head. And hold it there. Then she won't cry anymore. Ever." And she laughed again.

You'll never know the effort, the begging, and the pleading it took for me to get Mara to promise not to kill the baby until I got there. But somehow, she agreed. She would leave the front door unlocked and go upstairs to her room, and wait for me.

Today, if this happened, I would have called the police. But I was 16 years old, and I felt I had to protect Mara as well as your baby. Even this early in our relationship, I felt responsible for her well-being and her life. I simply walked out of school and ran to the train station. I had no money for a cab, and no car. I had to take the train to Hoboken, jump onto the PATH to swing back to Newark Penn Station, and take the other NJ Transit line from there; a direct link between where I was and your house did not exist. I was sweating with anxiety the whole way. Then from the Westfield train station I ran the 3 or 4 miles to your house.

I wouldn't say I had gotten there in the nick of time. From the looks of things, Mara could have waited another hour or so. But she explained she needed to make sure the baby was dead long before you got home, so she could call an ambulance and say she'd found her not breathing. And she wanted time to leave her dead before she started mouth to mouth herself, to make sure that didn't work. Mara figured that way there would be evidence that she tried to save her, rather than evidence that she'd killed her.

We talked and argued for an hour or so. Mara didn't want to disappoint you. In her crazed mind, at that moment, she felt killing your child would be the easy way out; quitting would require confrontation. The child was young enough that crib death would be accepted, she told me. Nobody would think she'd done anything wrong. In fact, Mara was angry at herself for telling me anything at all. She could have just done it and that would have been that.

Fortunately, I worked on Mara until she agreed to tell you, as soon as you came home, that she had to quit. That it wasn't working out. That she didn't like the job and needed to leave. She couldn't promise me she'd be able to make it safely while you found a replacement, or even two weeks. So, we compromised on one week.

I know you'll likely never see this letter. But if you do, I hope it reminds you how lucky you are to have what you have. You never know what can happen, or what disaster you sidestepped by inches. One day missing a green light and having to wait through a red one might cause you not to be killed by the speeding truck a mile down the road with brake trouble. Or you could be like the woman who went downstairs to the street vendor to get a bagel on September 11th, so she wasn't at her desk when a plane flew through the wall nine stories below her desk.

Or maybe – just maybe – you'll reevaluate your opinion of someone…like that stupid teenager who, to you, was playing at being an adult, and who had no concept of responsibility or commitment. Maybe you won't see him as that; you might even see him as the person who saved your daughter's life.

Chapter 8 - When You Play Monopoly, Never Trust the Banker

Among the various jobs Mara found after dropping out of college, one was working as a bank teller at a small bank in Union, New Jersey. It didn't pay that much but it was something to help her make her car payments and leave a bit extra. She was doing her best to save when she could, since we planned to move in together as soon as I graduated High School. Living at home with her parents was a very stressful situation for her, and after the disaster as an au pair I knew the only way she was going to hold it together was a complete change of scenery. She was obsessed with the idea of moving in together, having her own place…it was a combination of truly wanting to move forward with her adult life, and the childhood fantasy of "playing house." In the meantime, I was still working at the newspaper store, although my attendance was starting to slip. Mara demanded more attention and sometimes it was impossible to get back home and be ready for work at 5am. I knew I wasn't long for that job.

One afternoon Mara came by my house after work and said she wanted to go out to dinner. I only had about $10 but Mara said she would pay. We went off to a local diner, but not our usual place. This one was a bit more popular, and a bit more expensive. We ate and talked like usual, but before the tab came, Mara smiled sneakily and pulled out five $20 bills. "I'm paying for the dinner with **this**" she said quietly.

I knew she only get paid every two weeks, and even when she did get paid, she would never have $100 cash on her (this was 1985 after all, and she was only working part time, plus about five hours a week at a pharmacy). "Where the hell did you get that?" I asked.

She could see the sudden look of fear on my face. "Oh, don't worry about it. I stole it from work."

"You stole it from the bank? Are you crazy? That's a Federal crime!"

"It's fine, nobody will know. See, this one jerk comes in every day with a pouch and makes a deposit for his business. I always seem to get stuck doing his deposits. A few times I have had to recount the tens or twenties or whatever because I get a lower amount than he put on the deposit slip. When I do that, he can't resist making some snide comment about how he never makes a mistake."

"What does that have to do with stealing a hundred buck?" I asked.

"Well, today when he made his deposit, he put down that he had $640 in twenties, but when I counted, I got $740. So, I started counting again and he could tell I must have gotten a different total than him, so he made another remark about how he's right. I recounted, got $740 again, and looked him right in the eye and agreed with him."

"I don't get it."

"He gave me $740 in twenties, but put down on his deposit slip that he gave me $640 in twenties. So, I just decided to let him be right. I put it down as $640, and when it was time for lunch, I snuck the extra twenties into my purse and that was that. He wanted credit for $640 and that's what he got. Nobody knows anything, so stop freaking out."

I admit I'm no saint, and even in my younger years I did my share of vandalism and shoplifting. But this was something new to me: stealing from work, and a bank no less! But there was nothing I could do about it. I just told her I didn't think it was a smart thing to have done, and asked her never to do it again. With her fragile state, I could only imagine that if she had been caught it could have easily pushed her over the edge.

It had to be at least six months later, when Mara had been working full time at the bank, that she said she had something she wanted to show me. We went up to my bedroom, and she pulled a savings account passbook out of her purse. It was from a bank I had never heard of. I opened it, and the passbook had her name in it, and only one transaction: a deposit of $1,000.

"I wanted to keep it somewhere safe for now," she said. "I didn't want to have that much cash sitting around. I figured we could use it for stuff we'll need when we get our apartment, and the first month's rent."

"What the fuck?" I asked. "A thousand bucks? What the hell have you been doing?"

And she told me.

Now that she had been at the bank for a while, she worked her own drawer and was a full teller. As you'd expect, she handled deposits, withdrawals, cashing checks, money orders, and all the usual stuff. Over the course of a day, her drawer might begin to have too much cash in it, or not enough. When either of those things happened, she would call the Manager and they would do a transaction of currency from her drawer to or from the safe.

The process was pretty simple. For a deposit, Mara would use the counting machines and bundle each type of bill appropriately. Then her Manager would use machines to quickly recount the funds. The Manager would give Mara a receipt which was used to "prove" (or balance) her drawer and the end of the day. In a withdrawal from the safe, the process was faster because the money was pre-bundled with official wrappers. The Manager would count up stacks to the appropriate amount, the teller would do the same to make sure it matched, and a receipt was given.

According to Mara, one morning about a week earlier she had needed a $10,000 withdrawal from the safe. The Manager counted out the stacks, pushed them to Mara, and Mara had recounted. One, two, three, four, five, six, seven, eight, nine, ten...eleven. Mara had counted $11,000. Without a moment of hesitation, Mara had smiled and said "Yup, $10,000" as if everything was normal. She got a receipt and brought the money to her drawer. Fifteen minutes later she "accidentally" knocked a couple of bundles onto the floor, bent down to pick them up, and slipped a pack of ten $100 bills into her pack of cigarettes inside her purse. Then she picked up the other bundle and went back to work.

It was scary to me how easily Mara was able to work out the details of what she needed to do in only an instant. When it was time for her lunch, she went home and hid the money in her bedroom. Leaving during lunch was not unusual for her, as she did that a couple of times each week. When the day ended, the drawers all proved (minus any usual tiny imbalances) but the Manager was in a panic: the vault was short $1,000. She was the only one with access, and had no idea how this could have happened.

All the tellers were told they would need to stay after closing, while the corporate office was called and all the drawers were rechecked. Nobody knew what to do, as this had never happened before. The Manager was truly worried she might be fired if the money wasn't accounted for. In a manipulative and clever move, Mara started talking to another teller and voiced concern that the bank might try to blame one of them for a theft. The other teller suggested that everyone have the Manager search their purses and pat down their bodies to prove nobody had stolen it. Corporate was in favor of the idea, but said they couldn't force anyone to comply. Of course, all the tellers volunteered to subject themselves and their belongings to the search anyway...after all, they were all innocent and had nothing to hide.

When the safe was triple checked and the personal searches completed, corporate was out of ideas. So everyone was sent home, and a corporate official was scheduled to come by the next day. He spent the morning going over all the transaction records, receipts, transfers; anything anyone could think of. Nothing was amiss. He and the Manager had a phone call with corporate. She came out looking very upset, but told everyone that corporate was just going to write it off and not discipline or fire her. The best guess was that during the morning delivery from the armored car service, somehow the drop-off or pick-up had been miscounted by both the manager and the driver, and all day the bank had unknowingly been short $1,000 in the safe. At some point in the future the thousand dollars would turn up in the bank's system, most likely by someone who had no knowledge of this shortage at that one branch, and be marked as an overage of unknown origin.

"I waited over a week just to make sure the coast was clear,'" she explained to me. "Then I opened this account at another bank to hold the money until we need it."

She was actually proud of herself for what she had accomplished. For me, I was shocked, and more numb than terrified. The whole thing made me paranoid and sick to my stomach. After a lot of arguing and begging, Mara promised that she wouldn't do something like this ever again.

As it worked out, within a few months Mara quit the job because the hourly pay was so low, and because business was so slow, they had laid off two tellers and wanted everyone else to work extra hours. I doubt losing $1,000 helped matters, but then again, I don't think there was any correlation between the two. She also rationalized quitting by pointing out that we didn't know where we would be living yet, and in all likelihood that bank would be too far of a drive from our apartment.

I don't know; maybe she quit just because she didn't want to break her promise and knew she would be unable to resist stealing again if the opportunity presented itself. To the best of my knowledge she never stole from a job again, or from anywhere for that matter.

Chapter 9 – Why Did I Stay?

There is one question which I am asked all the time when discussing my relationship and marriage with Mara: "Why did you stay? With the infidelity, misery, self-destructive behavior, and everything else, why would you put yourself through that?"

It's a question that has many answers, depending on when you're asking about. And none of the answers are complete, or necessarily satisfactory. It was such a combination of factors, changing based on the situation or the year or the season.

To begin with, there's always love. I truly loved Mara, even when I wasn't really old enough to understand what love was. As my first kiss, my first love, my first sexual partner, and my first girlfriend, she held places in my heart that could never be filled by anyone else. She was beautiful, intelligent, driven, and had a very similar sense of humor to mine: terribly dark, combined with a childlike appreciation for the dumbest jokes.

My personal commitment to the relationship was very strong from the beginning. Even though I was just in High School, I don't remember every considering getting away from Mara and breaking it off, even during the craziest early stages. One additional reason for that was it never occurred to me that I could do better. And I don't just mean I was in a state of bliss that couldn't be matched. I mean, I couldn't imagine why any woman would be the least bit interested in me. I wasn't even sure why Mara was.

My full level of self-realization hit when I was around twelve years old. One day I was just living my life with my strange family, without regard for what the world was like for anyone else. I hadn't spent time comparing myself to everyone else, or being very self-critical. I had plenty of emotional problems growing up, but I didn't know other families were different. I always assumed that if I spent the night at a friend's house, their family was just on their best behavior because I was a guest. Sort of the way we tried to be normal at home when one of us had a birthday party and friends came over. We scaled back our behavior and it all seemed proper, as if that's what everyone did.

And then, one day, I instantly had a sense of the world and my place in it. And I hated myself. I was ugly, I had terrible acne, I was short (or average), and not very strong or athletic. I wore the wrong clothes, which were often dirty. I had thick glasses, and if they broke, I had to try to mend them. I didn't understand all the intricacies of personal hygiene, and my skin and hair were oily to begin with. Our house, and my room, were always a complete mess. My mother was a hoarder in many respects, and always seemed to have a beer or a glass of wine in her hand. I was loud, obnoxious, and I didn't feel like I had any close friends. I felt tolerated at best, but never really wanted.

My family grew up in wealthy towns with very good school systems, but we never had any money. After my parents divorced, the very thought of asking my mother for $5 was scary because you already knew what a rant she was going to go into about how "your father" hadn't given us any money to live. That was completely untrue, and we all seemed to know it, but there was no arguing with my mother. She had her own years of mental illness, and you never knew if what she was saying was a purposeful lie, or just her clouded version of the truth.

In Mara I found someone who seemed to really like, and love, me for whom I was. She thought I was brilliant, handsome, funny, and caring.

Instead of laughing at how I looked or what I wore, she tried to help me improve myself. She restyled and cut my hair, and tried mousse and other ideas to make it do something other than lay there.

Even the messy house wasn't such an issue for her. She seemed to genuinely like my siblings, and enjoyed hanging out with all of us. If things did get to her, she didn't blame me for not knowing any better. One time she locked herself in the bathroom for about ninety minutes and refused to come out.

I banged on the door and called to her. "Mara, are you okay."

"Go away!" she yelled back. "Leave me alone."

I tried about half an hour later and got the same response. I figured she was pissed off at me for something I didn't realize I'd done wrong.

When she finally opened the door, it turned out she had been cleaning it the whole time. "I just couldn't stand how dirty it was in there, and since I use it when I come over, I wanted it cleaner for all of us."

So, between the two of us there was love and acceptance. But as Mara's mental and physical problems grew over the years, not only did I feel it was my duty to stand by her, but the whole thing seemed natural to me. As a youngster I'd been attached to my mother despite how crazy she acted, and I was always ready to defend her. I'd learned to tiptoe around her moods and her problems, and doing the same with Mara was only too familiar.

Of course, there was also the sense of guilt and obligation I had. Mara had made it clear to me many times over the years that I was her reason for living. If I wanted to leave her, or to get a divorce, all I had to do was let her know and she'd end her own life. How do you walk away from someone when they tell you that? It wasn't an empty threat; it was a fact. And I felt guilty about being unable to get Mara into a better place in her life. I didn't make enough money, I couldn't find her the right doctors, I couldn't help her get over the sexual abuse. She didn't blame me, but I did. I blamed myself for everything. I set standards for myself I would never impose on anyone else, and those included it being my job not just to give Mara a reason to live, but to help her get better in every aspect of her life. Inevitably I would fail to meet those impossible standards, which only reinforced my own belief that I was a disappointment and a failure. A self-fulfilling prophecy, to be certain.

But through all of these reasons, Mara and I had a lot in common. We loved movies, and our tastes were very similar. We loved music. We loved animals. And most of all, we loved to laugh. Despite how sick Mara became, despite the days on end of illness or crying or mania or depression, there **were** good days. And there were good hours in bad days. And during those moments, or hours, or days, we laughed our asses off. We might be laughing at each other, playing pranks or teasing lovingly. Or with each other; we both had a childish streak that we'd act out without realizing. When we moved into our first apartment, while unpacking the car, Mara put our metal colander on her head and walked into the building like a robot. I was dying laughing watching her, but she wasn't even conscious of what she was doing until I told her.

We had so many favorite movies or television shows we loved to laugh at. The Simpsons, Seinfeld, Get a Life, Howard Stern's first TV show (on Channel 9 in New Jersey) …we'd lie in bed and get sore laughing so hard. And movies, both new and classic. When we weren't laughing at those, we'd be laughing at commercials, people on COPS, at our family members, or each other. Or the cats. Our cats were a constant source of amusement. And love; they kept us going through some of the darkest times.

Mara was also competitive, in a very fun way. Whether we were playing Mario Brothers or Gumshoe or RC Pro-Am on the Nintendo NES, or cards, or Boggle, or pinball, or strategy games like Kremlin of Enemy in Sight, Mara played to win. She delighted in killing off one of your crucial Politburo members in Kremlin with a roll of the dice, or setting fire to one of your ships in Enemy in Sight, or hitting your car with a freeze ray in RC Pro-Am. "Pew, pew" she'd call out, laughing hysterically, while the bolts shot out of her car. There was always *something* to laugh at. Individually those moments aren't that easy to remember, and they probably don't make for especially interesting reading. But they were crucial in giving us both the strength to keep going.

There was also our secret language, the private dialect any close couple develops or phrases and inside jokes and memories. When you are someone's world, and share everything with them, you have a verbal shorthand to refer back to moments in the past. In Mara's latter near the end of this book you'll see some of that. Things like "orange peel" or "we're alright, we can laugh about it now" or "tears of joy." So often being on the same mental wavelength can only keep two people closer than they otherwise would be. So, there were happy things that held us together. Sadly, there were also plenty of negatives that had the same sort of effect.

Over the years, for most of the last third of our relationship (if not longer), there was one other problem. It was no longer that I couldn't do better. It wasn't even that I felt a happy future was something I could never find, although I often did believe that. It was that I was convinced misery is what I deserved. If we were miserable, if I hated my life, so be it; that's all I deserved. Even if I could somehow find happiness, I didn't deserve it. The only way I could deserve to be happy was if I could make Mara happy too. Failing that, I was nothing but a piece of shit, and this destiny of misery was all someone like me was meant to have, or deserved to have. Whether it was fate or God or some other universal power, I belonged in this dark, desperate world. There was no sense in fighting it or pretending I deserved anything else. In a strange way, it was as though I felt happiness was a battery, and if I tried to take some energy from it when I hadn't earned it, I'd be depriving someone more deserving of that happiness.

It sounds foolish in retrospect, but it took me many years to understand and overcome those opinions of myself and my place in the world. I'm still not especially fond of myself, but I don't hate myself the way I once did. As for if I had the chance to do it over again? I don't have that chance, so I don't think about if I would or wouldn't. I still beat myself up for individual moments, bad choices or decisions, saying or doing the wrong thing at the wrong time. But, big picture? I can't put myself back in that place with the same mind I had then. So, I don't see how I could have done anything differently.

As a friend used to tell me, I did the best I could with the knowledge and experience I had at the time. Sitting here today, most of it still seems woefully inadequate. But it can't be changed, so I try not to dwell on that.

Chapter 10 - Moving Out

A few weeks before I graduated High School, Mara and I started the search for our first apartment. Since I wasn't going to be earning much to start at my new job, while she wasn't even working at that moment, trying to find someplace that we could afford in a neighborhood that was at least moderately safe was clearly going to be a challenge. It would have been a lot easier if Mara had stayed employed, but recriminations weren't going to do any good.

There were really only four requirements we had for a prospective apartment. The first was that it was in a neighborhood we both felt safe enough to walk in. Second, it had to be in our price range (which wasn't much until Mara started working). Third, it needed to have some kind of air conditioning, even if it was only enough to cool one room. And fourth, it had to be located somewhere that I could walk to transportation to get me to New York City. That meant near a New Jersey Transit train station, or close to a bus route that went directly to New York or Newark.

The first couple of places we looked at were better than I expected, but price-wise I couldn't see any way we could afford them (even if we were approved for the lease). Next on our list was a one-bedroom apartment in South Orange. Neither of us were that sure how to get there, so we took the highway out to South Orange Avenue all the way in Newark and followed that road towards South Orange. At the time, there were some very dilapidated neighborhoods along the way, and we both agreed that if things didn't start to look safer as we got into South Orange we would just keep on driving. Fortunately, the closer we got to the area the better things started to seem.

Eventually we found the building. There didn't seem to be any attached parking, so we parked at a metered spot down the street and walked up. It was an older building, but generally clean. Two elderly ladies sat in lawn chairs on the porch and greeted us as we walked inside. We made our way down the stairs to the basement, where the management office was, next to the laundry room. The super talked to us a bit and showed us the apartment, which was on the third floor. There was no elevator but the staircase was wider than you might expect, and I didn't much mind. The apartment was tiny – a small bedroom, a miniscule bathroom, and one larger main room that included the kitchen and living room in one. That room also had an air conditioning unit build into the wall.

There wasn't that much to talk over. The neighborhood seemed okay, the rent was as cheap as we had found, there was an air conditioner, and it was a ten-minute walk to the South Orange train station. The bank next door was the same bank we used, and Mara thought she might be able to get a job there as a teller. Parking was going to be a bit of a problem, but it was explained that if we bought a parking pass from the city every month, we could park in a municipal lot down the street a little. Some residents parked in the bank parking lot when it was closed but being towed from there was always a risk. Most importantly, if we could give them the security deposit and first month's rent, we were good to go as of July 1st. The search was over.

My Dad treated us to some furniture as a graduation present, so that was delivered directly to the apartment (a sofa, a bed, a coffee table, and a couple of wall units). We found an inexpensive table and chairs for the dining area, which was part of the living room as the kitchen area only had enough room for one person to stand in at once. The way Mara set the place up was pretty nice, all things considered.

At first Mara was rather happy about the whole arrangement. I'd go off to New York by train while she searched the papers for a decent job. She was able to get part time hours at the bank next door, but we needed more than that to make ends meet. She kept busy with the job search and the excitement she had playing house for the first time, cooking meals a few times a week and doing the laundry at the machines in the basement. One meal in particular stood out for years: spaghetti meat pie. I have no idea where she found the recipe, but the ingredients called for a can of spaghetti (this apparently referred to a can of pre-cooked spaghetti and sauce a la Chef Boy-ar-Dee). But Mara didn't catch that reference, so instead she put in a bunch of uncooked spaghetti pieces. "I didn't know exactly how much a can of spaghetti was supposed to be, since our spaghetti comes in boxes." I tried to play dumb and chew through these burned strands of uncooked spaghetti surrounded by ground beef, but one mouthful in Mara realized she must have made some kind of terrible mistake and took my plate away, throwing everything in the trash. Even she had to laugh at the results of this one.

The one problem we were experiencing was with the air conditioning. As big as the a/c unit was, it still couldn't cool down the living room very well, and the bedroom was always uncomfortable hot. Worse, we quickly learned that if you turned the a/c unit to higher than 3 on the 1 to 10 coolness setting, the fuse would blow. The first time that happened, Mara had to get the super to come up to the basement to show her how to fix it. She couldn't find the circuit breaker, and that's because as it turned out there wasn't one. The building was so old, the panel was fitted with the ancient glass screw in fuses.

The 15 Amp fuse had blown, so the super replaced it with another. As soon as Mara turned the a/c back on, it blew again. So, he replaced it with a 20 Amp this time. He also told Mara where we could buy our own boxes of fuses nearby. When I got home, I couldn't help but be troubled by the fact that he would so cavalierly replace one fuse with another designed to allow more electricity through the power line. After all, there must have been a reason all the fuses in that fuse box were 15 amps to begin with, right? But he seemed to think it was fine. "They won't blow as often this way" he explained.

I should pause to mention that while we never personally had any safety problems at the building (other than blowing the 20-amp fuses too), years later a strange thing happened. One of my sisters moved into the same building – in fact just a floor above our old apartment – without ever realizing we had lived there earlier. Sure enough, while she was at work one day the building caught fire and burned to the ground. I'm suspicious that the overloaded wiring may have been one of the causes of the fire, but it wasn't the primary reason the damage was so extensive. That can be blamed on someone (city, utility, or private individual) paving over the access to the main gas shut-off valve, delaying the fire department's ability to safely fight the fire. My poor sister lost everything she had.

After a few months, life in that apartment became rather claustrophobic. Mara had the car all day and could come and go as she pleased, but aside from looking for more work she rarely went anywhere except the bank next door. I'd return from the city and the atmosphere in the tiny apartment was simply heavy. There was no privacy, no personal space. We were short on money and in such cramped quarters that every little spark turned into a flame. And Mara was becoming randomly unstable; you didn't know what would set her off or why. She complained constantly about the two gargoyles on the front porch, about having to lug groceries up three flights of stairs...and about one of our neighbors.

The neighbor is one thing I agreed with Mara on. It had grown from a roll-your-eyes joke to a form of mental torture. We'd never seen this neighbor in person, but they were directly next to us. Every weeknight, we'd hear the door to that apartment slam. Presumably the neighbor had just gotten home from work. Within 90 seconds we'd hear the opening notes as Anita Baker began singing her song "Sweet Love." It's a great song, and Anita Baker has a beautiful voice. It's just that we both grew tired of the song after hearing it play over...and over...and over. This neighbor didn't just play it every time they came home; they played it nonstop for at least 30 minutes. Every. Weeknight. Without. Fail. We both grew to loathe that song. I fantasized about sneaking into the apartment and smashing the record to pieces. Instead, we just tried to block it out with our own music, or the TV. But you could still hear it. "With all my heart I call you baby...."

One week I had been invited to go to a coworker's apartment in the city on a Friday night to play spades with a group of people she knew. (Actually, it was the apartment of two coworkers who were in a relationship). I told Mara about it early in the week, and she was fine with the idea. I'd stay for a few hours but still be sure to leave early enough to catch a train home. I even asked if she wanted to come into the city herself and join us, but I knew the answer would be no. She hated New York City. It was loud and dirty and it frightened her.

Friday came, and I called Mara after work to remind her I'd be home late. It was a good time, and even though I'd never played spades before I was able to quickly grasp the concepts and my partner and I cleaned up. I'd met everyone there except for one woman, and she was very sweet so there was no feeling uncomfortable or unwelcome. Just cards, some wine, and a lot of laughs.

I caught one of the last trains out, and walked up the hill from the train station to the apartment. I remember thinking things seemed much different later on a Friday night. There were a few bars down near the train station that I had never noticed before, but with the lights on and the sounds of talking and laughter I couldn't miss them now. It gave the area a much livelier vibe, and I made a mental note to suggest that the two of us should visit one of them one day soon.

I walked up the stairs and into the building, and laughed to myself because this was one of the few times the old lady gargoyles weren't perched on their lawn chairs on the porch. It had become to tedious, being forced to say hello to them every time I walked by them, and then catching snippets of negative comments about me or both of us as we made our way down the hall.

I got to our apartment door, unlocked it…and stopped. The deadbolt was locked too. I couldn't remember Mara ever locking that. I was the only one who bothered, when I was getting ready for bed. But there it was; I couldn't get in. I knocked on the door and called Mara's name, but got no response. I tried pounding a bit, and still there was nothing. Frustrated, I left and went back towards the train station, stopping at one of the pay phones. I called home, expecting to find Mara had fallen asleep.

Instead, she answered the phone wide awake, and furious. "I can't believe you went and played cards. I don't want to see you, go away." And she hung up. I called back, and the line was busy; she'd taken the phone off the hook. What the hell was the problem now? She knew where I had been, knew the phone number there if an emergency came up, and I had even called her after work before heading over to their apartment, at which time she had been fine. Now, all of a sudden, I had committed some kind of Federal crime.

I didn't know what else to do. I had my keys to the car, but I didn't want to blow money we didn't have on a motel room. And I certainly wasn't interested in pounding on the door and having our neighbors get involved in this insanity. So, I went to the car – which I found parked in the bank parking lot – climbed into the back seat, and did my best to lie down and fall asleep. At least I knew I didn't have to go to work the next day, so there wasn't going to be an issue with be needing to find a place to shower and change if I couldn't get back in the apartment.

The next morning, I trudged back up to the apartment door (after saying good morning to the gargoyles) and tried to open it. Still locked. I knocked, and Mara opened it and walked back into the apartment without a word. She got into bed and was quickly asleep. I never got an apology for her locking me out, nor did I get an explanation of what offense I had committed. She was just distant and cold to me for a few hours that day, and then we went out to go to the grocery store and run a couple of errands. Life went back to normal, or the normal we were experiencing anyway.

Soon after, Mara's parents decided that they were going to sell their home in New Jersey and move to New York City full-time while they renovated their lake house to accommodate year-round occupancy. In the process, they offered us their two cats: Rags and Biff. Rags was a mix of Norwegian Forest

Cat and some other breeds, and while he was generally friendly, he seemed to have never fully recovered from being dragged around by the tail by Mara's brother when he was a kid. Rags had a habit of ripping most of the hair out of his tail, but otherwise he kept to himself and occasionally looked for some affection. Biff was a gray Persian, but with the attractive normal face instead of the smushed-in one. He loved talk and affection, but his long hair required daily brushing to avoid getting badly matted. Mara really wanted them, and as I'd never been allowed cats or dogs as a child, I was more than happy to agree. It meant the apartment was even more crowded than before, but in this case, it also helped make things seem more peaceful. Dragging huge bags of cat litter up three flights of stairs wasn't much fun, but they were worth the trouble. Ever since we adopted those two cats from Mara's parents, I've never had a time when I didn't have at least one cat.

Despite the very tight financial situation we were in, it became clear to us as we approached the end of our lease that we needed to find somewhere else to live. That's when Mara had the idea of looking for a larger apartment and asking my oldest brother Paul if he would be interested in sharing it with us. It seemed like a great fit: we all got along well, and Paul was looking to move back to the area. We'd find a two-bedroom apartment with a larger living area, share the rent, and we'd all come out ahead.

Paul was enthusiastic about the idea, and gave us carte blanche to locate and choose a place. After looking around we discovered a new building of six one-story condominiums a block off the main road in Maplewood. It wasn't a majorly residential part of town but that wasn't of great importance, since the bus line ran along that street and I could ride that into Newark and take the PATH train into New York from there. It would mean a slightly longer and more weather-sensitive commute, but it still seemed like a good location and a decent-sized unit. Two lawyers had purchased the condominium as an investment and were offering it for rent, so we decided to go for it. Living there would still be a bit more expensive than what we had been paying, even after subtracting Paul's share, but I just wanted less stress in my home life at this point. Besides, Mara was still looking for full-time work and one of these days she'd have to hit on **something**. It was worth a try. We said goodbye to our first apartment, and the new family unit – me, Mara, Paul, Rags, and Biff – prepared to move on to the next chapter.

As usual, it didn't go as smoothly as I hoped. Nothing ever does.

Chapter 11 - An Artistic Interlude

I thought I'd include a favorite art project Mara gave me in an attempt to apologize for a dalliance she'd had with another guy. I don't remember exactly when this occurred, but it was most likely while we lived in our first apartment, or just before we moved in together. Despite how mad I was about what she had done, I found it disarming and forgave her (as I always did), and have kept it ever since. I can't say exactly why it tickled me so much; it just did.

DEAR DOUGY

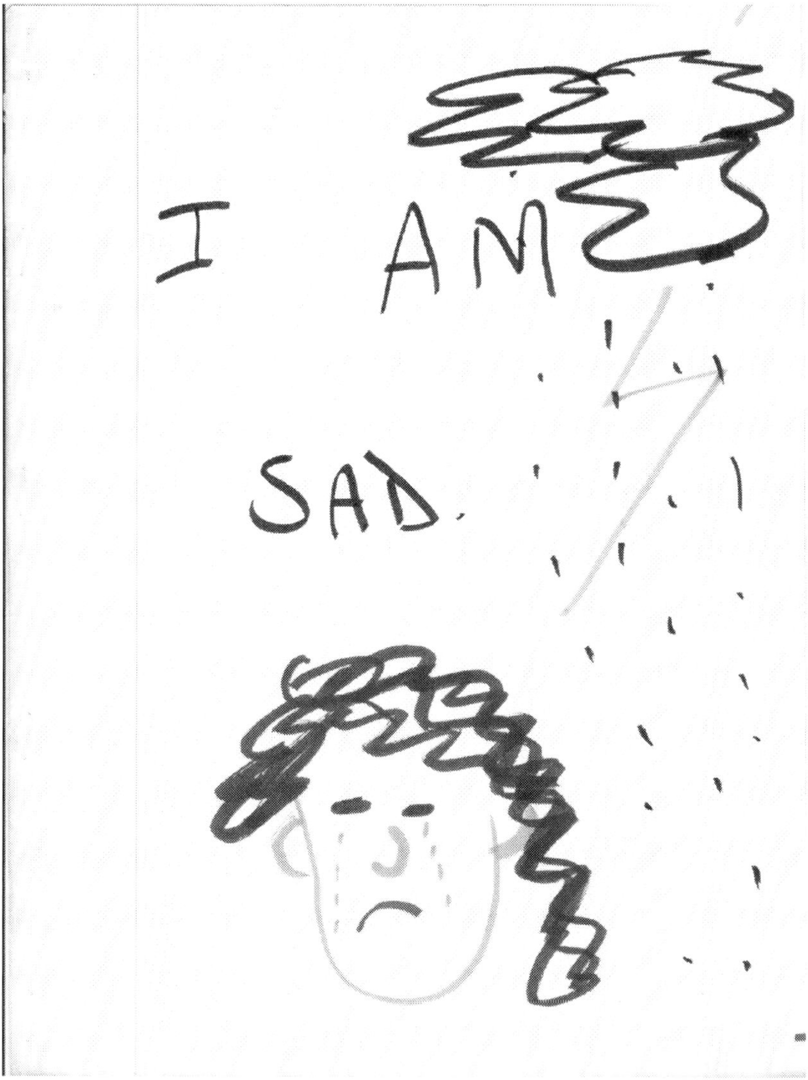
I AM
SAD

I MADE YOU MAD.

I AM SOOOOOO OOOOOOOOOOOOOO OOOOOOOOOOOO OOO..... (etc.)

SORRY!

I LOVE YOU.

Always!

(Sigh)
Doug

AND IF YOU FORGIVE ME.

Hmm... I think I'll forgive Mara

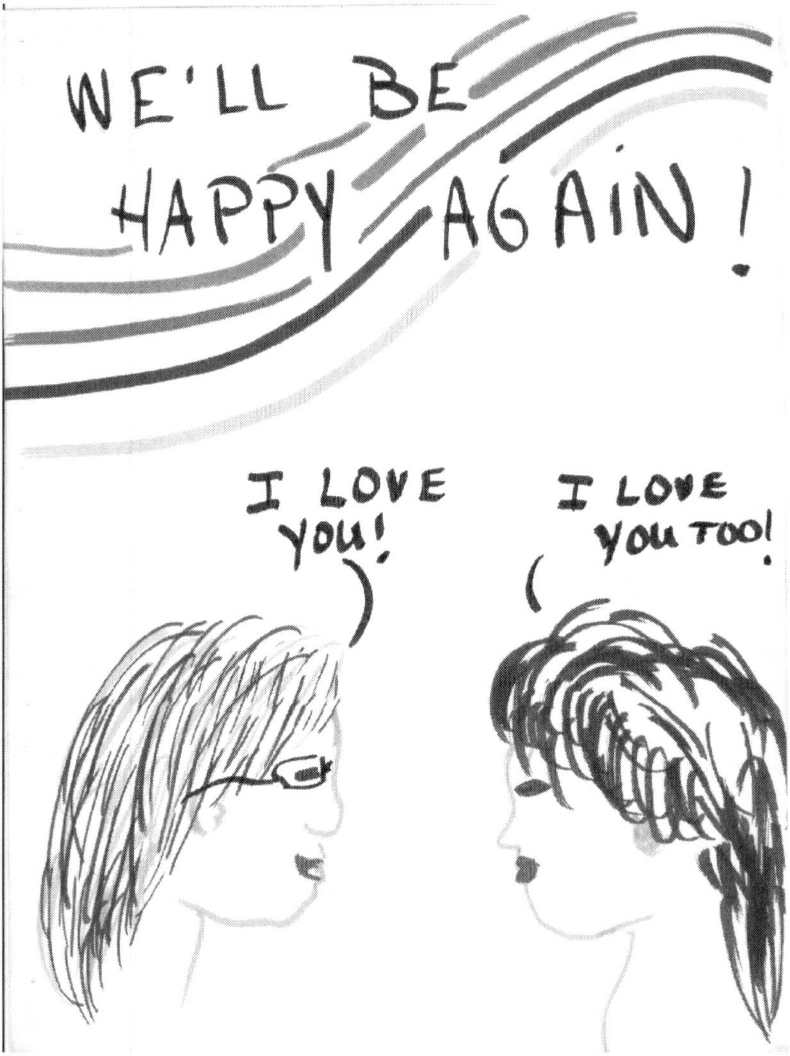
WE'LL BE HAPPY AGAIN!
I LOVE YOU!
I LOVE YOU TOO!

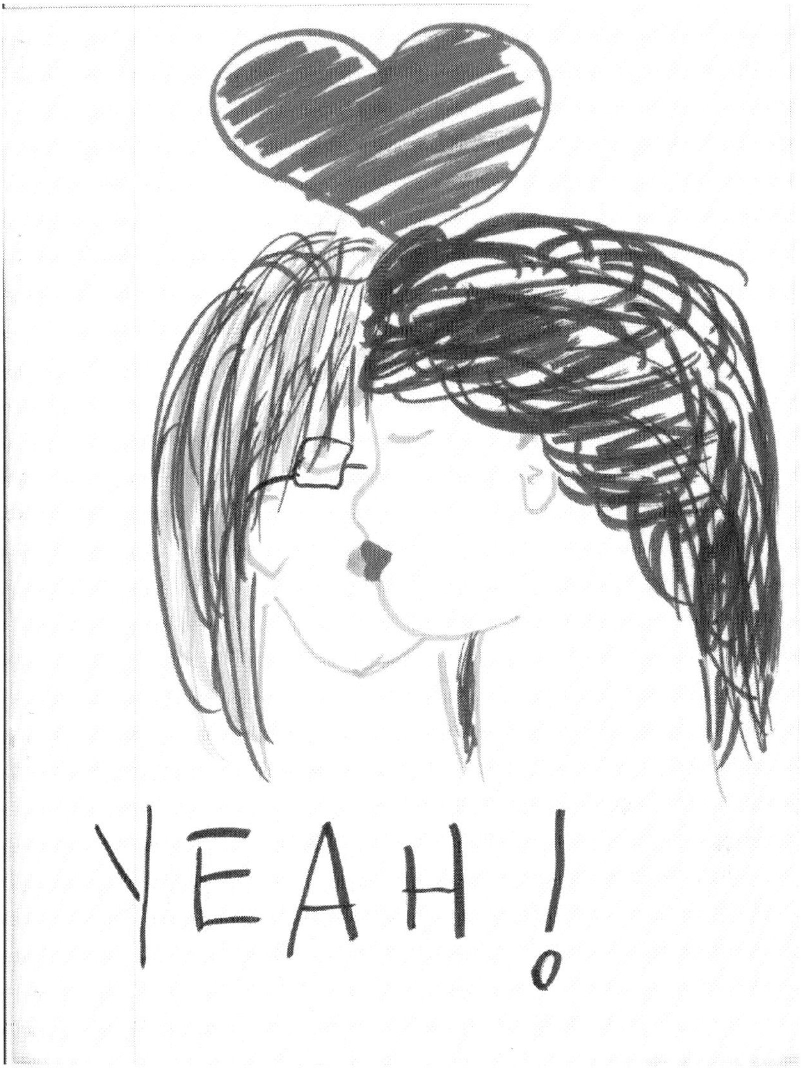
YEAH!

Chapter 12 - Can't Win for Losing

When we moved into the Maplewood apartment, things finally seemed to be going in the right direction. There was more space, everything was new (since it had just been built), and we had the cats to keep us company. Within a week or two, Paul arrived and things settled into a bit of a routine. It seemed to take a bit of adjustment but I felt like a cloud had been lifted since we got out of South Orange.

Mara even found some good news on the job front. She had worked full-time for a very brief period at some kind of coupon company, but that firm went bankrupt and she had to begin her search again. Sears had recently bought out Coldwell Bankers and they were opening a corporate office a few towns over. Despite not having a lot of experience with data entry, her time as a bank teller and other office work was enough for her to get a full-time position in the accounts payable department. Not only was this a good job with better pay (and with a 10% discount at Sears stores), but since the office was just opening Mara would avoid the whole "I don't belong here" feeling she fell into when she came into an established social group. She would be one of the very first people in the entire department, and so she would feel comfortable and welcome.

I was experiencing some growing pains at work, so to have Mara feeling more confident was a weight off my shoulders. There was so much to do at her office that she'd occasionally need to go in on Saturdays. I'd often go with her, just to hang out and read a book while she worked, before we went grocery shopping or did other errands. I tried to make myself useful by going out and picking up lunch if I was around. Certainly, I could have stayed home and rested, but I wanted to be as supportive as possible about Mara's job and the hard work she was doing.

With Paul living with us, we also found my other siblings coming by to visit more often, especially my two sisters. Allison liked to come over, visit with all of us, and then play Nintendo with Mara (the two of them were much better than me at those games). Even my mother came by a few times. Mara loved to tell the story about how she came to visit one day when I wasn't home from work yet. Mara offered her something to drink, and my mother pulled a jumbo-sized Heineken out of her purse and said "No, I just need a glass." Mara offered her a bottle opener, but of course my mother had that handled as well. That was Mom for you.

Yet despite the friendly atmosphere and her new job, Mara simply could not stay happy for very long. Soon Paul was becoming a major problem...in *her* eyes. It didn't matter what he did; she found a reason to complain about it. If he spent a lot of time in his room, Mara would bitch to me about how Paul didn't want to socialize with us. If he spent time with us in the living room, she acted like he was intruding on her personal space. If he left a rinsed-off dish in the sink for five minutes, Mara would go on a rampage, but she saw no problem in her piling up dishes wherever she pleased. I remember one evening in particular when she bitched to me for close to an hour about how Paul just did whatever he wanted and acted like he owned the place. Then she got up to go to the bathroom, and when she returned, she complained until I fell asleep about how Paul was pissing her off by behaving as if this was our place and he had to live by our rules. It made zero sense, but it was driving me crazy.

Mara did let up a bit when Paul developed terrible food poisoning, but in a way that just made him an easier target for her. He was too sick to care about anything except trying not to die (or wishing he was dead, depending on the moment). The heavy, dark atmosphere that had settled over our first apartment was reappearing here. When Mara wasn't complaining about Paul, she was miserable about any number of other problems. Physical affection was becoming exceedingly difficult for her, other than holding hands or kissing good morning or good night. On the rare occasion when she desired intimacy she cried afterwards. Even with no real understanding of the psychological issues involved, I was beginning to see that the years of sexual abuse had left their mark in ways neither of us were really prepared for.

I felt completely beaten down. Work was difficult and stressful, and I didn't look forward to coming home in the slightest. I wasn't sleeping well, which made everything worse. It all felt like a bad drug trip. I could see the writing on the wall, and it came quicker than I expected. Mara demanded that Paul had to move out; his name wasn't on the lease, and she seemed oblivious to the fact that if he left, we would be just as tight with money as we had been in our first apartment...or else she simply didn't care. I called my Dad to ask for advice, and he could hear my mental state was completely cracked. He offered to talk to Paul directly and try to explain the situation. I felt like a coward and a total failure, but I accepted his proposal. At least as an adult I've always tried to avoid confrontation. My priority was keeping Mara alive and trying to help her get her head straight. Paul would need to leave.

It didn't take long for that to be arranged. In the meantime, Mara's friend April had been coming over to visit more frequently. The two of them shared the strangest relationship I could imagine, especially given the fact that they'd known each other for a decade. Mara seemed not to like April at all when she wasn't around. She complained about her hygiene, her appearance, her eating habits, her laugh...but yet they remained friends. For her part, April couldn't have been more awkward. I don't know how much of what she did was just cluelessness and how much was a cry for attention. I remember one time the summer before Mara left for college. She invited April and me to come up to the lake house for the day. April drove, and just getting there was a near disaster. April had no sense of direction, to the level that when I said "turn left here" and pointed left, she still turned right. When we finally made it, Mara thought she recognized the shirt April was wearing. Sure enough, it was some short-sleeve college sweatshirt Mara had been trying to find for weeks. April was wearing it inside-out in a futile attempt to avoid detection. Mara also found her missing red umbrella with the name Mara embroidered on it in the back seat of April's car.

April had been looking for a place to live, and Mara introduced her to a very sweet girl named Karen that worked with her at Coldwell Bankers. Karen was very good at her job and was also thinking about joining the military sometime in the future if office work turned out not to be her calling. The two of them decided to get an attic apartment together and split expenses. The place was above a store downtown, but was kind of nice in its own way. Two bedrooms meant there would be privacy. I don't recall if April was working, or if she was relying on her Dad for money at the time (or both), but they decided to give it a go. They took a six-month lease just in case things were a disaster.

Karen tried not to put Mara in the middle of any roommate disputes, but because they worked together things were bound to come out. April was a slob; April was late with her share of the rent and expenses; things like that. The former didn't surprise me; I remembered coming out to the living room one morning after April had been over to visit, and finding her dirty panty hose in a ball on our coffee table. She had taken them off and just left them there when she went home. I hear you should bring something when you visit, but I think the general rule is more along the lines of a bottle of wine or some flowers. Dirty panty hose isn't in any Miss Manners column I've read.

April's financial decisions left a lot to be desired too. One week she begged Mara to loan her $5 so she could make it through the last four days of the week until payday (yes, $5 went a lot farther in 1987 than it does now). She obliged and loaned April the money. The next evening April stopped by with half of a sub sandwich and a can of Hawaiian Punch in tow. Mara went ballistic on her. "How can you blow $3.50 on that when you needed $5 to make it until Friday? You could have bought bread, peanut butter, jelly, and a few cans of soup and been set!" April just shrugged. She felt like having the sub and so that's what she ate. Mara swore that was the last time she would loan April any money, especially considering how we couldn't much afford to be loaning anyone anything.

One evening I came home from work a bit late. The bus ride from Newark was always a little iffy on timing, and depended heavily on traffic, weather, and how often people rang to stop the bus. The drivers on that system were a bit weird. Most stops along the way had multiple bus routes that stopped there, so if you didn't wave at the bus as it approached it wouldn't stop to pick you up. But sometimes it was very difficult to see what bus was approaching, especially when traffic was heavy or the weather was less than perfect. So, if you realized too late that the bus was yours, the driver sometimes wouldn't even slow down, and you'd be waving your arms up in the air, jumping up and down, as it sped past. I liked to imagine the drivers laughing to themselves when that happened. Somehow it made it more tolerable believing that someone got **some** enjoyment out of it. And if you flagged down the **wrong** bus, you were asking to be berated.

Anyway, when I got home it was already dark out. Mara was sitting by the phone and looked worried. I apologized for being late and she explained that it wasn't me; she was worried about April. She told me that April had been over and was very depressed, and talking about suicide. That was over an hour ago, and April wasn't home, or if she was, she wasn't answering her phone. I didn't think it was that big a deal; between Mara and April there was conversation about someone killing themselves nearly every day. April's seemed a bit more of a threat or a dare, but Mara's never was. Hers was just matter-of-fact, a discussion of why she wasn't doing it that day or why she might consider doing it in a week.

Mara got up and left the room, and when she came back, she seemed even more nervous. It seems that the bottle of migraine pills she had in her purse was missing, and Mara feared April had taken them and planned to use them to kill herself. Soon after the phone rang, and it was April's Dad (whom Mara knew but whom I had never met). April had tried to kill herself and was in the hospital, but was expected to make a recovery.

At Mara's insistence we went over to his house the next night for dinner. I didn't see much of the place, just the screened-in porch where we served us plastic trays of some cold chicken. A glance into the main house suggested April's Dad was either as messy as April was, or a hoarder as well. I didn't have much to say during the meal. April's father talked a lot about

April's problems over the years, although the conversation was mostly focused on himself. Mara was semi-supportive, but I did find it odd near the end of the conversation when Mara mentioned her missing bottle of pills and suggested that **someone** (April, her father, who knows) should be reimbursing her for the cost. It didn't seem to be the most appropriate time to bring it up, even if it was money we couldn't afford to waste. We left empty handed, and Mara complained about that the whole way home.

I don't remember if we ever saw April after that. Mara and April may have gotten together once or twice when I wasn't around, but it seemed she had dropped out of our lives entirely. The only contact between the two of them were phone games. Late at night Mara seemed to get a big laugh out of calling up April (this was in the pre-caller ID days) and playing "Mary Had a Little Lamb" using the buttons on the phone. One weekend we found a message on our answering machine of someone trying to do the same thing to us, followed by a raspy "fuck you" whispered into the receiver. Mara demanded we save that message to another cassette so she could listen to it and laugh later on. I never saw the humor in it.

Many years later, when Mara and I had moved to Texas, I asked her if she had ever tried to get in touch with April again after she had tried to kill herself. Mara just laughed and looked at me, and then stopped smiling. "Oh," she said. "I thought you were joking. I forgot you never knew what really happened."

"What do you mean *what really happened*? She tried to kill herself, went to the hospital, and the two of you stopped being friends after that."

"No, that was the story, not the truth" Mara said. And then she proceeded to explain to me what had really happened that day. I'd had no suspicion whatsoever that anything different had taken place, but it seems I (and everyone else) had been lied to.

According to Mara, what actually happened is April called her and was complaining about life, about how miserable she was, and how she wanted to kill herself. Mara hung up and drove over to April's place. She went upstairs and started an argument with April.

"I was sick of all her whining" she told me. "She was always talking about killing herself but I knew she had no intention of following through with it. It just pissed me off." So Mara berated April, telling her what a liar she was, what a drama queen, and how Mara knew she'd never kill herself.

When April tried to protest, Mara pounced. She grabbed some soda from April's fridge and gave it to her. "Here, you say you want to kill yourself? Prove it!" She then handed April her migraine pills, one or two at a time, and more or less bullied April into swallowing them. After ten minutes the bottle was empty. Then Mara dragged April by the arm into her bedroom, unplugged April's phone, and walked out with it, closing the door behind her. I think Mara said she tried to use a chair to keep the door closed, since the only lock was on the inside of the room.

"I figured she might pass out before she tried to get back out of the bedroom. She had taken enough pills to kill her, if she waited long enough. And there was no way she could call anyone with the telephone gone."

Mara's plan had been to wait until later that evening and then, "concerned" for April's well-being, go back over there and "find" the body. Obviously, that never happened. Instead April managed to get out of her bedroom and called 911, probably using the phone in Karen's room. Whether she had ever told anyone the truth was unclear, but doubtful.

That was what really seemed to still eat at Mara through all those years. "That stupid crybaby got all kinds of sympathy from her Dad because of her so-called depression, and because she had finally tried to kill herself. Except she never tried. She was a faker, and she still got love and sympathy, while I suffer every day and nobody in my family gives a shit now, or ever gave a shit." Mara had absolutely no remorse about what she had done, only regret that April had lived.

It's hard to say if this revelation changed the way I saw Mara, because by the time she told me this version of events she had fallen so far into despair and irrational thought that nothing would have surprised me. If nothing else, Mara was consistent: she didn't value her own life, and likewise she didn't seem to value the life of any other human beings. The death of an animal could bring her to tears and, in some cases, keep her crying for days; we'd had to block the Animal Channel on cable because too often she would flip by and see something about hunting or animal poaching. But for people? She barely felt anything.

Chapter 13 - Sick

Mara continued to work at Coldwell Bankers for a few more months. Despite all her other complaints, she seemed to enjoy that job overall. There were a few problems, as there always were. First was the crappy pay she got. She needed the job badly when she started, so she was fairly certain that she had undersold herself when it came to hourly wage. Now that she had been there a while, it was becoming apparent that there was no consistency when it came to who was being paid what. A new file clerk was hired, and Mara happened to ask her about why she decided to come work there. She was shocked to hear that the file clerk was making more per hour than she was, especially considering how her job required a lot more accuracy and access to sensitive information.

When Mara complained to her supervisor about the issue, the supervisor told her that it was against policy to discuss what you make. Mara countered her on that, pointing out that there was no employee handbook of any kind so how was anyone to know what was against company policy? The next day, Mara's supervisor pulled her aside. But it wasn't to criticize her for discussing pay. Instead, it was to complain to Mara about her own pay. "She isn't just making more than you, Mara. I'm her supervisor and she's making more than *me*! I complained to the corporate office and they said it was none of my business, and also that it was because she has a college degree. I *hate* this place!"

The entire operation had huge holes in it. Just after the first of the year someone called to ask about 1099's for people paid on commission. Oops! The company had never bothered to set up a system to do that. This left Mara and the rest of her department working late every day, as well as weekends, to throw the documents together before the Federal deadline for sending them out to the appropriate people (and the I.R.S.).

The late hours did seem to build more of a team atmosphere, and pretty soon there were regular happy hours after work. I was glad Mara was becoming better friends with her coworkers, and especially that she was socializing more. Unfortunately, this also soon led to a few **very** late arrivals home, sometimes long after midnight. I had already learned the tell-tale signs of Mara's infidelity (although exactly how far she was going with whoever she was messing with was still in question). Unlike previous occasions, Mara didn't come to me asking for forgiveness. She would just pass out in bed and not look me in the eye for a day or two. I figured it had to be someone (or multiple people) she worked with, and she was afraid that if she confessed, she would be forced to quit her job.

On one occasion she came home around 3am, and this time she cried and fell into my arms. She said a black man had hidden in the back of her car, held her at knifepoint when she left work, and then raped her. Afterwards he let her go. The whole thing sounded ludicrous to me; she hadn't called the police (and refused to now), the "rapist" had taken nothing of value even though she had nearly $100 in cash on her, and she said the whole thing had taken place in the car. This was a busy and well-lit parking lot, and I couldn't see how she could be held at knifepoint (and forced to have sex multiple times) for what was supposedly seven hours without anyone noticing anything. But I just held her and consoled her. Later she asked that I never mention it again, because it upset her too much. I dropped the subject, and so did she, forever. I never knew the truth - no matter what I suspected - and I never will.

About a month later, Mara began to complain of intestinal pain and frequent diarrhea. It wasn't every day, but it was a few times a week. We couldn't determine any kind of correlation between what she was eating and when she felt sick. Her father suggested Pepto Bismol and more vegetables, so we gave that a try. Mara already suffered from occasional migraines; those were terrible and would incapacitate her for an entire day. There was nothing she could do when she had one than lie in a quiet dark room and swallow painkillers. Those didn't really alleviate the pain, but they usually helped her fall asleep. Her mother had suffered from migraines for years, ones so bad that she needed an injection of strong painkiller to knock her out. Mara's migraines were awful but they didn't usually reach the point of her mother's, with hours of nausea and vomiting. And they only hit a few times a year. But this new digestive problem was a lot more frequent, and she was very sensitive about it. It's hard to call work and tell them you can't come in because you're shitting every twenty minutes. It's embarrassing and it also sounds like something you could find a way to work around.

Her Dad also gave her a prescription for some anti-diarrheal pills, and those would help for a day or so. But then she'd find herself in worse pain, because the diarrhea would start again but be trapped behind more solid waste, sort of like a clogged drain where pressure was building up behind the clog. Mara said that pain was ten times worse than it had been before, so she was reluctant to take the pills after giving them a try. Every time things in her tummy would calm down, we'd hope that was the end of it. But a few days later it would start again. Blood tests and parasite checks showed nothing.

This was Mara's first experience with the medical phenomenon I call "blissful ignorance." She would go to a doctor, who would find nothing wrong, and then they'd tell her "Aren't you happy? There's nothing wrong. That's good news." I suppose that's great news if you're concerned about a lump on your neck or you have tests done because of a pain in your chest. But when you're spending hours every day in the bathroom, **something is wrong**. "Nothing is wrong" is just another way of saying "I don't know what the problem is, and I have no ideas on how to proceed, so I'll just send you out the door." Granted, Mara was never the most agreeable patient. Having a doctor for a father led her to speak much more harshly and aggressively to other doctors than a typical patient, and usually that doesn't get you very good results. On the other hand, she tried to avoid doctors who were friends with her Dad because they would see her and then want to give their professional opinion to him instead of her. Her Dad tended to minimize her pain and misery, and massage whatever the doctors told him, so there was never clear communication from doctor to patient.

After a month of this, Mara said she needed to quit her job. The hours were too long, and the stress level there was way too high. She'd keep working, full-time if possible, but it would have to be something less stressful. General office work at a smaller company, or one where every problem didn't seem to be a crisis, sounded much more attractive to her. She felt that even with her illness, she could handle that. She bemoaned the bankruptcy of the coupon company where she'd had her previous job; she had been busy there but never stressed out or forced to work weekends.

Mara's resume was a bit thin, but she widened her employment periods to fill in empty gaps which had been left by periods of unemployment or jobs she didn't care to list. She wasn't about to use her au pair work as a reference, and she wasn't comfortable putting down the bank she had stolen from (even though as far as she knew, they had never discovered her theft). But Mara was still young, so having three jobs listed was a good balance: she had experience but didn't hop from job to job (at least according to the resume).

As I mentioned in the "Open Letter to Bart and Cheryl," it was at this point that Mara began her series of jobs. She seemed to be keenly skilled at job interviews, and would apply for (and accept) jobs that she had no business taking on. She'd claim any skill necessary to get herself in the door, and then she just hoped she'd figure out what she was doing as she went along. A few times she was actually able to handle most of the responsibilities assigned to her. But not always.

The most notable example is one I alluded to earlier. She was hired as a bookkeeper for a small company. On her first day they showed her around the office and gave her a set of ALL the keys. And when I say all the keys, I mean every last one: front door; master key to offices; key needed to open the safe (where the checkbooks were kept); and the key to every locking file cabinet and desk in the office. It looked like a janitor's ring, overflowing with keys. I don't even know if they had duplicates for some of the filing cabinets. She was told that the door keys, her desk key, and the safe key should be taken home with her each day, but the rest should be left locked in her desk or the safe.

She wasn't given any real training at this job, because according to her own description of her qualifications and skills, it should have been second nature to her. She sat down at a computer with a stack of receipts and invoices and a master ledger and put to work. Mara shuffled through the papers, reading some of the invoices. She wasn't even clear on what this company **did**, because during the interview she was too busy using whatever magic she conjured to get the job. She told me the secret was to ask a lot of questions about the person interviewing her, what they did, how long they had been with the company, and why they liked working there. People loved to talk about themselves, she reasoned, so if she let them do that for most of the interview, they would have a favorable impression of the experience. And being young, she wasn't seen as a threat or a possible nightmare. The other secret was **never** to ask about how much the pay was, vacation or sick time, and benefits. She let the interviewer bring those up, and sometimes they didn't until after she had accepted the job.

So, she sat at her desk until lunch, accomplishing nothing. Her boss stopped in and asked how everything was going, and Mara told her that it was going well; she had started a bit slow but now had her bearings. Then Mara got up and said she was going to run to a nearby fast food place to grab some lunch. She locked the door to her office and left.

…and then Mara drove straight home. She took the keys and never went back. They called the home phone, worried that she had gotten ill or had an accident. Mara wouldn't answer. When I got home, Mara explained what had happened. I begged her to call them and just say she had changed her mind about the job. She refused. I didn't know the name of the place so I couldn't call for her, and she didn't save any of their messages on the answering machine.

In the coming days the phone calls became angrier, then switched to actual begging. They didn't know what happened, but would she please just return the keys so they didn't have to go to the trouble of replacing every lock in the entire office? They even sent a few certified letters - which Mara refused to sign for – and a couple of letters by regular mail. I even offered to bring the keys there myself, but Mara told me she'd thrown them away. I don't know if that was true or not. All I know is they never got their keys, and eventually they stopped contacting her.

Nothing that outrageous happened again, but Mara continued a cycle of getting a job and then quitting within a few weeks. Each job was less responsibility, fewer hours, and less money. And through the cycle, her intestinal problems were getting worse. The frequency and urgency of her diarrhea increased, as did the pain. Some nights I would sit on the edge of the bathtub holding Mara's hand while she cried in pain and frustration. "Why is this happening to me?" she would ask. "I try to be a good person. What did I do?"

The last job she found was working the desk at a doctor's office, and she seemed to actually like working there. But she had to take one day off the first week, and two the next, and very quickly they called to tell her she was being let go. For some reason that really hit her hard. Maybe it was because her Dad was a doctor, and she made some kind of mental connection between her boss and him. Or maybe it was just that she thought a medical professional would be a bit more understanding about someone having medical problems. I'm sure they had some sympathy for her, but in the end, she had been hired to do a job and she wasn't showing up to do it. She had to be fired.

It was after this final job that Mara came to my crying one evening with her ultimatum. "We've been living together almost two years. We either have to get married or we need to split up." She gave no indication this conversation was even coming, and no further details about why she suddenly decided this was so important now as opposed to any other time. It really made no difference to me, because I wasn't planning on going anywhere. I'd signed up for this and now I was going to have to see it through until the bitter end, whatever that turned out to be; I was resigned to my fate. So, I agreed and said we'd get married. She made us go out to the mall the next day and spend a lot of money we didn't have on an engagement ring (which entirely ate up the available balance on a new credit card we had just gotten).

Next it was time to call the parents. I called my Dad and told him I had some news, and his actual response was "Please just don't tell me you're going to get married." In many ways I was following in his footsteps, and he did not want to see me suffer through mistakes he had made. But he didn't try to argue with me either; once I told him he resigned himself to my decision and that was that.

Mara's parents were a different case. I was surprised that they were so positive about the move, since they had never liked me and never felt I was good enough for their daughter. In retrospect I can better see that this marriage was to them a transfer of ownership: Mara had been their problem, and once we were married, she would officially be my problem. From that moment forward, I'd be around to take the blame for whatever went wrong.

Mara and her mother had never gotten along very well, but they were going to try and work together to assemble the big wedding Mara had always dreamed of, and the major social event her Mom would require from such an occasion. Numerous times since we met, Mara had told me how she'd dreamed all her life of walking down the aisle in a long white dress to "Here

Comes the Bride." If she could survive the inevitable disagreements with her Mom, at least she'd get that wish.

But first there was one more obstacle that had to be overcome. Mara's parents demanded a Jewish wedding, which meant I would need to convert. My Dad had been Jewish by birth but was now a self-avowed atheist. My mother was Presbyterian. In the Jewish faith, religion is passed by the mother: only if you are born to a Jewish mother are you Jewish at birth. For me, I'd have to look into conversion. A Rabbi that Mara's parents knew held a series of conversion classes, and while our timing was off by one week, we were able to enroll (you have to attend as a couple). As long as we passed the class and didn't miss more than one more class (you are allowed two absences, and we'd had one the first week) I could proceed to the next step. That would mean I could be officially converted in time for a wedding in May, which was the rough target they were all thinking about.

With Mara now unable to work, it was time to find somewhere smaller and less expensive to live. After looking around we located another condominium, this time in a five-story building right across the street from the Rahway train station. A married couple had bought the unit (as an investment, like last time) and wanted someone to rent to. It was only about $150 less than the Maplewood place but my commute would be easier and utilities would be less. The condo even had a small stackable washer and dryer so we wouldn't need to go to the laundromat any more.

In some ways the move felt like a step back. Smaller place. Mara was not working, and seemed to be getting sicker, but nobody could diagnose a specific problem. Her mental state was also weakening. We were going to get married, but that was nothing I was especially excited about; I knew it was going to be just another source if stress and disappointment for Mara no matter how well things went. The neighborhood we were moving to was noisier and a little rougher. But this was the path we needed to take. So, we packed everything up and headed off to Rahway.

I didn't feel especially positive, but as usual even my low expectations were not going to be met.

Chapter 14 - Rahway

For the second time, we were moving into a brand-new condo. But this one wasn't built nearly as well as the prior one. The building was an old factory of some sort, which had been refurbished. There was an elevator, which was a plus (especially during the moving process). Yet the entire apartment design was strange, and whether it was just the layout or also the way we chose to set things up, it led to another claustrophobic atmosphere.

The windows (one in the bedroom, two in the main room) all faced out towards the elevated train station. So, there was always a lot of activity and noise coming from that direction. They were also sealed terribly, and during the winter months you would feel the cold air blasting through the metal frames. Nothing about the place felt warm or cheery.

The kitchen was larger, which was a plus. It had a trash compactor, dishwasher, and the washer/dryer units. Having the trash compactor was a plus because it meant less trips down with garbage, but it also meant when it was time to bring the trash out it would be way too heavy for Mara to lift (not that she would have been expected to anyway). The real issue was the washer and dryer. They were tiny, noisy, and for whatever reason the condo had been built without any form of dryer vent. Instead the owners had supplied a plastic device which you fitted to the end of the dryer hose. By keeping the plastic thing filled with water to a certain level, it was supposed to catch the dryer lint in the water and just have the hot air blow freely. It was a cheap, badly-designed accessory, and the lint would blow all over the apartment no matter how much water we kept in there. A small amount of dryer lint would get caught up in it, but not much. This left a musty "dryer vent" smell to the place year-round.

The main room was positioned at a 90-degree angle to the kitchen, and was long but not very wide. It simply didn't lend itself to being a comfortable place to sit or do anything. It was obvious we'd be spending most of our free time in the bedroom, where our only color TV was kept (and where the cable for the TV was hooked up). Everything went in the bedroom: TV, stereo, computer desk, bed. The living room had the wall units and couch, but with no stereo or television the only reason to sit out there was if you were playing a game or something.

Despite our financial problems and Mara's health, Mara wanted to get more cats. Rags was getting old, and Mara wanted more feline company for while she was stuck at home. So, we adopted a black cat named Ubber, and a few months later a little tiger-stripe named Tigger. Ubber was Mara's favorite; when she was younger she'd had a black cat named Midnight who had been her "best friend." Midnight got outside and was run over by a car, and Mara never got over that. She still carried a photo in her wallet. Ubber was her new Midnight, and he obliged by having that cuddly lap-cat personality so many black cats seem to carry with them. Ubber and Tigger also became fast friends, with one of them running out into the living room crying for the other one to come play, which the other immediately would.

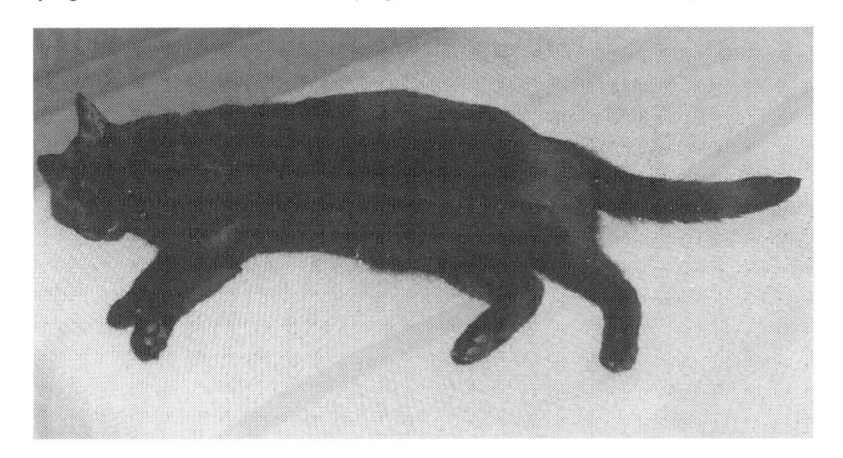

Biff liked Tigger, but he was not a fan of Ubber. He'd chase him, trap him under a table or chair, and swat at him with his paws like a boxer. Ubber was very passive and never tried to fight back. Biff also tried to bite Ubber when he had the chance. He was really a bully, and it made Mara upset since Ubber was never anything but sweet to everyone.

For me, work was very stressful but I was doing okay. The commute required me leaving around 530am every day but at least I only had to walk across the street to catch the train. The only trick was the PATH trains were timed in such a way that if you didn't get off the NJ Transit train quickly when it pulled in to Newark and jog or sprint to the PATH train to make it before the doors closed. Sometimes you would have five minutes, but often you'd have less than one, and if you missed that PATH train you had to wait twenty minutes for the next one to leave. It became a bit of a contest to see which regular commuters would get up and stand near the train exit first. Week after week people would stand up earlier and earlier to be closer to the front of the line. It bordered on the ridiculous.

Since I took the train to work, Mara had the car for whenever she needed it during the week, although she rarely went anywhere at this stage. She would go on occasional job interviews, but she must have lost her magic touch. Suddenly there was nothing out there for her. It was just as well, because she was spending at least one day out of every four in the bathroom. There's no way she could accomplish a job in that condition, and it wasn't like she could work part time and schedule her sick days around that. She never knew when it was going to hit...and we still had no idea what *it* was.

Twice a week when I got home from work we would rush off to conversion class. It was rather simple: learning some Biblical stuff I was already generally familiar with, some history, ceremonies and prayers, and how to write and read simple Hebrew. The class had a sort of group feeling, but we didn't seem to belong (as usual). Some of the other people in the class were downright rude, or even denigrating what they were learning. It made me wonder why they were going to the class at all. A man in his 40's was making his wife go, but he himself showed up late every week, yawned, loudly opened or crumpled bags of food (which we weren't supposed to be eating in there), and got on everyone's nerves. He also seemed to enjoy arguing with the Rabbi, and saying the "hocus pocus stuff" in the religion was pointless to him.

Mara hated the class. She didn't need to learn anything (since she wasn't the one converting and she had gone to Hebrew School and learned it all years ago), so it felt like a waste of time to her. I would have been fine going by myself, but the rules required both of us to attend. When there were about four weeks left Mara put her foot down one night and refused to attend. "We're not going tonight, we're staying home." When I pointed out that we only had this one absence left, and she could easily get sick and force us to miss one of the remaining classes, she crossed her arms, put a determined look on her face, and started shaking her head back slowly from side to side. The entire time she kept declaring "I don't WANNA go, I don't WANNA go!" At first it was annoying but by the third minute of this I was laughing hysterically. For some reason she had hit on just the right level of outrageous humor in her childish stance.

"Okay, okay, you win. We'll stay home."

She ran over and hugged me. It had been a while since she seemed that happy. I guess she just wanted to feel like she won in something again. Later that night when the Rabbi called to warn us that we could not miss any more classes, Mara acknowledged that but also pointed out that she felt that was arbitrary and unfair. "Two couples in there show up 45 minutes late every week. Even after missing two classes we've spent more time in there than they have." But she knew we'd have to attend the rest of the classes. And we did.

The only other time Mara seemed to leave the apartment was when we occasionally went to the movies, or when she had to accompany her mother on some wedding planning business. Those plans were going about as badly as I had anticipated. Mara and her Mom were oil and water, or more accurately gasoline and a match. They couldn't agree on anything, and that would lead to the battle of "it's my wedding" versus "we're paying for it." Mara's parents were going to foot the bill for the wedding, as was tradition, but because of that they wanted to control almost every aspect of it. More than once she came home in tears, and I figured she would threaten to cancel the entire wedding a minimum of three times before everything was over.

In the meantime, whether it was stress or not, her intestinal problems were getting worse. She was going to the bathroom at least eight times a day, and each trip in there was painful and long. Surprisingly, she wasn't losing any weight in the process, which I couldn't really understand. How could she have diarrhea again and again without suffering some kind of weight loss or malnutrition? I made sure she drank plenty of fluids so she would become dehydrated. Mara "couldn't" drink water by itself, so she was drinking a lot of Sprite or other soda instead. I knew that amount of sugar wasn't healthy, but it was better than winding up the hospital with an IV in her arm. But at the rate things were going, that was exactly where she was going to wind up.

Finally, on her third gastroenterologist (all of which were friends of colleagues of her Dad), Mara was scheduled to have a colonoscopy. The doctor had decided that at least that way he could get a better idea of what was going on inside her. We scheduled it for a Monday so that I could keep an eye on her the day before and make sure she followed the pre-procedure instructions. That was a battle in itself. There were two steps involved. First was a gallon jug that had some white powder in it. It was to be filled with water, and then Mara was supposed to drink eight ounces every 20 or 30 minutes until it was all gone. This would clean out her intestines in advance (which I didn't think was especially necessary given how much she was going, but the doctor knows best). She was allowed to have a few popsicles along the way to hide the taste, but only ones with no real fruit so she was sticking with clear liquids.

I set the kitchen timer and kept bringing her glasses of the stuff whenever the timer went off. I quickly noticed that the two times I didn't stay in the living room with her, Mara's level of complaining about the taste was much less. A quick examination of the plant next to the couch confirmed my suspicions: Mara was dumping the stuff out if I didn't watch her drink it. It was like I was dealing with a little kid, but as usual I couldn't help but laugh. So, I had to babysit and stood over her as she drank each glass, her nose plugged, and then grabbed for the popsicle to cover her tongue in flavored sugar. It was a slow process, but eventually she finished the whole jug. I think I aged a year or so before it was over.

Then the vile stuff began to do its thing. Mara could hear loud gurgles and bubbling from her insides. It was loud enough to hear over the television. It immediately reminded both of us of the noises from "Lard Ass" Hogan's stomach in the movie "Stand by Me" during the pie eating contest. Pretty soon Mara had to run to the bathroom, and I was ready for a disaster.

Surprisingly, while the urgency was tremendous and the results gross, Mara was happy to report there really wasn't much pain involved for a change. It all came out so easily, I guess aside from how sore her intestines were, there wasn't enough work involved to result in the agony she had been experiencing. For the rest of the evening there were countless quick dashes to the bathroom, but at least Mara wasn't crying. She was embarrassed, but not in great distress.

The next morning Mara endured a bit more embarrassment as I had to give her a pre-packaged enema to finish the job. I tried my best to be as calm and nonchalant about it; for me it wasn't a big deal, despite never having done it before. It was just something that had to be done, and that was that. Mara felt utterly humiliated by it. I guess it was simply a violation of a very private thing. If we knew how things were going to work out, she would have tried to get used to the idea.

I took off work that day, and Mara and I went to the hospital where the colonoscopy was being done. I think her mother had offered to go as well, but Mara wasn't going to have any of that. The presence of anyone in her family could only make things worse. Her father was on staff at the hospital so he'd be around at some point afterwards to discuss the results with the doctor, but Mara had been pretty strong expressing to him that she wanted any news explained to her first, and to her Dad second. This gastroenterologist had a very good bedside manner, and seemed to quickly grasp the dynamic of the family. He knew he would have to give a medical version to Mara's Dad (and she had no real issue with that), but he would also treat her as a patent first and the daughter of a friend second. That was a very welcome change from the prior two doctors.

I paced in the waiting room while Mara had the colonoscopy done. I wasn't that familiar with the procedure. All I really knew was they'd put Mara to sleep and stick a long scope up her butt, and look around. I didn't know what they were looking for, or what they might possibly find. That had never really been discussed. I suppose the doctor didn't want to list various results; no reason to make things worse until he saw whatever he saw.

We had been warned that it could take three or four hours, but I think the doctor was back in only ninety minutes. He greeted me and told me everything went fine. "I was able to see the problem almost right away," he said. "Mara has Crohn's Disease. I took a few biopsies to confirm it, but I'm certain that's what we're dealing with. I'll explain more later when she is in recovery, but it's not cancer or anything like that."

I had no idea what to think, because I'd never heard of Crohn's Disease. I didn't even know how to spell it. Today you see occasional commercials for new medications meant to treat the symptoms, so I suppose more people have heard of it, and associate it with diarrhea. But back in 1988 it was a complete unknown to me.

When the three of us met an hour later to go into the results in more detail, there wasn't a lot more that I learned. Crohn's was a chronic inflammation of the intestines accompanied by often painful diarrhea. Nobody knew what caused it, and there was no cure. The only two medications sufferers used to try and control it were corticosteroids and sulfa drugs, along with anti-nausea and anti-diarrhea medications to try and alleviate the digestive symptoms. The doctor mentioned that weight loss often accompanied the disease, and at that Mara sarcastically exclaimed "well at least I'll have that to look forward to."

"No, you probably won't have that" he replied. "Your Crohn's appears to be only in your large intestine, and most of the weight loss occurs when it is in the small intestine and interfering with the absorption of nutrients. Besides," he added, "the steroids will probably made you gain some weight, among other side effects."

There really wasn't much of a treatment plan. Mara would start with a high dose of the steroids and immediately begin a slow tapering off, with the hope that she could adjust to either only take them during extreme bouts of Crohn's, or at worst maintain a low dose. She'd also take the sulfa drug (Sulfasalazine) daily. With luck she would see improvement and alleviate most of her pain and diarrhea, with the help of anti-diarrheal drugs used in moderation (to avoid any constipation). But unless it went into remission, the problem wouldn't completely go away.

Long-term, there was the possibility she would need some kind of resection of the large intestine (a colectomy) if one particular area became too damaged or sever ulcers appeared. She'd also need to monitor her foods to see what correlation there was between diet and the severity of her symptoms. Anything that made her sicker would need to be avoided.

The doctor also told us about the Crohn's and Colitis Foundation, which was a group that was raising money for research and tried to educate sufferers and the public about the disease. He gave us a flyer from the Foundation and suggested we order the book they offered which gave an overview of the disease and offered some tips on living with it and dealing with it (both for the one with Crohn's and for family members).

We went home and ordered the book, and set about filling Mara's prescriptions and beginning her treatment. We had to mark up the calendar with her daily steroid doses because the tapering process was complicated and it had been strongly impressed on us that it was imperative to do it properly. The steroids were not good for her long-term, and if you cut back too quickly you were sure to start a flare up of Crohn's. On the other hand, if you stayed at too high a dose for too long you could become steroid dependent and be unable to stop the medication or even lower your dose very much.

I'd give Mara her morning pills before I left for work, and her evening pills before bed. She felt much more comfortable leaving me in charge of it. This was the procedure we would use for the rest of our time together. She had a general idea of what to take and how much she needed to take but she preferred to leave the counting and doses and precision in my hands. That was fine with me as it also let me feel assured that she had taken what she was supposed to *when* she was supposed to.

A week or so later I found Mara looking in the mirror, poking at her face. The medication seemed to be helping so far, at least to the point where she wasn't in agony all day, every day. "What's going on?" I asked.

"I don't know. There's something different about my face but I can't figure out what it is."

"Well, I did notice your skin is looking a touch yellower. Remember the pharmacy said that sulfasalazine might do that to you. You're also supposed to avoid getting too much sun, although I don't remember what happens if you do."

"No, I saw that too. But that's not it. There's something else. I just can't figure it out. I look **wrong**."

A few days later the book on Crohn's Disease from the Foundation arrived, and Mara sat in the bedroom reading it while I was making some dinner. After a while I heard her yelling. "Get in here! Get in here!"

I rushed in and found her back in the bathroom, glaring in the mirror. "Look at me. Look!"

"I don't see it, what's wrong?"

She held up the book and thrust it towards me. "Moon face! That's what I have. These fucking steroids give me moon face!" And she threw the book across the bedroom.

And once she had said it, I could see it. I could see what had been wrong, but which neither of us could decipher. Her face had gotten rounder, mainly around the bottom and near her chin. It was bigger, and rounder, like a big moon.

And while Mara laid on the bed sobbing to herself, I knew deep down that this was only going to be the first of many revelations about the disease – and the treatment – that would upset her greatly.

Chapter 15 - And the Hits Just Keep on Coming

Mara had never been thin. I learned later that some people in High School used to tease her about being fat, but at that age I never saw her that way. She had beautiful curves and very large breasts, so naturally she wasn't going to seem svelte. But her large chest was always an issue for her. She didn't like how big they were, and especially how heavy they were. A doctor had told Mara that her breasts had a lot more flash and less fat than was typical, which made them heavier. She had long had worries about how they might affect her back in the long run, and how stretched out they'd get. As a result of these fears, and the general feeling of being overweight, after graduating she decided to have a breast reduction.

I'm sure there have been advancements in breast reduction surgery since back then, and also more standardization of pre-operative procedure. I was against the surgery, simply because I felt there were too many things that could go wrong. But Mara's parents supported the decision, and this was before we ever lived together. As usual, Mara's mind was made up and she wasn't about to change it.

The surgery seemed to go without any major problems, and other than caring for the incision areas and the drainage bags she had to have for a few weeks afterward, Mara was pretty happy with things. That didn't last. The scars were much larger than she had ever imagined; they not only went under her breasts (along where a bra's underwire would be) but also around her areolas and in a vertical line connecting the areola to the incision underneath the breast. She also realized that she had lost nearly all sensation in one of her breasts, at least at the skin level. On top of all that, she didn't think they were small enough. But there was no way she was going to go through that all over again, especially considering these unexpected issues.

Now, a few years later, her worst fears were being realized: she was gaining weight and watching her breasts grow as large as they had been originally. This new weight gain could be attributed to a few factors. First, Mara was not exercising, partly out of how sick she's been and partly because of how depressed she was. She had joined a gym soon after she started working at Coldwell Bankers, but only went once or twice before all the problems with Crohn's started. Instead she spent a lot of time fighting with the gym to cancel her membership and get some of the money back (which she was eventually able to accomplish with a few medical notes).

Second in the list of factors was her new dose of steroids. They can make you retain a lot of water, lose weight slower, and in some cases (including hers) they can increase your appetite. Mara felt as if she was blowing up like a balloon. The more she read about steroids the more she hated taking them. Long-term there were great risks associated with them, but even in the short run she had to deal with her moon face, a sudden increase in acne, and many other sources of unhappiness. Unfortunately, it seemed her body was not going to allow her to stop taking them, or even cut the dose as low as her doctor preferred. Every time she dropped below a certain level, the Crohn's would flare up terribly. After a while it was decided to stop with the yo-yo of her dosage and just leave her at 20mg a day until she had time to adjust. Then she would try a very slow and gradual tapering again, with hopes that it would work at last.

The third factor was Mara's diet. It was never a thing of perfection, but with Crohn's it quickly turned even further south. One of our earliest discoveries was that fruits and vegetables, especially uncooked, were a major wrecking ball to her digestive tract. That meant one of her favorite foods – and one of the few healthy things she ate on a regular basis – was out: salad. Mara could go on a salad kick for says, and wouldn't even need to smother it with dressing. Now that was forbidden for her. Even cooked vegetables were a problem, but less of a disaster. But raw fruits and vegetables would need to be avoided at all costs, at least for the time being.

In fact, what we soon discovered was that the more processed or unhealthy a food was, the easier she could tolerate it. Chips? No problem. Cookies? Keep them coming. Crackers or snack mixes? Better than real food. Things like Twinkies would actually seem to settle her stomach down. Maybe it was something in the white filling, I don't know. But junk food went down easily and came out with less trouble than anything else. So she started to lean heavily on that. No pun intended, that made her weight a bigger issue.

In an effort to counteract some of the dietary issues, Mara decided to cut out soda. She had been told that carbonated beverages could aggravate her stomach pain, so except for the occasional Diet Cherry 7-Up, she started drinking a lot of Crystal Light drinks that she mixed in a pitcher from water and their prepared powders. I was as encouraging as I could be about that, since dehydration was a danger, and also because the more sugar she avoided at this point the less weight she'd put on, regardless of what the steroids were doing to her.

Sadly, as the Crohn's medications began to at least lessen her distress, her migraines because a much more frequent occurrence. This was a different kind of suffering for Mara. She'd take anti-nausea pills and spend the day in bed with a black cloth over her face, swallowing painkiller after painkiller. I don't think they really did much to alleviate the pain; it was more just that she hoped they would make her so woozy and drowsy that she would be able to sleep. On those days I spent my time reading if at home, because the slightest noise could set her head throbbing again.

Mara visited a few neurologists, but none had any new ideas for her other than to try an assortment of odd medications that had no FDA approval to treat migraines but which had gained a reputation for occasionally helping. One was a sinus medication, one a different form of painkiller…they didn't make any difference. Her latest neurologist suggested she keep a food diary for him, to try and narrow down if there was some sort of food triggering these. Mara did it despite her insistence that she was avoiding everything she had been told: red wine, nuts (especially tropical nuts), chocolate, even MSG. These days you don't find monosodium glutamate (MSG) in much of anything, but back then it was an ingredient in many snacks and chips, and a regular ingredient in Chinese food. Some Chinese restaurants had begun to advertise themselves as "No MSG" as public perception to the "flavor enhancer" was growing more and more negative. That was a far cry from just a few years earlier when you would find it included in the spice section of every grocery store; a brand name, "Accent," had even been regularly advertised on television. We checked labels to avoid it, because it was clearly a trigger for her.

At Mara's next appointment, the neurologist went over the food diary and could find very little to comment on. Everything seemed to be in order. But he did realize Mara had said nothing about what she drank all day. The "food" diary was supposed to include food and drink, not just solid food. Mara apologized and explained what she drank most days: a bit of flavored seltzer water (only a bit, to avoid the carbonation), one cup of coffee (which wasn't great for her stomach, but caffeine was thought to help with migraines), a glass or two of diet soda, and plenty of the Crystal Light drinks. They were sugar-free after all, and therefore a great substitute for the sugary drinks she used to consume.

The neurologist looked a bit unhappy at having to break some news to Mara. "Those drinks, and the diet soda, all have NutraSweet in them. For a lot of migraine sufferers that's a definite migraine trigger. I'm afraid you've been giving yourself all these terrible migraines by drinking that stuff. I suggest you cut all artificial sweeteners out of your diet for the time being and see if there is any improvement. I think there will be."

On the drive home, I expected Mara would be happy about finally having a possible solution to the sudden increase in migraine frequency. But she wasn't happy at all. She was miserable, and angry. Angry that she had been taking pain pills with drinks that were causing the headaches. Angry that her one successful attempt to keep some of her weight gain under control was being taken away from her. And angry that she had to be so careful about everything she ate and drank, all the time. I think that was the biggest source of her anger: that she was losing the little bit of control she had over her life.

"I am **not** going to get *stuck* drinking plain water for the rest of my life" she hissed to herself as I drove along silently. "Real fruit juice makes me sick. I can't have anything diet. Fine. I'll just go back to soda, fruit punch, and whatever kind of sugar water I can find."

I didn't have anything I could say, and I didn't want to set off her anger to a worse extent. So I just drove us home. She sat and seethed quietly, tears slowly running down her cheeks.

"I hate being alive" I heard her mutter as we pulled into our parking lot.

Chapter 16 - Breakdown

Things just seemed to be going from bad to worse for Mara, and for me. She was depressed, in pain, gaining weight, and didn't want to do anything but lie in bed. Her only happiness was spending time with the cats, which was being dimmed a bit as Rags was really showing her age. Ubber was her constant companion, sleeping with her in bed at all hours (when he wasn't playing with Tigger or hiding from Biff's bullying).

While a terribly sweet and intelligent cat, Ubber had one problem: he would not crouch when he used the litter box. It wasn't intentional, but half the time when he peed it would spray out of the box and onto the surface below. We weren't really sure about how to handle it. Covered litter boxes weren't a common thing back then, so we didn't have that as a choice. The best we could do was move the litter box into a closet, and cover the floor below with shower curtain liners and trash bags in multiple layers to protect the carpet beneath. They we scattered litter around here to assist in soaking up his mess. Over time he got a bit better, to where he would start in a crouched position and slowly raised his hind legs. It wasn't a great situation, and the smell was not pleasant when he missed, but there was no way we were going to get rid of him.

I kept trying to convince Mara to go for psychiatric help, but she wasn't interested. She had spent some time going to a therapist that her parents hooked her up with, and that was a complete waste of time. Her problems were far too deep for this woman to handle, and because the therapist also communicated privately with Mara's parents there were things Mara didn't feel comfortable discussing with her (such as her sexual abuse, since her Dad didn't know anything about that). As far as Mara was concerned, no therapist was going to help. And the idea of psychiatric medications was something she rejected completely when I suggested them; she'd heard too many horror stories about MAO inhibitors and similar drugs. I didn't want to push that side of the idea, because if she got her back up, she'd never change her mind later. It was better to leave the door open for the future.

One day while I was at work Mara called me in a panic. She said someone was in the apartment with her. She was in the kitchen and someone was in the apartment because the bedroom door was closed and she didn't close it. She refused to go open it and look. She wouldn't even call the police – or let me call them – because she also thought it was possible a ghost or some kind of demon was hiding in the bedroom. I could hear in her voice how unhinged she was. I had to leave work and come home. By coincidence (and exactly as I would have expected, given the way I always felt luck was against me) leaving the office that day cost a good deal of money in a project I was working on. Her timing was tuned to be **perfectly** terrible. The day prior or the day after would not have mattered.

I made some excuse about a water leak or something else that Mara couldn't handle, left work, and spent the next couple of hours making my way home. I was angry and very frustrated. When I got home, Mara was standing in the kitchen with a knife in each hand, shaking slightly and looking like a crazed killer from some horror movie. "I know there's a ghost in there. Or a demon. **Something** is in there. It closed the door and thought I wouldn't notice. But I did, haha. I did. It's not going to get **me**."

I told Mara to wait and I walked over to the bedroom. The door **was** closed, as she said. The door to the bedroom opened inwards, so to me there would only be two possible ways for the door to close without Mara having done it herself. The first was pulling the bathroom door closed; they were only a few feet apart and sometimes closing the bathroom could cause a bit of air suction that pulled the bedroom door closer to being closed. But I had never seen that cause the bedroom door to close fully, only to make it move a few inches. The second was that someone – or something – had closed it from the inside. In that case the culprit would still be in the bedroom, as there was no other exit from the room except the bedroom window (which was three stories up with no fire escape).

The other possibility was that Mara had closed the door herself and forgotten, but even with her crazed state I didn't see that as likely. We never closed the bedroom door; there just wasn't any reason to. It was situated so the only way you could see into the room was by walking into a small hallway that also allowed access to the bathroom, and even if you walked into that hallway you could only see a very small amount of the bedroom – the area where the dresser and television stood. So not even privacy concerns would make anyone close the door.

Under normal circumstances I would have been laughing as I approached the bedroom door. But between being so angry about having to come home for this, and the wreck Mara was at the moment, I was somehow stuck between nervousness and confusion. There were too many emotions and thoughts at once. I crept forward stealthily and grabbed the doorknob. Slowly and silently turning it, I kept the door pulled closed so if there actually was anyone in there, they would be unaware of my presence. Finally, with a deep breath, I pushed the door open and walked quickly inside.

The television was on, but muted. The window was closed. The light was on. And there, staring back at me, were three pairs of confused cat eyes. One of them brushed by me quickly to get to the litter box. I checked the closet, just to be sure, but there was nothing. It was pretty obvious to me: the door closed slightly when Mara closed the bathroom door, and then the dopey cats had been playing and pushed it the rest of the way closed. Reality had returned; Mara was acting crazy and had completely overacted to something benign.

I tried to comfort her and explain what had happened, but she remained unconvinced (although she did put the two knives away). At first, she protested that we should leave and stay at a motel for the night. Then she changed that argument into an insistence that she would sleep on the couch in the living room so she wouldn't be within reach of whatever demonic being had closed the bedroom door. As the night wore on, she came in to watch television, and finally went to sleep despite herself.

This episode was just further evidence that Mara's mental state was getting worse and worse. I was at a loss of what to do. I tried suggesting a psychiatrist, medication, and even her being hospitalized to make sure there was nothing physically wrong with her (since she seemed to reject the idea that she was losing her grip on reality; I would have preferred hospitalization in a mental facility until they could stabilize her). I asked if she wanted to call her parents or someone, but not only wouldn't she do that, she demanded I not call them, and threatened to hurt herself if I did. I did call her Mom to let her know about Mara's unstable state of mind, but she seemed to brush it off as most likely Mara just being a drama queen.

I kept working on Mara and trying to wear her down over the next few days. Then one day I arrived home from work and found Mara's mother in the bedroom with her. Mara had been crying, and her mother announced that Mara had agreed to go check herself in to a well-regarded mental hospital in the area. Her Mom wanted her to go that night, but Mara said she wouldn't go until the following evening but that she would go voluntarily.

This was very good news, although it was scary in its own way. I didn't know what Mara's diagnosis would be, or if she'd get the kind of help she needed. I was both relieved and nervous. Of course, I was also a little suspicious that Mara wouldn't follow through with going the next day. I started convincing her it would be better to go immediately. It was a Thursday, and checking in on a Friday might mean sitting around doing nothing therapeutic all weekend. I explained that it had nothing to do with trust, just with it being better for her to check in tonight instead of waiting. Plus, she needed to have them approve and organize her Crohn's medications, and she didn't want them cut off for a few days, did she?

Deep inside, I also found myself a bit angry. Mara's mother was giving me all kinds of dirty looks, as if this was somehow my fault. Either I had made her this way, or I had allowed her to get this way and done nothing to try and get her help. I didn't know what she thought, or what she had been told, but the whole attitude about going to the hospital was one of it being something Mara's mother (or parents) had come up with and presented to Mara. There was no recognition of all the work I'd been putting in just trying to maintain her life, and desperately moving her closer to accepting treatment or hospitalization. Instead of receiving any credit for my efforts, I felt like I was being blamed. Blamed for everything.

We packed up a bag for Mara and drove out to the hospital. Mara's mother followed in her own car. Mara was especially worried about the cats and how they'd be, but I assured her I would take good care of them. There was no way of knowing how long she would be gone; Mara had this mental picture of a few weeks, and I didn't want to say anything to break that over-optimistic view. The key was to get her to check herself in. Everything else could be dealt with afterwards.

Mara was still on her Dad's insurance at this point. Because he was a doctor and affiliated with many hospitals, his policy was especially good and allowed children to still be covered a few years longer than normal (if they had no insurance available from work or some other source). The cost would almost entirely be covered up to 45 days, with another 15 days possible if they deemed it necessary. This was the last time we'd approach a situation like this – or any health problems Mara would have - without cost being a primary issue.

The check-in process was an emotional roller coaster in itself. Neither of us had any experience with mental hospitals (my mother had been in them numerous times but I had been too young to know anything about what had gone on there) so the administrator had to go over all kinds of information with Mara. Not surprisingly, she fought or complained about every issue.

I have to commend the gentleman who was doing her initial intake. The man had the patience of a Saint. Obviously he had been through this routine many times before, and kept focused on the goal at hand: get Mara to sign the paperwork admitting herself for a 72-hour evaluation. All of her nasty remarks, complaints, and rude comments were met with a syrupy-sweet smile and a calm, reasoned tone. He mentioned she might want to have some money for the snack machines; Mara starting bitching about charging for snacks considering what it cost to be there in the first place. He explained they needed to go through her belongings carefully to look for contraband; Mara threw a fit and accused him of not trusting her. They removed some nail clippers and other such items and said they would need to be held by the staff and she could sign them out and use them with permission; Mara bitched about having to get permission to use her own property, and that she wasn't some little kid. No matter what she said or did, he just kept moving the process along. At last it was all done, the paperwork had been signed, and Mara was officially admitted. We hugged and kissed her goodbye.

Outside I gave her Mom a hug and started driving home. There was less blame hanging over my head at that moment, if only because seeing Mara falling apart bit by bit during the intake process was enough of a shock to make her stop thinking about how everything was my fault. By the time they had finished going through her stuff, Mara was clutching one of her shirts and muttering "this is mine, this is mine." At that moment nothing was ever clearer than the fact that she truly belonged in the hospital, at least until they could stabilize her and figure out what course of treatment was appropriate.

As I made my way back to Rahway I started to cry. The stress of the whole situation, and being forced to keep my fears and emotions inside so I could focus on Mara and her needs, had been eating me up. Now I was finally able to let a bit of that out. It wouldn't be the first time I cried on the way to or from the mental hospital.

I got back home and gave each of the cats a hug and a kiss. I knew they'd be fine; they were used to having Mara home during the day, but they were cats and they didn't require constant supervision. Poor Rags felt bonier than usual. I made a mental note to see about taking him to the vet. I wasn't sure when I would have the time to do that, and money had been very tight lately, but obviously he needed to be checked out. I didn't like the idea of him suffering needlessly, and on the other hand I wanted to do what I could to make sure he was kept comfortable until Mara came back home. It was just another thing to worry about.

For now, the focus had to be on Mara and her mental health. I didn't know what was going to happen, how long she would be gone, or what her prognosis would be. I also had no idea that this hospitalization would soon open up an entirely new can of worms.

Chapter 17 - It's a Madhouse!

Mara wasn't allowed visitors over her first weekend, but I did speak to her on the phone a few times. She was more coherent than she had been during intake, but still very angry and resistant to being in the hospital at all. I recognized that this was going to be a constant battle during her stay, and I would need to use whatever leverage I had, at least until she reached a point where she saw a bit of progress.

I had already figured out two paths of leverage. The first was that she had no choice for the first 72 hours. She had signed that right away, allowing herself to be committed for assessment during that period. It didn't matter how much she hated the place, the staff, or anything else. She had to stay at least for three days. They were legally permitted to restrain her or even sedate her in order to keep her there and stop her from harming herself or others. As much as Mara was unhappy about that, she understood it and wasn't threatening to try and escape or anything of the sort.

The second piece of leverage I had was one I put on the table very quickly: if she left the hospital against medical advice, insurance would decline to cover the hospitalization. That would mean we would owe thousands and thousands of dollars in medical bills, with absolutely no way to pay them. Considering Mara's opinion of her parents and their reluctance to ever do anything she considered helpful, she knew better than to believe even for a moment that they'd pay for the bill, despite the fact that they could afford it. So, the threat of financial ruin was an effective deterrent.

But it wasn't enough to keep her from complaining and arguing. And Mara had plenty of things she wanted to complain about, with varying degrees of legitimacy. The first was the fact that the hospital had decided to place her in the eating disorder ward. They had unofficially diagnosed Mara as a bulimic because of her weight gain and her tendency to binge when she was unhappy or upset. Mara wanted to argue that since she didn't purge, she couldn't be bulimic. And she preferred to operate under the delusion that only her medication and limited choice of foods were to blame for her weight gain. Binge Eating Disorder was not an official diagnosis back then, but it was clear that she used food as a mechanism to fight emotional pain, so I saw some logic to it.

Mara wasn't just upset at the idea of having an eating disorder. She also did not want to be on that ward because the rules there were much more restrictive. There was higher security, closer inspection of personal belongings, and just basic intrusiveness of every inch of your personal space. This was mainly due to all the anorexics on the ward. They were always trying to sneak laxatives or other items in so they could eat the minimum they were ordered to and not have it affect them physically. There had been a recent scandal about some kind of laxative tea making the rounds between patients, so all the security measures had just been tightened before Mara got there.

Because she was in the eating disorder ward, it was also going to take longer for Mara to earn passes for a few hours off the hospital grounds. There was simply less trust given to those patients, so it took more work and more time to earn privileges. Mara wasn't even allowed to have the door to her room closed during her first week or so (the doors had no locks, but staff wanted to be able to see everything at all times, so nobody could secretly purge or take medications they weren't supposed to).

If a patient argued too much, caused trouble, or had an emotional outburst, they would be put in the dreaded "quiet room." I guess nearly every mental ward had its own version of a quiet room. Padded walls, a bed with straps; it was meant as a place they could put you until you calmed down. If all you needed was time, they just restrained you. If you were more out of control, sedation would also be given. I've learned that a lot of eating disorders are partially based on the need to have control over a part of your life. When everything feels beyond you, you can still control what you do – or do not – put in your body. The quiet room was the antithesis of that: a room where you had zero control over what you did or what happened to you. It was a place nobody wanted to go, even if the patients didn't fully understand why the idea was so frightening.

I started coming to visit Mara after work on each night that had visiting hours. During the day there was group therapy, some other activities, and one-on-one time with some of the staff. Patients didn't spend much time with the doctors or psychiatrists. They had quickly put Mara on a dose of antidepressants to try and stabilize and boost her mood, but it was too early for those to have any noticeable effect. According to Mara, group therapy provided insight into a few of the other patents but wasn't doing much for her. The best progress she was making came though talking to one particular nurse on staff, and a few of the patients directly.

One night a week there was family therapy, which I was invited to attend since we lived together. Mara's parents decided we shouldn't all go together, but that I would go one time and they'd go the next. I don't know if that's because they were worried about blame being tossed around, or if perhaps the hospital had suggested it. Attending the family therapy was eye opening for me for a few reasons. First, I realized that a sister of one of my High School classmates was a patient. That was only important in that it made the entire experience seem a bit less scary, or perhaps less freakish. "Normal" people and their family members could wind up in the mental hospital too. It also made things a little uncomfortable for me once or twice when I saw people I knew come to visit this patient. I didn't want them to see me...it wasn't that I was embarrassed that Mara was there, but they weren't people I knew well or was friends with, and I wasn't in the mental mindset to have pleasant small-talk with people that wouldn't have given me the time of day a few years ago.

The other thing I learned because of this particular patient, in family therapy, was a lot about enabling and minimizing. Her parents were adamant that their daughter wasn't "sick" like these other patients. It was something else, something minor that could be dealt with without medication or therapy. One week her mother came with an article describing this new theory on seasonal depression, caused in rare cases by not getting enough sunlight in the winter. "I'm sure this is what she has. She's always better in the summer." It made me feel sad and sorry and roll my eyes all at the same time. Denial can be a powerful force.

My routine seemed both physically and emotionally exhausting at this point. I'd get up at 5am, care for the cats, walk across the street, and take the train into work. When I got home I'd go upstairs, check on the cats, and drive out to the hospital to visit or attend group sessions. It was dark when I left home and dark when I returned. My diet was terrible: for dinner I would either grab a Big Mac at McDonald's (which I have never liked before and never wanted since this time), or stop off at the Summit Diner after visiting for eggs or a burger. If I stopped, I was almost always the only customer there. Work was busy and that kept my sanity during the day, but nights were long and lonely. I generally cried in the car on the way back to Rahway. By the time I walked into the apartment I was spent, and collapsed in bed.

      One night I returned from work to find an evil odor in the apartment. Rags was lying on the kitchen floor on his side, purring, and next to him was a huge pile of vile-smelling diarrhea. I knew the purr was some kind of endorphin release to alleviate pain and discomfort. His time had come, or had come days ago and I was simply too damn busy or oblivious to notice his rapid decline. I felt sick and guilty. And now I had to call the hospital to let Mara know that Rags was dying and I needed to take him to the vet immediately to be put to sleep.

      As you can imagine, that was a conversation which did not go well. Mara was hysterical, and wanted me to wait at home while she tried to convince the staff to let her come outside so I could drive by the hospital first so she could say goodbye. It felt like two hours, but I think the negotiations were simply an excruciating thirty minutes. First they threatened to put Mara in the Quiet Room if she didn't calm down. Then she worked on them and worked on them until they agreed to let her wait on the lawn (with a staff member) so she could say goodbye. And finally, after all that, it was mutually decided between Mara and one of the nurses that having me drive all the way out there would be unfair to Rags. Our normal veterinarian was actually near the hospital, but that were closed for the evening. I'd be going to the emergency clinic in a different direction. Instead Mara had me hold up the phone so Rags could hear her say goodbye. Then I scooped Rags up in a towel (at which time he looked up at me – the first sign of recognition he'd made since I found him) and raced off to the clinic.

Our veterinarian was a very skilled, thorough professional, and despite the ragged looks of the place (and the vet) the emergency clinic was as well. I had to wait nearly an hour for my turn, during which I tried to pet Rags gently and comfort him. He didn't seem to be in pain; he was simply lost in a haze of brain chemicals and illness. The vet wouldn't just put Rags to sleep. First he needed to do a general exam on the miraculous chance he could be saved and achieve a decent quality of life. It became quickly obvious after the exam and an x-ray that Rags was beyond help. Cancer or something or the sort was ravaging his insides, and it was time to say goodbye. I stroked him as he closed his eyes for the last time, and cried. I had never needed to put a pet to sleep before. I did not want to be in that antiseptic-smelling room, but I wanted to give Rags every bit of love and comfort I could as he left. Then I petted him some more for a few minutes; his body was lifeless and stiff and no longer seemed real.

By the time I finished paperwork, made arrangements for Rags to be cremated (which Mara had insisted on), and found a combination of credit cards that could cover the charges, it was after midnight. I got home after 1am. The apartment smelled like death, and I could barely keep my eyes open. I poured a huge pile of clean cat litter on top of the diarrhea Rags had left in the kitchen, sprayed air freshener all over, and stumbled off to bed. There was simply no way I could clean it up until the next day.

Of course, I woke up late for work the next morning and had to rush out of the house without even a shower or washing my face. I made my train with maybe sixty seconds to spare. All day I was miserable and did my best to keep busy, and to make things worse I felt greasy and filthy. After a day in New York City I always felt a bit grimy, but starting off such a mess to begin with greatly compounded my discomfort.

My plan was to get home, clean up the kitchen, and then go out and visit Mara if there was still enough time. I was running on fumes but I didn't want to leave Mara to her own devices. Especially now that Rags had just died, I felt it was very important for me to be there for her. I got home and went up to the apartment. The stink wasn't anything like it had been the day before, but it was still noticeable. There was no point in taking a quick shower until I tackled the mess in the kitchen.

And that's when the doorbell rang, and from the other side of the door I heard our landlords (the husband and wife) calling my name. Great, just great. I already knew what was going on: our neighbor to the left (who was a tremendous busybody and constant complainer) had probably walked by the door and smelled the odor, and then called them to bitch about it. I couldn't blame them for reacting (I figured they were waiting in the parking lot for me to get home, if they hadn't been in the apartment already). It was a lot for me to explain. They were upset and the smell, and a bit shocked at my disheveled appearance. I told them about Rags. Their big concern was that it wasn't going to happen again, which was easy to assure them about since Rags was dead now.

Then they started asking about Mara. I suppose Nosy Neighbor had mentioned she hadn't been around much lately. They wanted to know if we had broken up, and started asking all kinds of personal questions. Since I was the one who was working and paying the rent, I didn't think it was really any of their business, but this was their first rental property and I imagine they were nervous that they'd rented to a disaster waiting to happen. I told them Mara was in the hospital with Crohn's and Crohn's-related depression, and wouldn't be home for a few weeks. When they asked what hospital I lied, and told them one of the ones her Dad worked at. I wasn't embarrassed more than I felt it wasn't their concern (unless Mara wanted them to know). Eventually they left, but only after stern warnings about possible eviction proceedings if things like this happened again. I wasn't sure if they felt sorry for me because of the tears in my eyes and deep circles in my face, or if they thought I was abusing drugs. Either way, I was just happy to have them leave so I could clean the place up and take a shower.

    I spoke to Mara on the phone and let her know I just had to take the night off. I'd barely have time to sit down with her before it would be time to leave, and I needed to get some sleep so I could try to function normally the next day. She was surprisingly understanding about it. Her favorite nurse was working that night and Mara said the two of them needed to talk about something important. I asked her what was going on, but she just said she'd tell me about it later. It was something the nurse thought she should do, and Mara wasn't sure if she was ready. She agreed to fill me in the next day when I visited, and also to tell me what the decision she made about it.

    When I came by after work the next day, I knew things were about to become a lot more stressful for everybody.

Chapter 18 - Blame, Denials, and Recriminations

I went to visit Mara the next day and we sat on her bed and discussed her latest decision. She and the nurse had a long talk the night before about this being the perfect opportunity to finally reveal to her father the years of sexual abuse she had suffered at the hands of his father, Mara's paternal grandfather. Not only would this be a quiet, safe environment to disclose her experiences, but on the off chance her Dad wanted someone to talk to about this (being a doctor, he felt he knew everything about everything) there were professionals available standing by.

I was worried about Mara's Dad dealing with this for two reasons. The first, and most obvious, was learning that his own father hat perpetrated such terrible things on his daughter. That's the kind of information which shatters a lifetime of beliefs and point of view. You think you know certain things, and certain people, and in an instant, everything is thrown upside down. He would probably start to question a lot of other things he'd been told throughout his life, and wonder what other lies or skeletons were hidden along the way.

The other thing I felt bad about was whether this would affect his marriage at all. After all, he'd been kept in the dark about this for years, but Mara's mother knew at least some of the details. Mara had described for me how one day she sat down with her mother, cried in her arms, and told her about what her Grandad had done to her. It felt so good to be able to stop keeping it all a secret, and her mother promised she would never let Mara be alone with him again.

But that conversation was also a source of great pain and anger for Mara, because she said that from that moment onward her mother began to slowly minimize what she had been told, to the point of almost acting like it had never happened. True to form, Mara was sent off that very summer to spend a few weeks at her grandparents' home. She had a very difficult time understand her mother's actions, and forgiving them.

As strongly as Mara believed the conversation had taken place, I might have hesitated to believe she had really told her mother if not for a conversation that took place in front of me soon after we met. We were at Mara's house, and her grandparents were coming over. Mara told her mother we were going to go get some ice cream and then over to my house, and her Mom began to insist that she be home for this family gathering.

"I'm going to Doug's house. I'm not going to be here when **he** is here."

"Why not?" her mother asked.

"You **know** why not, Mom" Mara replied. And the look on her Mom's face – coupled with the fact that the subject was immediately dropped – told me all I needed to know. Mara **had** told her mother about the sexual abuse. How much she told her, how much was believed, and what her Mom had convinced herself of in the years since were all in question, but there was no doubt in my mind: she knew. There was no other time in all the years I knew her that Mara's mother clammed up and backed off the way she did that day, at that moment.

In terms of Mara's Dad, all of this information would suddenly come to light. His daughter had been abused by his own father. His wife knew about the abuse but never told him, which he might hold against her. And then there was the whole matter of her action – or lack of action – which failed to protect Mara from additional abuse. That's the kind of shock which could rip a marriage apart. I felt like Mara's parents loved each other, but they weren't really that close, and they argued quite a bit. If sides were drawn up, there was no telling who would wind up where.

I have memories of being at the meeting in the hospital, but all these years later I am no longer sure they are real. They may just be my visual creations of what I was told, much in the same way that experts say most of your earliest childhood memories are not your own but based on photographs and stories you were told. Logically it seems the odds are better that I wasn't there. Mara would have wanted me to be present so she had support if things got ugly, but I think the two of us agreed that to have me present would be an intrusion on her parents' privacy, and would also make it harder for her Dad to deal with what he was going to learn. Also, it would keep her parents from acting normally. Everything was a show when someone else was around. Now and then I'd seen them with the masks off, but appearance and what other people (their friends, their social circles, society) might think were a driving force in most everything they did. Social media works wonders for that purpose these days, but back then everything was more based on social contact, and what someone would tell someone else, who would tell someone else. All things considered, I believe I wasn't actually there. But memory does play tricks on us all.

I know I got all the details from Mara afterwards, both on the phone and later in person. From her perspective things went better than she feared. Her Dad said that he believed her, which was a major worry for Mara. She still couldn't be certain if he did truly believe her, or just believed that **she** believed it, but either way his position was that she was telling the truth. He hugged Mara and let her cry in his arms. He did express a lot of concern over what his own mother knew or didn't know, and Mara told him truthfully that as far as she could tell his mother never knew anything about anything. Mara had always been told to keep it "our little secret" and that other people "wouldn't understand" or would get mad at her. After all, she was special; adults wouldn't like him making Mara his favorite, and other children would be very jealous. It's the same twisted logic so many abusers use to build a shroud of loyalty and secrecy over what they're doing.

In a sad way, the dynamics of Mara's family had fed right into the abuse and hiding it. Because of the constant concern about maintaining appearances, all her life Mara had been told not to tell certain people certain things. Don't tell Gramma that your cousin came over, because she will be upset you didn't all go to her place. Don't tell your brother about being allowed to use the car. Don't tell the neighbors about what your mother and I were discussing last night. Don't tell Dad about what Mom and her best friend said. It was a family filled with secrets, big and small, and would have taken multiple filing cabinets to keep track of who was supposed to know what, and who wasn't. So the idea of keeping this sexual abuse secret, the "special treatment" she received, must have seemed quite natural to Mara as she grew.

When the subject of Mara's mother knowing about the abuse came up, her Mom denied it entirely. She did admit to having a conversation with Mara some years back, but explained that she thought it was just Mara being upset about something innocuous, an innocent touching that she needed reassurance about. This was the moment when things could have taken a very bad turn. Mara got angry, partly by her Mom's minimizing and also by her denials.

"You thought it was innocent when I told you he put me on his lap and liked to slip his fingers in my pussy? Was that just something I misinterpreted?"

I think it was the look on her Dad's face that made Mara back off and just leave that topic alone. There was no going back to that day to prove anything, and even if Mara was correct about everything, she knew her mother could have slowly convinced herself that whatever happened wasn't what she had been told. Time would have also let her lie to herself and believe she hadn't been told some of it at all. In the midst of yelling at her Mom she looked over at her Dad and it seemed he was about to collapse. Mara's Dad was private with his feelings, and not one to cry. Mara couldn't bring herself to shatter him that way. She quickly apologized to her Mom and they moved on.

It's just as well, because when Mara started to yell, one of the staff members began to approach. Yelling was not allowed on the ward. The idea was to keep everyone calm and mindful of what they said and how they were saying it. Even knowing the kind of conversation they were having, it wasn't allowed to get loud. The Quiet Room waited patiently for the next person who didn't obey those rules.

The remainder of their discussion focused on the normal family dynamic: who to tell, and who to keep this a secret from. Mara was in favor of letting everyone know; because her parents were sort of the social center of the families, people from both her Mom's and Dad's sides frequently celebrated holidays or other occasions together. So her fear was that other children may had been abused along the way. Nobody was even sure if

Mara's sister had suffered abuse at all (although I suspected she hadn't; she had a much less passive personality, and therefore was less of an attractive target for a predator). Certainly her sister would have to be told; there was no real disagreement about that. But that was the only item on the agenda everyone felt the same about.

Mara's mother didn't even want to tell Mara's younger brother. She explained that since he was in High School it would upset him and take his focus of his studies and basketball. Mara thought that was ridiculous; while it was doubtful that he had ever been abused he should still be asked. Certainly as her only brother he had a right to know what had happened to her, even if they didn't provide all the sordid details. And wasn't his sister being in the nuthouse a distraction already? It was eventually decided that he **would** be told, but that Mara's mother would be the one to tell him.

On the other hand, Mara's father was hesitant to tell his own sister (Mara's aunt) about this. She would be very upset about the whole ordeal, and he didn't want to destroy her view of their elderly father. But here Mara's mother was more adamant; the aunt had children, and they needed to be asked about their experiences. The danger of not saying anything was far greater than the angry or emotional reaction she might have about the revelation. Mara's aunt would **have** to be informed. And, in all likelihood, regardless of what they asked her to do, she would in turn tell Mara's grandparents. Mara felt awful about hurting her grandmother, and at this stage she wasn't prepared to confront her grandfather directly and see what he would say and if he had any remorse. That had to wait for later, when she was both physically and mentally stronger. But the fireworks were going to go off as soon as the information started to get passed around.

As for her Mom's side of the family, Mara's parents didn't want to tell anybody anything yet. It was agreed that they'd need to tell one of her aunts on that side in the future, just so her cousins could be kept safe and talked to (they were both very young and the limited exposure they had to Mara's grandfather made abuse unlikely). The rest of that side could be decided on a case by case basis as time went on. That is, except for one person: Mara's maternal grandmother.

Gladys, Mara's grandmother, was the eternal wild card. You never knew what was going to come out of her mouth. One moment she could be calm and coherent, and the next shrieking about something she knew was true because she "saw in on the media." When a conversation started about secrecy, and who to tell and who not to tell a given topic to, it was almost a guarantee that "don't tell Gladys" would be one of the first things mentioned. Everybody knew that they had to keep Gladys in the dark about anything that went on, but it was still important enough to mention as a reminder. This was almost like reminding the family "don't forget to breathe today."

This complicated web of secrecy when it came to normal topics made conversation very difficult in larger groups. As soon as someone would start to talk about something, you'd hear coughing, panicked topic changing, or a kick under the table, all to control the information flow. But if Gladys was part of the conversation, the only way to talk was to let her take the lead, and then make quick comments (or strange jokes) when she left the room or got distracted. If she was told about Mara's sexual abuse, there was no telling what she would do. Everyone she knew would hear about it, even neighbors she barely spoke to, and it was likely that each day she'd be telling a different version of the story, with a new version of fact and false mixed together, and perhaps with Gladys bringing opposing opinions on random occasions. One day she might cry about this, and the next day gnash her teeth over the lies her granddaughter was spreading. In was inevitable that someday she'd hear something about it, but at present job number one was to keep Gladys out of the loop. It was hard enough just keeping her from finding out Mara was in the hospital (let alone a mental hospital). Involving Gladys wasn't pouring gasoline on the fire; it was stacking hundreds of boxes of explosives all over the place and lighting random fuses.

So now the cat was out of the bag. Mara's parents both officially knew about how she had been molested for years. It was no longer a dark secret (to her family, that is…I'd known for years now, and so had a number of Mara's High School friends. Mara even put "PG" in her cryptic long yearbook message which referred to "perverted grandfather"). As they hugged and said goodbye at the hospital, Mara's Dad made one of his typical optimistic-but-minimizing statements. I know he didn't say such things to be hurtful; they were merely an expression of what he wished would become the truth.

"Now that you've told us," he said, "that's 90% of the battle. It isn't a secret any more, and you'll be able to move on from this and never think about it again."

A nice dream, but as far from reality as anyone could get.

Chapter 19 - Running Through a Minefield

The shit started to hit the fan almost immediately. Mara's aunt was outraged at the accusations being directed towards her father. She didn't believe any of them, and wasn't even willing to consider the patronizing view that Mara believed them but was wrong. No; Mara was lying, knowingly and purposely. She didn't offer any sort of motive Mara might have for doing this and making up such horrible stories, other than Mara was an evil bitch who enjoyed the suffering of others and wanted to destroy the entire family because of some perceived slight her own parents had committed. She was willing to still communicate with her brother – Mara's Dad – but not anyone else in the family. The only positive was that because she was so convinced none of these things had ever happened, she wasn't going to tell her own father or mother about them. She wanted to wait for Mara to recant her claims and admit what a demonic liar she was.

I imagine Mara's Dad felt some anger at Mara for causing this disturbance, but he remained surprisingly supportive and did not give in to his sister's beliefs or threats. It must have been a terrible spot to be put in. A week or two ago his middle child checked herself in to a mental hospital, which was painful enough. Now his father was a child molester, his daughter a victim of abuse, and his sister was steaming like a teapot. I had formed the opinion of Mara's Dad that he tried to keep his emotions to himself; he was more old school who didn't cry, and who needed to maintain the appearance of being in control of things (this also fit in with his being a Doctor). He was overweight, worked long hours doing rounds at three hospitals, and always looked worn out physically and emotionally. The last few weeks had been one gut punch after another for him, and I'm really not sure how he managed to fight through it. I imagined a lot of quiet sobbing in the shower, if he allowed himself that much.

A day or two after the big meeting, I called to speak to Mara. There was a pay phone on the ward and if nobody was using it, it would ring until a patient would answer to see who it was for. One of the girls I had met – a cute but frighteningly thin anorexic – answered and told me Mara couldn't come to the phone. I asked if I should call back in a little while (figuring she was in a group or session) and she told me no, I probably should just wait until I came to visit that night and hopefully she could see me then. Mara was in the Quiet Room.

I didn't know what could have happened, since Mara seemed to be making slow but steady progress. She'd gotten through that tense and painful meeting with her parents without falling apart. She was feeling the early stages of results from the medication they had put her on. Mara was even making some friends on the ward and trying to help some of the anorexics deal with the pain and depression which were driving them to try and melt their very lives away.

Obviously there were some things Mara hated about the ward. She found group therapy very frustrating, because for many of the patients there appeared to be no way to reason with them. Some were confined to wheelchairs because they did not have the strength or muscle tone to walk easily. It was through Mara that I first learned about how many eating disorders are much more about feeling out of control and wanting to grab on to some aspect of life that could be conquered. The ones with terrible body image issues were easier for Mara to deal with; she hated the way she looked as well, and she could understand how society may have warped their views of what a healthy person looked like. But the ones who were desperate to feel like they had some control, some choice in what direction their life was taking…Mara could never find a way to get them to loosen their grip. It frustrated her. I think if she hadn't been so overwhelmed in life by her own problems, Mara might have made a very good therapist. But life had led her to the opposite side of the spectrum.

When I came to the hospital that evening, I was told Mara was allowed visitors, but only in the public areas, not in her room. And I could only visit for an hour. If she maintained her decorum and followed the rules those restrictions would be lifted in a day or two, either gradually or all at once. I was advised to keep her calm and remind Mara of her restricted status if she started to get excited or loud.

Mara was sitting on a couch when I walked into the ward. She looked at once pale and exhausted and furious in some strange combination. Clearly the anger was something she was holding inside and controlling, but it was there and it looked deep. Something had really wounded her since the prior evening. I didn't know how much to attribute to the Quiet Room and whether she had been sedated.

I asked Mara to explain what had happened if she could, and why she had been set off so badly that she had to be strapped down. Apparently they hadn't sedated her; it was more protecting herself from herself, and giving her a chance to calm down and even scream out her anger if necessary. That was probably why she looked so pale: from yelling and screaming until she was so exhausted that she fell asleep.

It had started when a staff member had given Mara a book to read on sexual abuse survivors. The meeting with her parents had gone well enough, and it was thought she might like to learn more about sexual abuse and how it affects people. Mara didn't see much reason to read the book, but agreed to. After all, the abuse gave her some bad memories, and keeping it a secret from her father (and then revealing it to him) had been a source of angst for years. But it hadn't affected in her any other way that she could recognize, besides obvious ones like hating her grandfather.

As I've already mentioned, when Mara told me she had been sexually abused by her grandfather I felt bad for her. I was sorry she had that awful experience. But to me, and to her, and to the other friends she had confided it, it was like a car accident. It happened, it was a bad memory, and you might have an occasional ache or pain in the future but it was just something you moved on from. Mara and her friends had joked about it privately in High School. "Something About Amelia" was a very well-regarded TV movie a few years earlier about incest and abuse, but even there the focus was on the pain caused by keeping it a secret and the necessary damage caused by revealing it to others. There had just started to be a panic over sexual abuse at day care centers a few years earlier, but they were mixed with Satanic rituals and sounded outrageous (and, again, there was no consideration given to the effects of such abuse in the media. As a very strange coincidence, I should point out that Mara had applied for a job – and been turned down – at the Wee Care Nursery School in Maplewood, NJ after she dropped out of college. This school would become the scene of one of the best-known cases of sexual child abuse on the east coast during the hysteria). The world seemed to agree with the assessment Mara's father had given: getting it out in the open was 90% of the cure.

As we sat there, Mara explained to me what had happened, and why she had fallen apart. Even then, a day later, she was shaking as she told me.

"I started to read the book, just because I was bored and had nothing else to do. You know I don't like reading any more, ever since my Dad made me go to that stupid speed-reading course. Now I read slower than before but remember less. So I was making my way through the book. I didn't think there would be anything for me to learn in it. I already know what it is like to be sexually abused and molested, why do I need to read about it, or read about it happening to other people?"

"Then I came to this one chapter. A woman was talking about being molested by her uncle. And she started to talk about how it had affected her. And it was me. Don't you get it? That was me on those pages!"

I was trying to keep Mara calm the best I could, and she was trying hard as well. She was half-whispering, a quiet scream of anger. Nobody was looking over which was a good sign. "I don't understand," I said. "What do you mean it was you?"

Mara took a breath to try and compose herself. "The things she was talking about. Not the abuse, but everything she said about herself. Living with secrets and lies. Seeing sex as the way to give and get love. Hating herself. Being driven to do things that made her hate herself even more. Wanting to be dead. Sick thoughts in her head. Not being able to focus or concentrate. Even eating terribly and getting fat, trying to drive men away. And so much more, Doug."

"I thought…" She was crying silently now, with tears rolling down her cheeks. I reached over and wiped some off, but she barely noticed. She was focused on an invisible point in front of her, trying to concentrate on what she was saying and how she was saying it.

"I thought, I mean I knew. I **knew** he fucked up my childhood. I knew that, right? But I didn't get it. Now I see it. Everything. Everything about me, everything I do, everything I think, everything I hate about myself. All my instincts, all my reactions to everything. It's **all him**. It's all because of him."

Mara clenched her teeth and looked at me, so angry and so fragile at the same moment. "I fucking hate him. I hate him. He didn't mess up my childhood. He's fucked me up. He ruined my whole life. I don't even know who I was, or who I was going to be. I'm just this fucked up person because he broke me and reprogrammed my whole brain. I've been living as the person he built for years. I'll never be **me**; I'll always be just the pieces he left behind. I'll never be free of him. Even when that bastard dies and rots in hell, I'll be left behind, always reminded."

I wanted to explain to Mara that this wasn't the end, that she could learn to heal herself and get beyond what happened to her. Even as I wanted to do that, I was absorbing what she had explained to me, and so many things seemed to suddenly fit into place. It was like making some kind of scientific discovery, and it all seemed so obvious to me now. Why hadn't I seen the connections? I was beating myself up at the same moment I was trying to comfort her. It was frightening how much of her behavior and trains of thought which had appeared erratic and random now fit a defined pattern.

"I just felt like fainting," Mara continued. "It was like being in a Twilight Zone episode. And then all at once, I wanted to rip my face off, tear at my flesh. Anything to stop my brain from thinking and realizing and understanding. I didn't want to know all this, and it was too much too fast. I think I screamed and threw the book and knocked something over. I can't remember clearly, I was so crazed, I just remember what felt like ten sets of arms dragging me into the Quiet Room and strapping me down. And I was terrified that being like that would trap me with my thoughts, but I screamed and cried and it sort of drowned out some of my brain. And then I woke up and my face was set and scratchy from salt, and my throat was sore."

Telling the story seemed to calm down Mara a bit. I asked her if I could see the book, but she didn't know where it was. "Don't bring that thing near me right now" she said. I understood what she meant.

"No, I just want to get the name of the book so I can get a copy and read it myself, so I can understand you better. Maybe it will help if you know I can see what you're going through."

Mara actually smiled for a moment, and then started to cry again. I held her as she quietly sobbed and talked to herself. "I'll never be okay. I'm damaged and broken. He ruined my whole life. My whole life."

I wanted to believe that wasn't true. Certainly, some people had gotten through this (and much worse) and found a way to the other side. I so badly wanted to be the positive voice of reason. But in the back of my mind I could also see the other path: the one where Mara never did truly recover. She wasn't exactly strong to begin with. Could it be possible that she was too damaged to heal?

I didn't want to believe that. I stopped thinking, and just listened to Mara sob and talk until it was time for me to leave.

And then I cried all the way home.

Chapter 20 - Hurry Up and Wait

While sparks were flying outside the hospital, Mara slowly made some progress as an inpatient. Her medication had lifted her out of the deepest portion of her personal hell, and despite the collapse of her psyche when she realized the destruction the sexual abuse had been causing her for years, she recognized that she had found a starting point and with work (and a bit of luck) she could start to slowly walk the long staircase towards a happier and more stable life.

As I expected, once she found her footing, Mara began to push towards getting out of the hospital, or at least finding an approximate time frame until she would be let out without having to leave against medical advice. To me this was a positive sign, not just because she wanted to come home, but because she had enough mental energy to think about things like this. Unfortunately for Mara, after discussing the matter with a number of patients (including a few repeat customers), she learned there appeared to be one firm rule when it came to leaving: you were "well enough" whenever your insurance ran out.

Almost by magic, a few days before any patient's insurance was due to run out (assuming any appeal for additional covered inpatient days had been denied), that's when a release plan was put together and discussions about outpatient psychiatric care took place. Obviously in some cases this makes perfect sense; there were certainly patients that were not truly ready to re-enter their old lives but had used up whatever number of days that insurance was willing to cover. It would be in their best interests to stay longer if at all possible.

But for roughly half the patients, once they had been stabilized and educated about their illness and contributing issues, they weren't going to gain anything by being stuck on the ward for an additional week or two. There's only so many group therapy sessions you can attend, and only so many arts and crafts projects you can complete. Aside from some anorexics with a firm intent on starving themselves until they collapsed and died, the eating disorder ward was much more about keeping patients busy and marking time until you were no longer a source of income.

I'm not trying to suggest that the daily staff there didn't care about the patients. On the contrary, the nursing and orderly staff seemed to care quite a bit. Mara always said that outside of being prescribed medication, the only help she ever got from anyone in the hospital was advice and assistance from the staff, especially the ward nurses. They were the glue that help everything together, and they had the knowledge and experience to notice when someone's behavior was off. When that happened, they would try and talk the patient through the problem instead of running to the doctors (who would either do nothing or adjust medication levels).

Now that Mara had been on the ward for a few weeks, she started to be allowed occasional one-hour and two-hour passes. There wasn't a lot to do on such a short pass, but we would drive to a nearby park or just walk around the grounds. On one pass, she arranged to meet a woman she'd made friends with in the hospital who had been released. We shared a park bench, and I read a book while the two of them talked. On the drive back, Mara was shaking her head and rolling her eyes.

"What's the matter? Is she not doing well?" I asked.

"Oh, it's not that at all, she's doing very well," Mara replied. "She's back at work and doing the right things. It's what she told me about the bills she saw that had been sent to the insurance company. This place is just one big racket."

Mara explained that this woman worked in the medical field – I think she may have actually been a nurse – and even though her insurance covered her stay, she took it upon herself to look over the bills carefully to make sure things had been charged properly. What she discovered was that the hospital bent – or broke – every rule in order to squeeze every dime they could out of each patient.

For example, when this woman arrived at the hospital, she was dealing with a badly sprained ankle, and had to walk on crutches. Her doctor spoke to the hospital and asked she be allowed two over the counter painkillers every four hours (up to 8 pills a day), as needed. But because she was on a psychiatric ward, she couldn't keep that medicine on her person. Instead she would need to go to the desk, ask for it, have it approved, and then they would provide her the pills. It was all sounding like a big pain in the ass so she never bothered to get any. Instead she toughed it out until it felt better.

Now, having left the hospital, she found they had billed her insurance for eight pills a day, every day she had been there...even though she had never taken any. Not only that, they charged an extra fee on top of the medication for "administration of medication" four times a day. The charge would have been a bit over-the-top even if she had taken the pills, since we're talking about medication that costs a few cents per pill retail. But the institutional cost for the medication - plus having to have a staff member administer it – was simply outrageous.

While she dug around and made phone calls trying to get her insurance company to dispute those charges, she found a single line item charge that completely blew her mind. On her final invoice, for services rendered at discharge, there was a charge for $249 for a pair of crutches. The crutches she needed to walk around with during her first two weeks on the ward. **The crutches she brought with her from home when she arrived at the hospital.** Someone saw her with them as she left and threw a charge for them in the middle of all the other miscellaneous items. It is entirely possible that person thought they'd given them to her and the charge had slipped through the cracks, but either way this was a true shake your head moment.

Situations like these are what was souring Mara on the hospital. She was stable, and she didn't think they were going to do anything to make her better from that point forward. She wanted to get back home, get on with her life, and focus on outpatient treatment.

And our wedding. That was still a major concern for Mara, from multiple perspectives. First, she was afraid that I would back out now that I knew I was marring a "crazy person." This was a silly view, especially since I knew she had numerous mental issues long before she was ever hospitalized. If anything, this breakdown was a positive sign, because she learned a lot about her condition and was even taking medication now. I did my best to put her mind to rest whenever she brought this up. I don't think either of us considered ourselves much of a prize at that point, but I understood the basis of her insecurity.

And then there was planning the wedding itself. This was becoming a growing source of stress for Mara. Through conversations with her mother, it seemed that planning was moving forward with only the slightest bit of input from Mara herself. Her Mom was already out making some preliminary decisions about possible locations, florists, photographers, and even the date. Nothing had been finalized of course, but Mara didn't even want her Mom eliminating possibilities without her say-so. "It's our wedding, not hers! I don't mind us making decisions together, but she shouldn't be deciding anything on her own."

Being a guy, I didn't much care one way or another. As long as Mara got her way enough times to keep things from being cancelled, that was enough for me. In the meantime, I was spending my energy trying to keep the peace. Mara had now worked her way up to four-hour passes, which allowed us to go to a movie one weekend, and then for me to take her home to visit the cats for an hour or so on another. Without question, that was her favorite pass, as she had missed the cats terribly. Ubber nearly jumped up into her arms when he saw her. The sadness of Rags being gone wasn't hanging over the apartment that heavily, especially since she had the happiness of being reunited with the others.

While Mara waited for her insurance to run out – and therefore for her to be "ready for release" – she spent most of her time sitting around the common area making friends. Or having people walk up and make friends with her. There wasn't much else to do, and it gave her a chance to be giving to people who didn't have the family support that she did. For example, Mara had asked me to bring her some nail polish and other nail supplies. She was allowed to have the polish, but the polish remover was kept by the staff for safekeeping. One day a girl named Courtney came by and asked if Mara would paint her nails. Courtney was not doing very well: she was morbidly obese, didn't bathe often, and talked to herself quite a bit. Mara had tried to be kind to her, and since nobody else was willing to even go that far, Mara was now her "best friend."

Mara went ahead and started painting Courtney's nails while they sat and made small talk. About halfway through the first hand, Mara noticed how dirty Courtney's nails were. There were all kinds of brown matter under them. It wasn't until she got to the second hand that Mara realized the "dirt" was also visible at the tips of her fingers, and it wasn't so much dirt as actual shit - feces. Mara did her best not to grimace, and went on painting Courtney's nails (being careful not to touch them directly with her own hands). When she was done, Mara exclaimed "Oh, that color looks so great on you." She pushed the polish bottle across the table towards Courtney. "Here, you should keep it!" It was a win-win: Courtney was touched by the gesture, and Mara didn't need to throw the bottle away, as there was no way she ever wanted to use the polish again.

Pretty quickly Courtney's fondness for Mara became an issue. One day Courtney came into Mara's room and closed the door behind her, which wasn't allowed. Mara was lucky not to have her passes taken away as a result, but Courtney explained she did it by instinct and the staff decided to leave it alone. She also made it a point to try and eat every meal with Mara, and to pepper her with questions about every little detail of everything she did. "Did you like your tea?" "Are you going to watch anything on television tonight?" "How many pairs of socks did you bring with you? I have extras if you need to borrow any." It was just a bit overbearing, but Mara didn't want to make a fuss and hurt Courtney's feelings.

One night things crossed the line. Mara was asleep in her bed, and woke up to find Courtney standing in the doorway, rocking from side to side. Mara sat up, startled, and whispered to her.

"What are you doing Courtney? Go to bed, you're going to get us in trouble."

"I need to tell you something Mara."

"Ummm, okay, make it quick."

"I love you, and I want us to be best friends forever. I think before you go home, I'll kill us both so we can be friends in heaven until the end of time."

Mara didn't know exactly what to say. She just looked at her and said "Go back to sleep, we can talk all about it tomorrow." Courtney wandered off and Mara tried to get some more sleep, which wasn't easy.

The next morning Mara met with a few staff members and explained the situation. It was decided to move Courtney to a more secure wing of the hospital, "just for a few days." They promised Courtney she'd be back on the eating disorder ward long before Mara went home. Obviously, that was a blatant lie, but at this stage they simply preferred to avoid any outbursts. Courtney gathered her belongings and that was the last we ever heard of her. I did occasionally sarcastically suggest over the next few years that we should try to find out where she lived and give her a call.

In retrospect, I did find some irony in Mara being so frightened by Courtney, especially when I compare it to how she treated April (and how she would talk about killing me in later years). It's all a question of when somebody is in their right mind, and when they aren't. Crazy ideas seem sane and reasonable at the moment when you're fighting your demons and losing.

A few weeks later Mara's insurance coverage for psychiatric hospitalization was finally getting close to running out, and a release plan was written up for her. This was another point when I could see the hospital wasn't exactly knocking themselves out to facilitate outpatient care. They gave Mara a list of a few suggested psychiatrists, a prescription for three months of her medication, and a pep talk. They didn't speak to me or her parents about how best to support her, or what to expect when she came home. They didn't even suggest Mara go see a therapist outside of the psychiatrist. Maybe they just believed more in pharmacology for the treatment of mental illness. Or maybe once the meter stopped running, they didn't care what happened. Who knows?

On the "big day," I came and helped Mara pack up her things and we drove home. Mara seemed apprehensive, but overall she was happy to be a bit more stable. Most of all, she was glad to be out of that place, and looking forward to being home in her own bed, with the cats to keep her company. As I drove back to Rahway, Mara dug around in a plastic bag of things they had placed in safekeeping for her. She pulled out the bottle of sulfasalazine we'd brought from home and shook it at me, laughing. "How much to you want to bet they charged me for these pills?"

I didn't expect things to be great, but at least life could get back to *our* version of normal. And now I could stop eating so many disgusting Big Macs.

Chapter 21 - Here Comes the Bride

The focus of life at this point centered around Mara's battle with Crohn's Disease, planning for the wedding, and trying to keep her mental outlook positive while she dealt with the continued ramifications (and surfacing memories) of sexual abuse. Now that she had told her Dad, and the secret was out in the open (or as open as things got in her family) some of her memories of past events were becoming clearer. It wasn't that she remembered things that she didn't have any memory of, but more that (as she described it) ghosts in her mind were taking solid form.

This experience wasn't easy on her, to say the least. Mara's moods swung wildly from content and happy to sobbing to angry fits. Her happiest times were when we are bundled up in bed with the cats and watching a video or one of her favorite TV shows. She also loved going out to the movies when she was able to handle it, which was once every two to three weeks. She loved all the cats but Ubber remained her true companion and the mental replacement for Midnight. I was never clear on exactly when she had Midnight, but I figured one black cat was around for at least a portion of the sexual abuse, and now another was there to comfort her during the healing process. Her happiest moments seemed to be when we were lying in bed for a Sunday nap and Ubber climbed on top of her and joined in.

Mara's Crohn's Disease was now somewhat stable, but for her that just meant if she avoided the foods she couldn't handle she would only need to go to the bathroom four or five times a day, and of those usually one would be agonizingly painful. She said it felt like something was on fire inside of her. The best I could relate to what she was telling me was something akin to when you eat something bad and it has to wait to work its way through your digestive system, stuck in the traffic jam behind the food that didn't disagree with you. Her gastroenterologist thought my description sounded rather perceptive, and had Mara do a few tests in his office (which thankfully didn't involve drinking that jug of "poison" Mara hated so much).

Afterwards he announced that Mara had a variety of what he called something like mucosal prolapse. At the time this was used to describe a variety of problems, but the net result was this: Mara had been straining when she went to the bathroom, and as a result (in combination with other factors, known and unknown) she had damaged her rectal walls and the muscles involved in elimination. In layman's terms, when Mara pushed, she was now unwittingly pushing **against** herself. While her intestines were trying to eliminate the waste, Mara's attempts to push and move things along were actually forcing everything back inside. So the harder she pushed, the more painful it was and the bigger the traffic jam became. The best treatment for this was to simply stop pushing, and to take fiber supplements to firm things up slightly which would in time allow the muscles to strengthen. If things were simple too painful and she couldn't be patient, application of a warm water enema would get the immediate matter out quickly (although he warned the pressure during application would likely be painful since her colon was so sore and irritated).

Dealing with Crohn's Disease was strange for me. If you had told me five years earlier that my daily life would focus on someone's bowel habits, I would have laughed or made rude comments. Instead, there I was, day after day, and trying to help Mara manage both the disease and the whole issue of taking a shit. It never bothered me, and I was never grossed out by any of it.

On the contrary, I had to be overly calm and polite and nonchalant about all of it, in an effort to spare Mara and unnecessary embarrassment or misery. I have no children, but I imagine this mentality is similar to what parents go through with a sick child. When you love someone, your mind turns off the area that might otherwise make you feel disgusted or repulsed. Whether it was simply discussing what kind of poops she had during the day, or giving her an enema, or checking for hemorrhoids, or applying creams to sore and red areas, or helping her clean up when her back muscles were in too much pain to wipe properly...you just did it. I think it was easier on me that on Mara; she'd sob and feel utterly useless and humiliated. That's a very personal and private bodily function, and having someone so involved in whatever was going on there must be terrible.

Now that Mara was out of the hospital, she became much more active (and assertive) about wedding plans. When we first announced our engagement, Mara's parents had offered to give us some money instead of a big wedding. I suggested we take the money – we sure as hell needed it – but Mara had dreamed of a big wedding her entire life, so I knew my opinion would be ignored. I found myself caught in the typical male trap of a wedding: I was asked to give opinions about many things that I had no preference or interest in, otherwise I wasn't participating. But my opinion would inevitably mean nothing when it came to making a final decision. Mara and her mother were the two heads of this operation, and those heads butted more often than not.

It became clear rather quickly that Mara's mother was pulling the "we're paying for this, so we'll get our way" card on just about every hand. Where to hold the wedding; what food to serve; who was going to be invited;

what band was playing at the reception; even the bridesmaids' dresses were all decided by her Mom. The wedding dress itself was a bit of a compromise, but Mara didn't fight too hard on that front. She knew there was no way she would look the way she wanted to on her wedding day.

Mara's eating habits were still terrible (75% by necessity, 25% by choice), and between that and her constant diet of prednisone she continued to gain weight. Her wedding dress needed to be able to accommodate her size **and** be adjusted larger at the final fitting if necessary. Mara was always hot, and sweating had also become a very embarrassing problem for her. It wasn't underarm sweat either; everything would sweat. Her arms and her legs were issues, but for Mara the two areas she was most self-conscious about were her face and her palms. We were hoping that with a handkerchief she could control both areas, or at least keep the sweat to a minimum. Makeup would need to be lightly applied, because there was no way Mara wasn't going to have a damp face all day.

The only things we seemed to have any choice on were our pattern selections for china, crystal, and silverware. This presented two problems for me. First, I **didn't care** what patterns we chose. There were a few options that I *hated*, and those I spoke out on. But for the rest, whatever Mara wanted was fine with me. That led to the same arguments about me not showing an interest. But there was a bigger problem: I didn't want to register those or select patterns at all. Why did we need expensive fine china or silverware? We didn't entertain (hell, we barely cooked real meals), we had no room for the stuff in the apartment, and I much preferred we limited the gift choices so there would be more cash coming our way and less money spent on foolishness we would use once or twice in our lives. To be honest, I preferred guests give nothing as a gift over a place setting of some china pattern. This position really upset Mara, and I believe the arguments over it led to the only time Mara threatened to cancel the wedding over anything *I* said or did (as opposed to her Mom, who made Mara threaten to cancel at least once a week). As usual, I finally backed down and kept my mouth shut.

In the midst of all this planning, Mara's parents kept bring up how they were "hurt" that my Dad and Stepmom weren't more active in planning the wedding. I couldn't quite understand why they wanted them around, since Mara's Mom was making all the damn decisions anyway. Eventually it came out: they wanted them to "participate financially" in the wedding.

The focus of this participation was paying for the photographer. I'm not sure why that particular item was chosen, but that was the one Mara's parents kept telling me about. "We expect your father to pay for the photographer." My Dad was barely earning a living at this point, relying on my stepmother Barbara's earnings to get by. He was also still paying my Mom monthly child support and alimony. I knew there was about a zero percent chance he'd be willing to put up even a hundred bucks, if he had the money to spare in the first place.

I'm not trying to imply my Dad was cheap. Quite the contrary, he was generous whenever he could be, and Barbara has always treated myself and my siblings as her own children. But their financial situation was a mess and slowly collapsing. Downsizing to a smaller home and trying to make ends meet – while paying for my Dad's substantial medical bills – meant contributing to this wedding was the last thing on their mind.

Then there was the whole matter of the marriage to begin with. Despite his misgivings, my Dad was doing his best to be supportive about

Mara and me getting married. He knew I was repeating mistakes he had made in his own life, and it made his heart hurt. He wasn't going to try and stop me from screwing my life up; it was more important to him that we maintained our close relationship so he could be there for me in the future as I dealt with the repercussions. Still, if he had been able to pay for the photographer or anything else, he would have done it. But it just wasn't going to happen.

I told my Dad that Mara's parents kept bringing it up, and told him that I'd explained his situation numerous times. Yet they were still insistent. They also wanted to meet him and Barbara for dinner, since they would be "part of the family" now. My Dad told me not to worry about it; just give them his number and he'd make his position clear. I already knew he had no interest in being "part of the family" but he was willing to suffer through a dinner with the in-laws to confirm what he already suspected: he wasn't going to like these people. And we both knew that when he didn't pony up the cash, they weren't going to like him either.

Something I didn't think about until years later was the contradiction in the way Mara's parents were treating my Dad. On one hand they wanted him to pay for part of the wedding and supposedly become family, but on the other hand they never once asked if he or Barbara wanted to include any friends on the guest list. I can't say I was surprised though, since it seemed Mara and I were barely able to make the cut. If there was a way to do the wedding without either of us being there, Mara's parents probably would have opted for that.

As the guest list for the wedding began to form and grow and reshape, like a giant amoeba, a few things became clear. First, aside from my immediate family, Mara and I were limited to only a few guests each. Second, just about every family member Mara had ever heard of (and some she didn't know existed) were being invited. And third, the rest of the guest list was being taken up with guests of her parents. Family friends, social friends, business associates, neighbors, former neighbors…I had no idea who 90% of these people were. Mara had a slightly higher recognition factor, but most of the ones she did know were people she wouldn't have chosen to invite.

In short, this wedding was a get-together and party for Mara's family and her parent's friends. The wedding itself, and the bride and groom, were simply distractions from the social event.

On my side, it was rather simple. My brothers, sisters, grandmother, Dad, and Barbara were invited (and if any of them didn't want to or couldn't attend, it wasn't an issue with me). I also invited my boss and his wife, and a couple of friends from High School that I had kept in touch with. From what I remember, only two of those friends even bothered to RSVP, and of those only one said he was attending. Again, I didn't take offense to that. I hadn't stayed that close to them in the couple of years since graduation, and they were busy with college and their own lives.

As for my mother Susan, I knew I couldn't invite her. There was no way she and my Dad could be in the same room at the same time without there being a scene, and there was **no doubt** that she would make the scene, not him and not Barbara. I called Susan and was blunt but polite and calm about it. I asked her if she truly believed she could promise not to do anything to draw attention to herself or start an argument, and she admitted that while she could *try*, that was nothing close to a guarantee. She didn't seem that hurt when it was presented in that logical and sterile display: Dad could behave, she probably couldn't, and therefore he was going to go and she wasn't. I don't think she took it personally, especially as we were communicating regularly at that point in my life and she had been discussing the possibility of staying over at our place one or two nights a week in the future if she got a part time job somewhere in our area (while she lived in south Jersey). Susan just accepted it: whoever couldn't control themselves wasn't invited.

On Mara's side, there was only one issue, and it was a huge one. Nobody knew what to do with her Dad's side of the family. Mara's aunt wasn't speaking to her at all, and if she agreed to go it would only be out of loyalty to Mara's Dad. And then there was the question of Mara's grandmother. How do you explain to a woman that she is welcome at her granddaughters wedding, but not her husband? The story was going to have to come out eventually, and it seemed like that was going to need to happen before the wedding, or the whole family was going to go ballistic. If prominent family members were not invited (or didn't attend) with no reason given, that would be as complicated - or more complicated - than the stress and pain of telling Gram about what Mara had gone through (no matter how much detail was omitted).

That conversation was left to Mara's Dad, with help from her Mom I imagine. Mara felt a lot of guilt about it, and wished she could come up with a way to invent an excuse that could keep her grandfather from coming to the wedding without hurting her grandmother. But there really was no alternative. Unfortunately, Mara and I both knew the reality was her grandmother wasn't likely to believe the accusations anyway. Even if she felt a drop of truth in them, between her husband and her daughter (Mara's aunt) they would convince her that Mara was sick, was crazy, or was just plain evil. I didn't anticipate her taking the evil angle, and when Mara and I talked about it I predicted she would take the "I believe you believe it, but it didn't really happen" position. Mara said she could handle that; she loved her grandmother and whatever she needed to do to reduce her distress and pain, Mara wasn't going to push it. With a family where the general rule was "don't talk about anything" we both assumed once the initial shock went away, it was going to be an untouchable subject with that side of the family anyway.

A few days later Mara's parents reported that they'd spoken to Grandma. They were very vague about how it went, or what they said to her or what she said back. Mainly they just said that she wanted to talk to Mara on the phone about everything, and they'd agreed to a day and time for that call (without checking with Mara first, as you'd expect). This call was to be between the two of them, and nobody else. Mara's parents wouldn't be on the phone, I wasn't allowed to be on the call, and her grandfather would not be a part of it either. Just Mara and her grandmother, in an attempt to discuss things calmly and quietly. This call wasn't meant to be a confrontation between the two of them, and certainly not a call to demand her grandfather admit what he had done to Mara.

The call was scheduled for an evening, so at least I would be home. Initially I just wanted to be there to help Mara through the emotional stress: hold her hand, make sure she knew she wasn't alone, and then be available to talk to her face to face when she got off the phone. Mara tended to feel very isolated and alone, and when you add that to believing everyone is on one side and you are on the other, it can lead to a volatile mix. So that was one situation I was anxious to avoid.

As he day of the call approached, Mara decided on her own that she would also like me to be on the call, but secretly. I was to be on the other extension but with the mute button on, and under no circumstances was I to say anything, no matter what happened. She had two reasons for wanting me to listen in. The first was it would simply make it a lot easier for her to tell me what happened without forgetting anything. I'd have already heard it, so we could move straight into discussing it and how she felt about it. Mara was bound to forget what some of her points were, and to let her emotions take the front seat.

The other reason she wanted me on the phone was so I could serve as a witness. Mara was far too aware that when her parents – and certain other people – heard something they didn't like, they would just wave it away as a misunderstanding. "I'm sure she didn't say that" was bound to be heard after the fact, if Mara felt she had been wronged. "You probably got confused" would be another; after all, she had been in the mental hospital, so how could they take her word at face value about anything? I'd be there to serve as her corroboration for anything she discussed with her parents later (and, on the other hand, to offer a different opinion on what was meant by something if I felt she took it the wrong way).

I wasn't looking forward to listening in on the phone call, or even just having the phone call take place. My parents fought and argued for years when I was a child, and Susan was famous for her multi-hour rants at the kitchen sink, yelling at nobody and singing rude songs she made up as she went along (a skill I'm actually pleased to have picked up). My stomach hurt just thinking about it, and I believe I was more nervous than Mara. Or maybe I just didn't expect it to go as smoothly as everyone seemed to be thinking.

I arrived home on the big day and found Mara rather calm. She just wanted to get through this as easily as possible. She was already thinking ahead to the wedding and the possibility of having her grandmother attend. While we waited for the phone to ring, Mara even started wondering if there was any way she could have her grandfather attend but not interact with him or see him, if only to make things easier on her grandmother and her aunt. That really wasn't a feasible option, and I reminded Mara that by the time the wedding rolled around she wasn't going to want any distractions going on, taking the focus off of what was supposed to be a celebration of our marriage. Just being around all those family members of hers, plus people she barely knew, was going to be stressful enough. It was better that she stopped worrying about how to best accommodate everyone else and spend a few minutes on accommodating herself. After all, in the end it was **her** wedding, no matter what her parents said and forgetting that there had to be a groom for the thing to take place.

We sat around for a bit, playing with the cats and glancing at the clock. Finally, at a few minutes after the appointed hour, the phone rang. Mara reached for the bedroom receiver, while I went and grabbed the extension across the room by the computer desk. I moved to the edge of the bed and reached out, grabbing hold of Mara's hand before the rollercoaster ride started (if there was going to be one...I was pretty sure there would be).

I could tell right away something was a little off. I could hear her grandmother but she sounded further away than you would expect. "Mara? Mara, what's wrong sweetie? Whatever it is we want to help you. Just tell us what's wrong?"

Mara opened her mouth to respond, and at that instant I realized why her grandmother sounded different: she was on a speakerphone. My brain made instant computations and inferences, but I had no time to warn Mara. Instead I just squeezed her hand, hard enough that she started pulling back instinctively. And then she got it.

"You lying bitch!" her grandfather yelled. *"You fucking lying whore! I hope you die!"*

"Mara sweetie, just tell us why you would say these things?" added her grandmother.

"You stupid fucking cunt, do you want to kill your Dad? Do you want to destroy your family with your lies? You're nothing but a whore."

I'm sure Mara tried to say something, and maybe got a word or two in, but only enough to keep her grandfather going.

• Her grandfather didn't let up. *"I never touched you, you're nothing but trash. Stupid fucking spoiled brat. You fucking lying bitch!"*

"Are you angry at us? Did we do something wrong?" It was good cop-bad cop with her grandmother being the "understanding" one.

"I hope you're happy, you fucking whore. I hope you rot in hell!" I couldn't even picture this old, frail man yelling these things, but it was happening.

As hard as it was to hear these insults thrown at Mara, I stuck to my agreement: I kept silent. To hear that kind of language coming from her grandfather was very shocking. He was a frail, tall, thin man in his late 70's (or so I guessed, I'm not great about knowing how old people are). His gravelly voice burst out in claps of thunder, pausing a few seconds in between to catch his breath.

Eventually Mara had enough, and gave up on the idea of a real conversation. She just started yelling back at her grandfather. "You know exactly what you did to me. You didn't care, you sick bastard. You told me it had to be our secret. Now everyone knows what a sick monster you are. You're a pervert and I'm going to make sure the whole world knows it!"

"I'm going to kill you, you lying bitch!" I started to wonder if he'd suffer a stroke.

I hung up my receiver and tapped Mara on the shoulder. She looked over at me, tears streaming down her face, and did the same. The anger Mara felt was keeping her together. There was some satisfaction in being able to yell back at him a bit, enough to pump her adrenaline and stop her from bursting into tears. Instead we just sat on the bed holding hands for about five minutes, saying nothing. A few of the cats who had run out of the bedroom when Mara finally let loose came back in and jumped on the bed. Mara pet them, scratched them under their chin, and felt them purr. She was breathing deeply, but trying to keep it slow. I told her I was very proud of her for standing up to him, and not letting her emotions tun wild.

"Come give me a hug" she asked, and I did. After a minute she let her arms drop from around me.

"I want to call my mother."

I knew that was coming too. Mara wanted to report to her parents what had happened, and see what kind of reaction she got. If sides were being drawn, she wanted to know who was with her and who was across the line. I'm pretty sure she had told her mother she would call afterwards anyway, but after all the stress of the phone call with her grandparents there was no question she wanted to call now.

If Mara had asked me to write down how that phone call with her parents was going to go, I would have been 100% correct. I saw it all before it happened, in almost the same sequence of events and the way it would move from topic to topic. It was so obvious it almost felt surreal.

First Mara started to tell her mother about what happened. Then she had to hold on while her Dad got on the phone too. There was some shock and surprise about her grandfather being on the call, but it was mostly minimized by Mara's parents. "I'm sure they just got confused about whether he was supposed to be on the phone or not. You know they're older."

Then the real trench warfare started. As Mara recounted the things he had said, for each statement there was a rebuttal. "I can't imagine my father saying that." "You must have let your emotions rum away with you." "Are you sure you didn't curse and yell at him first?" "That doesn't sound like him at all."

Eventually Mara was forced to play her trump card, and tell her parents that I'd been listening in on the conversation and could verify everything she had told them. That's when the real sparks flew. "I can't believe you would betray an agreement like that and have him on the phone." "Maybe that's why Grandad was so angry? What did Doug say to him?" "What would make you do a thing like that?" It didn't surprise me in the slightest that all the attention was suddenly focused on me and on how "wrong" it was for me to listen in, while no blame had been spread in the other direction for having her grandfather not just listening in, but actively on the phone call screaming obscenities.

Things dragged on for a little while, but eventually Mara's parents had no choice but to say things like "I'm sorry you had to go through that' and "I can understand why you would be so upset." No clear admission of wrong, but that was as close as it was going to get, and we both knew it. They would stay on Mara's side of the line, but they weren't about to take up arms and defend it.

If nothing else, that phone call ended any dream of Mara's grandmother being invited to the wedding. Her aunt would wind up making it clear she did not want to attend either, nor did she want to have anything to do with Mara any longer. That side of the family now saw Mara as persona non grata, except for her Dad. I would like to say that's a terrible thing to do to someone, but in all honesty, I can't fully blame them. It was easier to believe the man they'd known for all these years and take his word over the claims of a woman with mental problems. That's just a sad reality when it comes to abuse victims: they're often left with psychological damage and mental issues from their experiences, which in turn makes them less credible. A vicious cycle, but it would have been worse…her parents could have chosen not to believe her as well, which they didn't. Not openly anyway, and I really never got the sense they felt it was all a lie. They just would have preferred it was all swept under the rug, another little secret kept within the family.

Chapter 22 - Maybe Things Will Go Better at Your Next Wedding

No matter what else happens, time marches on. In this case, that also meant the wedding continued to approach. Arguments about how the guest list was shaping up – including the very small percentage of guests that me and Mara were allowed to invite – had already taken place, and the ones pulling the purse strings won out. In fact, they won out on just about every topic. Our input was rather minimal.

There were a few things we were allowed to offer opinions on. One was our wedding song, the song which would be played for our first dance. Mara's parents had hired a small band to perform, some typical wedding band, the kind you find in every town. We batted a few song ideas around; Mara even suggested demanding the Guns n' Roses song "Paradise City" just to confuse her parents and annoy the band, if nobody thought to veto it in time. In the end we settled on the old Phil Phillips classic "Sea of Love," which had recently been covered by Robert Plant's band The Honeydrippers. Other than that, we had only one demand: the band was not allowed to play the Kool & the Gang song "Celebration." Mara hated that song, and she also felt it was the most generic musical choice a band like this could make. She even told her parents to put it in the contract with the band: if they played "Celebration" they should forfeit whatever they were being paid. Her parents just looked at her weird.

I left all the discussions and debates about the food to Mara and her parents. Nobody really cared what I thought anyway, so there was no reason for me to get involved. When Mara would complain that I wasn't showing an interest, I would sigh and explain that to her, and I'd also point out that I really didn't care, as long as she was happy. Whatever she wanted, that was the decision I was behind, despite the fact that her parents were likely to overrule her.

"I *do* want things to be perfect," she told me, "but it doesn't really matter. All I really want is to be married to you, and to finally walk down the aisle in my wedding dress and hear Here Comes the Bride."

For the honeymoon, we were restricted in our choices. First of all, we didn't have much money to spend. Second, we didn't want to be gone for more than four days since Mara refused to board the cats and didn't trust anyone to take care of them in our absence. Her plan was to leave the morning after the wedding, and return four days later, so they would only be alone for three days. Sufficient food and water could easily be left out for that period. And third, Mara didn't want to travel more than a half day's drive, in case her health forced her to return home sooner than planned.

With those limitations, we started looking around for place that might be relaxing and peaceful. Mara wasn't especially interested in doing much during our honeymoon except for relaxing and perhaps a little light hiking or swimming if she was feeling up to it. She liked the idea of a woodlands setting, but not the social aspect that you might find at a Bed and Breakfast. Mara wasn't into socializing, especially with people she had never met before. What she wanted was privacy and a little seclusion.

At that time in the late 80's, you couldn't watch a television show in the New York area without seeing an occasional commercial for Mount Airy Lodge and Poconos Gardens Lodge, two resorts in the Poconos Mountains in Pennsylvania. At one time considered the "Honeymoon capital of the world," Mount Airy Lodge had fallen on harder times but still managed to drum up a decent business. You could rent your own cabin, complete with heart shaped beds or bathtubs, champagne glass-shaped hot tubs, television, wall-length mirrors, or whatever kind of thing you were looking for. Mara sent away for a few brochures, and decided staying at Poconos Gardens Lodge was the way to go. We could get our own cabin with heat, central air, and even our own private indoor swimming pool. Between that and room service, Mara would never have to go outside unless we wanted to walk around the woods. Sounded good to me. With luck we'd get a bit of cash mixed in with the wedding gifts to help pay for it. One more thing settled; amazing how easy it was to decide when her parents had no say in the matter.

The wedding dress was a whole other matter. I know it is a big ordeal for many brides, but for Mara it was complicated by her weight gain, her sweating issues, and her desire to have some sort of train on the dress (although not a very long one). I accompanied Mara and her mother to one bridal store; that was enough for me. I told them they'd have to do it on their own, or with Mara's sister's help. It was like the worst kind of relationship argument. First there was the tension in the air. Next, after five minutes of peace, somebody would be short with somebody else. This is known as the "starter's pistol" in these arguments, because it alerts all participants to the fact that the fight is on. For the next ten minutes or so terse responses would be mixed with snide comments. Whenever possible there needs to be three people involved, so the extra player can jump back and forth from one side to another. This allows the argument to last longer before somebody winds up in tears. Eventually "yelling whispers" lead to shouting, and at long last recriminations from offenses a minimum of two years old get brought up. The only positive to this kind of arguing is that the ride home is completely silent. Well, there's also the unofficial competition to see who can slam their car door the loudest. Good times!

Eventually – after visiting three or four bridal shops - they settled on a white dress with a train, that had some kind of hooks on it designed to hold the train up when the wedding march was over. I always thought trains were removable, but perhaps this was a cheaper way to go about it. I sure as hell wasn't going to ask! Of course, after more arguments, it became important that the veil was purchased from a *different* store. I guess they were veil experts or something. My suggestion to Mara that she "leave the tag on the dress so you can return it after the wedding" wasn't met with much appreciation.

A few weeks before the wedding, Mara was hit with a huge flare up in her Crohn's Disease. It was bad enough to require hospitalization to try and get it under control. Mara was weak, dehydrated, in excruciating pain, and spending most of her waking hours in the bathroom. At this point there was some discussion about contingency plans for the wedding. There really was no option: either Mara would get better in time, or what was effectively a party for her parents' friends and family would be just that...the subplot of the wedding ceremony would be dropped altogether, and we'd just get married later on at a courthouse or something.

Those conversations never went too far, because Mara's doctor assured all of us that she would make it to the ceremony. If she had flared up a week later there might have been a doubt, but there was enough time to get it under control. As he described it, the worst-case scenario would be he would pump her full of enough intravenous steroids just to get her through that one day, and then have her return to the hospital. But he really didn't think that would be necessary. She **would** be full of steroids and very sensitive to additional flare-ups, but it looked like she would be out of the hospital five or six days before the wedding.

It was around this time that Mara's parents finally went to meet Dad and Barbara, travelling to Staten Island to get together in their home. By now I don't think anyone was really looking forward to that meeting, but I suppose it had to be done for form's sake at the minimum. As before, the subject of paying for the photographer was brought up but quickly put to rest, much to the chagrin of Mara's parents. They were not pleased with the statement they were presented with: "We can't afford to pay for anything, but we will work to give Doug and Mara a cash wedding gift." Still, having things explained to them in person, first-hand, seemed to mollify them to the point that they accepted his explanation. It probably only reinforced the idea that I was not a worthy match for their daughter; no matter how they might have seemed to disregard her feelings and needs, they still wanted her to marry someone in the appropriate social class. But it was too late for them to do anything about it. And while I wasn't likely to be a storied professional or a tremendous financial success, they did see that I loved their daughter and that I was willing to go through a great deal of heartache to try and make her life as comfortable and pleasant as possible. I still believe they never liked me, but they both knew Mara could have found someone a lot worse.

Mara came home from the hospital about a week before the wedding, which gave us time to try and find solutions to some of her problems. The high level of steroids she had been on (and would continue to be on, tapering slowly) had her sweating even more than usual. She experimented with different face make-up, trying to find what combination looked good and didn't melt too quickly off her face. Fortunately, her eyes weren't that big of a problem, as long as she kept mopping the sweat off her brow. I went out and bought her a few lacy but thick white cotton handkerchiefs that she could hold and use as needed.

One of her other problems when it came to sweating was how damp her palms got. Normally that wouldn't have been a big issue, but at the wedding she was going to have to stand at the receiving line after the ceremony and hug, kiss, or shake hands with so many people. Even though she didn't know some of them very well, she didn't want to be gripping them with sopping wet hands. Just the thought of watching the looks on their faces made her nervous. The best solution we were able to come up with for this was a jar of antiperspirant. It was some major brand, but instead of being a stick, spray, or roll-on, it was a jar of cream for the same purpose. Mara tested it out and it while it felt strange it kept her palms mostly dry. She decided she'd quickly apply that before the ceremony, and it should last through the handshakes and hugs. Between the handkerchiefs and the cream, it seemed like she'd get through the day damp, hot, and generally miserable but still in one piece.

Most of the out of town guests were staying at the same hotel, a Hyatt. My relatives were all staying at my Dad's and Barbara's house on Staten Island, and would drive over together for the wedding. When the topic of bachelor parties and such came up, Mara was adamant she didn't want me going off to some strip club. That wasn't about to happen anyway, as I had only a couple of friends coming to the wedding. My brother Andrew was my best man, so we planned for him to come over to the apartment and play wargames with me the night before the wedding. Mara would stay at the hotel with her family and go to the wedding from there, making hanging out with her sister and her friend Sue her version of a bachelorette party. Considering how sick she had been, it was just as well that nothing major or exciting had been planned. We both needed the rest. Things had reached the level where there was no real celebration left in either of us, just some "let's get this damn thing over with" attitude.

And then it was the morning of the big day. I was alone in the apartment. Fed the cats, took a shower, started to get ready. I wasn't nervous; I was lonely. That apartment was full of life and laughs when the two of us where crammed in that small space, even though Mara was sick so often and in a bad state some of the time. Just lying in bed watching television, with the cats in and out of the room, we could spend hours laughing at some dumb show or some funny movie, or become completely engrossed in another. I sat around thinking for a bit before I left. This wasn't a great life, but there were enough moments to make it worthwhile. And we did love each other, despite all the problems. If we could maintain this level of happiness it would be okay. Nobody has a perfect life, but the key is finding the good moments in between the bad ones. When we were both there, it was a home. When I was there alone, it was just a place to hold stuff.

The wedding ceremony and party were a bit of a blur to me. There was some question as to whether my sister Antonia would make it, and while she was a little late, I was very happy she was able to join us. My Dad was rather stoic beforehand; it was a cross between being proud and walking his son to his execution (not a terrible interpretation, all things considered). There were a lot of handshakes and advice from friends of Mara's parents whom I didn't know or had met once casually. My grandmother Isabelle was there, which was a bit of an occasion as I had only met her a few times in my life. I was happier about that for my Dad. As they day wore on, he seemed to get happier; he loved spending time with his kids, dancing with Barbara, and enjoying a few moments of happiness. I made a mental note of that; I was a lot like him that way.

Mara spent most of the wedding forcing a smile and wiping the sweat from her face. It felt like another occasion of her and me in our own world, everyone else in another. When it was time for her to walk down the aisle, I saw her gritting her teeth as she smiled; instead of the traditional wedding march, "Sunrise, Sunset" from Fiddler on the Roof was being played. I didn't know if that would really set her off or not, and I had no idea who changed it or why. I just remembered how often she mentioned walking down the aisle to the wedding march was her dream. I simply smiled at her and hoped it was more walking down the aisle that mattered, and less the music.

After the ceremony, and before the party, it was time for photographs. That seemed to go on forever. I didn't even feel like I belonged in any of the photos, not even the ones with my own family members. I was twenty years old; I should be getting drunk at a college party or planning what club or concert I was going to go to that weekend. Instead I was working full time, getting married, and struggling to make ends meet. And now that we were married, her medical bills were entirely our concern. I had insurance at work but it wasn't that great. I suddenly felt a lot of weight on my shoulders.

At the party Mara was testy and irritable, but only let me see it. She was pissed off about the music during the ceremony, hot and "sweating like the big fat pig that I am," and didn't want to move from her chair. We had to do a first dance – awkwardly, as neither of us knew anything about dancing – but she only wanted to do the bare minimum. Sitting down again, she explained that her mother had done up the train of her dress on the hooks improperly and then when they started to argue about it her Mom had walked off. She was afraid of tripping every time she took a step, as the dress would get underfoot. I told her it was fine, it was her wedding, just sit there if she wanted to. I'd get her food and bring it to her, and she could just let guests come up and congratulate her at the table.

The rest of the wedding passed without any major incident. The guests seemed to have a good time, and Mara did her best to smile and be pleasant despite not feeling all that well. She was having some discomfort from Crohn's but luck was with her for once, and she was able to make it through the ceremony and celebration without having to run to the bathroom. She had taken some anti-diarrhea medicine the day before, which meant she was going to pay for that decision in the coming days but it was important to her to enjoy the day the best she could.

Overall Mara did enjoy herself in the moment, especially when her two young cousins (who were the flower girl and ring bearer) hung around the table. Of all the kids in the world, those were the two children Mara seemed to actually like. They were cute and funny and smart, and they had almost the perfect balance between childish innocence and more mature good behavior. And they had always taken to Mara, which children usually didn't do (for good reason at times). Having them around the table seemed to lighten Mara's mood, and also kept strange folks from staying in her proximity for too long.

At one point we were sitting at the table by ourselves and Mara started to laugh and shake her head. "See, if my parents would have listened to us, they could have saved some money" she told me, wiping more sweat from her brow. She saw the confused look on my face and laughed again. "Listen" she said, pointing off in a vague direction.

That's when I heard it. Despite being asked not to, the band was playing "Celebration." Her parents had refused to have that added to the contract as a stipulation; if they had, they could have demanded a refund. As it was, Mara seemed to enjoy laughing about it more than she was irritated. That was a good sign.

Soon it was time to drive home. My brothers and sisters had tied some two-liter bottles to the back of our little Hyundai Excel, and written "Just

Married" on the rear window. We jumped in and drove off, leaving everyone from the wedding behind us. We drove home, smiling and feeling happy and free at last. Some people on the highway honked and waved, and Mara uncharacteristically waved back. Two goofy smiling faces – one in a tuxedo and one in a wedding dress – driving back to our apartment in Rahway.

We made it home safely, and Mara went inside while I removed the bottles tied to the car. When I got upstairs, she had already switched out of her wedding dress and was packing some items for the honeymoon. We had plans to leave first thing in the morning (once rush hour was mostly over) and drive out to the Pennsylvania mountains. It wasn't going to be a bad drive; just a few hours, enjoying the late spring views. There were some really nice views along the way. I would have preferred seeing them in the fall, but we had already discussed the possibility of staying somewhere else for a weekend when the leaves started changing colors if we enjoyed our honeymoon (and if Mara was feeling up to it at the time).

Mara finished packing and then settled on the bed, petting the cats, while I changed packed some clothes and personal items myself. There was a notable silence in the bedroom, a bit of a cloud hanging over everything. I let things settle while I busied myself, and then climbed up in the bed and said hello to the cats as they walked all over me. Mara still sat quietly, petting Ubber but staring off into space.

"So that went pretty well, I thought," I told her, hoping to figure out if I had done something wrong or if her venom was reserved for someone else.

"It could have been worse," she replied. "But it was all about them. The whole fucking day was really about them. Not us, not me. Them."

I was relieved that it wasn't me she was pissed off at, but I didn't really have a response. I just sat there and waited. Eventually she spoke again.

"I can't fucking believe she had them play Sunrise, Sunset. She knew how much the wedding march meant to me."

"Is it really that big a deal?" I asked. "I mean it's just a song."

"It's not the song,'" she said. "It's *which* song. That song was all about them. Just like the wedding was. My own wedding and I was a sideshow attraction."

I just sat and started to think. "Sunrise, Sunset." It seemed harmless. From Fiddler on the Roof, right? Jewish wedding, Jewish musical, slow measured beat; a natural. And then I started remembering the lyrics. Mara was right. It's a song written entirely from the point of view of the parents, minus one or two lines from siblings. It's all about how the parents are standing there, wondering how time passed so quickly and the children have grown so fast.

In a way, it was the perfect choice for that particular wedding. A party for Mara's parents and their friends and relatives, with a few undesirables thrown in for good measure (my family and our friends). On the surface it was an innocent choice, but the more I thought about it, the more I understood why it bothered Mara so much.

"Don't worry," I told Mara. "You can use the wedding march at your next wedding."

That didn't seem to console her.

Chapter 23 - The Honeymoon- Part I

(What follows is a letter Mara and I sent to the management at Mount Airy Lodge/Poconos Gardens Lodge a few weeks after our honeymoon, and the response we received.)

Dear Sirs:

My wife and I were just married on May 28, 1989. We looked forward to this date for many years. Our honeymoon was planned six months in advance. Our plans were to stay at your Poconos Gardens Resort. We opted for the four-day/three-night package deal in one of your Nestlewood Chalet units. We were **very** disappointed with what we arrived to.

After a two-hour drive, we arrived at Pocono Gardens on May 29. We checked in and were led by a bellhop to our chalet (following his car with our car). The cabin itself was a major disappointment. Not only did it in no way resemble the picture from the brochure we were sent, but there were many things wrong with it in addition.

We first noticed the bed. There were stains all over the bedspread and the surrounding walls. The pillows could not have been more than one inch thick, one per person. The sheets were worn, thin, and cotton, in no way resembling the satin sheets in your advertisement. The "headboard" was merely a box covered with appeared to be carpeting not unlike a cheap car mat.

We then examined the rest of the cabin. The bathroom consisted of nothing more than a toilet; no mirror, no vanity, not even a garbage can. The air conditioning was completely inoperable, a matter which I will discuss later in this letter. The television reception was so poor, fully half of the channels were unwatchable. The "living room set" seemed to consist of nothing more than worn patio furniture.

Not only was the room completely unsatisfactory, the service we received was just as horrid. I made a total of three calls to the lobby during our one hour stay at your resort. The first was to complain about a huge wasp nest in the swimming pool room. In response, one of your staff came by the cabin about ten minutes later to present me with my very own can of ant and roach spray. I found this quite insulting, as I expected better service for over $250 a night. The next phone call was no notify the appropriate persons that the air conditioning was inoperable. This was a major concern for us, as my wife has a medical condition which among other things gives her a constant low-grade temperature. A cool room is vital for her comfort. When I booked the room, I specifically asked if each cabin contained individual air conditioning controls, and was assured that they did. When I confirmed the reservation a few days in advance I requested that the air conditioning be checked before our arrival, and was told that was standard practice.

The third and final call I made was to inform the manager that we were completely dissatisfied and wished to leave. I made this call after having waiting forty minutes for someone to come and address the air conditioning issue (nobody came, and nobody called). When I was finally connected to the manager, he informed me that Pocono Gardens had a strict "no refund" policy. This infuriated me, and I laughed sarcastically as I pointed out to him that I had seen another couple checking out early when I checked in, demanding and receiving a partial refund. He told me the best they could do was move us to another chalet. I had no intention of risking one more minute of our honeymoon on a resort that had failed so spectacularly in every imaginable way. I informed the manager that I had already made new arrangements to stay at a reputable hotel in New Jersey, as far away from their resort as I could get on such short notice. The manager reiterated the "no refund" policy to me. When I questioned the legality of charging me over $800 for a room in horrible condition that we had spent less than an hour in, during which we had used none of the room's facilities except the phone, he put me on hold so he could "speak to his superior." When he picked the phone up again, he announced that I should pack up our belongings, lock the chalet, and return to the lobby.

When I arrived there, the manager excused himself to go downstairs "to call the head of all three resorts." Upon returning he informed me that Poconos Gardens was willing to refund all but a $100 deposit. While I found this completely ridiculous, and told him so, I decided that the loss of $100 would be less painful than wasting any more of our precious Honeymoon time. I signed the refund slip, we got back in the car, and we drove as fast as we could back to New Jersey.

As things stand now, I am left with a terrible taste in my mouth and a very negative view of your resorts and your company. You give a bad name to the entire Poconos area. Every time we see an ad on television for a Poconos resort – or even offering real estate in the area – we get knots on our stomachs. We've told a number of people about our experience, and most of them were very surprised. They said they would have guessed that the Poconos was a nicer area with more reputable resorts based on all the advertisements they'd seen. They also expressed great doubt as to whether they would ever risk their time and money on a trip to your resorts, based on our experience.

For all of the reasons stated in this letter, I am once again demanding a refund of the additional $100 deposit. My wife and I made good on the reservation; it was only your complete failure to deliver that caused the cancellation. We plan to recount this episode in detail to major travel agencies and vacation information services, so that they can decrease the number of suckers who fall into your trap.

It's a horrible thing to have your honeymoon ruined, because a honeymoon is once in a lifetime. I would never wish it upon anyone, and I wish it hadn't happened to us.

Dear Mr. Kent,

I was sorry to read about the difficulties which you had encountered while you were here at Poconos Gardens Lodge.

Deposit money is taken to hold a room for our incoming guests. This was done in this case. If a room is not satisfactory then we will bend over backwards to find a suitable room for our guests. We have a no refund policy within our organization. Our room sales are by reservation only, therefore, when a guest leaves this gives us an empty room which cannot be sold. For this reason, deposit money is not refundable.

Again, I apologize and I hope you will give us another chance to host you in the future.

Chapter 24 - The Honeymoon – Part II

The disaster in the Poconos had been very stressful for me, and emotional for Mara. I kept hoping things were going to work out, but I already had a bad feeling when I saw a couple demanding a refund in the lobby as I checked us in. I was just happy Mara had waited in the car so she didn't hear that conversation. My goal was to keep her in a positive mental attitude as much as possible. We both knew it was likely her Crohn's Disease would flare back up during the honeymoon, but it seemed we should be able to relax and enjoy some relaxation and beautiful country in the meantime.

Her dissatisfaction with the chalet was immediate and complete. It really looked – and felt – like the cheapest of filthy motel rooms. Stains all over the walls and bed, worn low-quality furniture…I tried to keep Mara calm while she grew more and more upset. When the employee showed up with the can of bug spray as the solution to our wasp problem, she went absolutely ballistic. I knew that was the worst thing that could happen, so I suggested she just sit down and turn on the air conditioning, cool off and relax. And then, of course, the air conditioning blew nothing but warm air. I should have guessed that was coming!

It was while we waited – and waited - for someone to come check on the air conditioning that I offered the first solution that came to mind. We would bail on this place entirely, and I'd call the Hyatt she had stayed at the night before the wedding and see if they'd be willing to give us the same group guest rate they'd given people attending the wedding. She had enjoyed her night there, it was clean and fancy, and even with room service it would only cost about the same as this dump. I was able to use my MCI card to call and talk to the manager there, reserve a room for two nights (as Mara didn't think she could make it three nights away from home any longer), and then get back to arguing with the people at Pocono Gardens Lodge. I knew we could dispute the newest charge with the credit card company if they tried to bill us for the room, but the $100 deposit had been paid months earlier and if they didn't want to give it back, there was very little we could do about it.

By the time we made it back to the Hyatt, Mara was starting to feel a bit sick, but emotionally she was doing a little better. I suggested we go enjoy the swimming pool for a while; it was midday on a weekday, so it seemed likely it would be empty or nearly empty. We had our bathing suits with us since we had planned to swim in our chalet, and it sounded like a good way to relax and get Mara's mind off of worrying about getting sick again.

We hung out there for an hour or two, completely alone, enjoying the peace and solitude. Then it was back upstairs for a nap, and afterwards Mara wanted to order an early dinner. "I know I'm going to get sick soon; I can feel it. I want to have a good meal before that happens. I'm going to be paying for the wedding and the medication anyway, so I may as well enjoy myself until the shit hits the fan." We both laughed at this unintentional pun.

Since it was our honeymoon, Mara was more willing to be experimental with food. She wanted to eat in the room, and ordered herself some mushroom soup, fresh asparagus, and filet mignon. For whatever reason, she savored every bite as if it was her last meal. Mara swore this was the best mushroom soup she had ever tasted. After a piece of cheesecake to finish things up, she sat silently on the edge of the bed, enjoying the slowly fading tastes. "I don't care how sick I get," she said, "I am not going to throw this meal up. It'll hurt on the way out, but everything does anyway."

It couldn't have been more than twenty minutes later that the pains began to hit, and Mara knew her medication-induced holiday was about to end. She'd made it through the wedding, the party, and driving back and forth to Pennsylvania, and even got to enjoy half a day at the hotel. But now the honeymoon was over, in more ways than one.

We were fortunate enough to have a bathtub in the room, so Mara spent the rest of the night moving back and forth from the bed to the toilet to a warm bath. I dozed on and off; when things got really bad Mara would call for me to come and help her through the worst of the pain. She barely slept that night, and I was certainly wiped out by the morning.

Mara decided we should go eat breakfast in the restaurant, and forget the rest of the honeymoon. If she was going to be this sick, she preferred to be at home. I wasn't about to argue; I was planning on checking on the cats that day anyway, and we weren't locked into our reservation at the hotel. Breakfast was pleasant – I'd forgotten how much I loved real maple syrup compared to the watered-down name brands we bought in the supermarket – and then we packed up and headed home.

The cats were very glad to see us, and vice versa. I checked with work and things had been rather busy, so I decided I'd relax the rest of the day and get back to the office the next day. Mara expected to be sick or sleeping anyway, but at least now she would be able to feel comfortable in her own bed, the cats at her side (or on her side, depending). In a way, I was relieved Poconos Gardens had been such a disaster. I didn't want to imagine what Mara getting this sick would have been like out there. At least I knew we wouldn't have run out of toilet paper; we'd packed twelve rolls for emergency use.

It probably goes without saying, but the marriage wasn't consummated for two or three weeks. It wasn't important in itself since it wasn't like we had abstained since we met, but we did laugh about it in the months that followed. It always helped to have things to laugh about.

Chapter 25 - Life Goes On, and On, and On

After the wedding and the honeymoon, life moved into a steady routine. Weekdays I'd go off to work and Mara would stay home, watching television and keeping the cats company. When I got home we'd "argue" about dinner, and more often than not we would wind up eating peanut butter and jelly sandwiches, pizza, Chinese food, or fried chicken (or leftovers of one of those). On the rare occasion Mara cooked it would be during the week, and consist of either a cheap steak (cooked under the "broil" setting in a toaster oven a friend had given us as a wedding gift) or what she called Mexichips: individual tortilla chips with a spoonful of mild salsa and a thick slick of mozzarella cheese baked in the oven until the cheese melted.

On weekends, if Mara was up to it, we'd try to go out and see a movie on Saturday. Then on Sunday we'd stay in and nap all day while I cooked something of greater substance, like a roasted chicken. Unless Mara was feeling especially adventurous, she'd avoid all vegetables and have sides of instant mashed potatoes and stuffing. Meals seemed to be the high point of Mara's day, as she had little else to look forward to during the week. The few friends she still had were quickly disposed of, for whatever infraction she decided they had committed or just by default if she didn't talk to them for a few weeks. Mara had effectively isolated herself, and me. If it wasn't for work, I wouldn't have had any social contact either. I spent all my time commuting, working, or with Mara.

One of the only two real hobbies Mara had was scanning the TV Guide for movies, which I would then record on video tapes for us to enjoy later. They would wind up two or three to a tape (since each one had six hours of recording space). Which ones wound up on which tapes was random, but soon she got into the habit of turning one on when we went to bed, allowing her to stay up all night watching movies if she couldn't sleep. We built up quite a collection: more than 100 tapes with over 300 movies to choose from. Mara numbered each tape and build an index card system so she could flip through and choose one without digging through piles of video cassettes.

Mara's other hobby was Howard Stern. She would get up with me in the morning and record parts of his show on tapes, which she would then record over if there was nothing worth saving, or else transfer bits from one tape to another to save for later listening. I still have four or five of her Stern compilations. Besides the designed bits, her favorite parts were early in the show when Howard would complain about life at home. For some reason she loved listening to him complain about his wife.

One evening we were lying in bed watching some TV show when Mara muted the television during a commercial. "I just want you to know," she told me, "you never need to worry about getting a divorce."

"What the hell are you talking about?"

"If you ever get tired of being married to me, all you have to do is tell me and I'll kill myself. You don't need to get the divorce. You're the only reason I bother staying alive."

Then the show came back, and Mara unmuted the TV and went back to watching, without further comment.

It is very difficult to put yourself back into a moment, and remember exactly what you thought or felt. But clearly this moment had a strong impact on me. Mara had talked about suicide before. We lived a rather morbid existence together on a normal day; "when I'm dead" or "when I get hit by a bus" were common expressions used by bother of us, making jokes about how life would be different for the other when we died. "When I get hit by a bus, you'll already have your crazy cat lady starter kit all set up." "When I die make sure you use it for some sympathy sex with a few hot women." Things like that were said often, always in jest but also with the understanding that one of us would die before the other. That's part of life.

At this moment on this day, there was no joking. And this wasn't meant as a cry for help, or a threat, or anything like that. I understood what Mara was saying, although I knew she didn't see the ramifications of it from my side. For her, this was simply a truthful admission: if you want to end this marriage in the future, I'll willingly end it for you. Mara meant is as a sort of kindness, letting me know that there was no reason to stress if I decided I didn't want to be married to her, or if it had been a mistake. She meant to give me a "Get Out of Jail Free" card of the highest order.

Obviously, from my perspective Mara's statement carried a much different weight. But all it really did was put into words what I had known all along, and the challenge I had accepted. I had known for some time that it was my job to make Mara's life as tolerable as possible, with whatever happy moments we could put together. I was trying to give her reason to live, and to enjoy life despite her problems. Mara's blunt statement simply put the ethereal concept into solid form: as long as I stayed on the job, Mara would try to stick around. If I gave up, she would too.

It's a lot easier to see in retrospect how this one comment stayed on my mind for years to come. In many ways it's a terribly unfair thing to say to someone. It's effectively saying "my life is in your hands, and if you fail or quit you have allowed me to die." At the same time, I know she didn't say it meaning to be a burden or to lay constant fear and guilt on me. From her point of view, she was being kind by saying what she did. Sadly, her good intentions could never be taken in that way; in the darkest moments of my life I would have that knowledge whispering to me: keep going or she dies.

One of us was going to wind up being a martyr to the other, if things continued on this path until the bitter end. It was just going to be a question of who it killed first.

As Mara became lonelier and more isolated, she longed for some kind of personal interaction that didn't require leaving the house or committing to any type of friendship or relationship. It was with this in mind that she started participating now and then on my Computer Bulletin Board System (or BBS as they were known) called Zooman's Zoo. This was in the days before the internet, where computer users would use their modems to connect over the telephone line to other computers. A BBS was sort of a message clearing house: it was problem into different forums where registered users could post and reply to posts publicly, as well as send semi-private messages. Each forum would have its own topic: jokes, politics, sports, cooking, and the like. There were also areas to upload and download programs and pictures, and a few games you could play.

In general people tried to only call BBS's in their local area, so the call would be free. But you weren't limited to only messaging with people local to you, because of the BBS networks that had evolved. They were like a daisy chain of BBSs, with one computer calling the one above it in the chain or pyramid every day or two to upload messages posted by their users and download all the new ones from elsewhere. This let you communicate with people all over the nation – and the world, in some instances – with only a local call. Mara liked to participate but she didn't want to spend money calling long distance to my BBS, which was in my office in New York City. Besides, there were only a few forums she was truly interested in: mostly the more social ones. She would have me print off some pages of messages, and then she would write her replies out longhand for me to type in. It was tedious and it made her less interested.

    I wanted to encourage Mara to have some kind of socialization, even if it was just on the computer. I suggested that I create a new BBS at home that she could message on without making any phone call at all. Instead, people would call and connect with our computer. That seemed to please her, but after a few days she decided that if I was going to set one up for her to use, why not make it one tailored to her specific tastes? For starters, no kids. So many BBS users were teenagers, but she only wanted to talk to adults; people she might want to become friends with online, or even in person someday. And then she realized that if we were going to restrict it to adults, why not make it a true Adult's Only BBS with forums on dirty jokes, sex, S&M, fantasies, and other risqué topics in addition to a few tamer ones. I ordered a second phone line, set up all the software, and posted some free ads on other BBSs. Heart Throb BBS was born.

    Mara wanted to maintain some anonymity in the forums, so she decided to adopt the moniker of Voluptuous Violet. Under that pseudonym, she then took charge of most of the conversations and became a driving force behind user participation. She tried to post messages multiple times a day, greet new users, and loved to see a number of new messages when she logged back in after being away for a few hours.

In a way, the BBS replaced Mara's need for a job, as it allowed her to think, gave her a reason to get out of bed, and kept her communicating with the outside world. She also looked at it as office work: she would call each new user to voice-validate them (to confirm their age and their sex), she kept notes and made folders for what was going on in each forum and ideas she had for new ones, and even took to writing out some short stories in the Fantasy forum. Verifying sex was more important back then compared to now; there were always a lot of men who tried to set up a profile as a female, and not because of sexual identity. They just liked to mess with other guys and waste their time. On one or two occasions Mara would call a new user and discover they identified as a female, and if she thought they were sincere she would allow it.

The other reason Mara liked voice verifying new users is it gave her a chance to talk to other adults on the phone, but with no real relationship. More than 90% of the users were men, and they frequently would flirt with Mara (or in this case, Violet) and compliment her on her sexy voice. She seemed to love the attention. I wasn't jealous at all; in fact, I was happy to see her excited about it. Her interest in anything physically sexual was infrequent at best, and occasionally would end with her sobbing afterwards. Too many things reminded her of her grandfather now. I figured the attention of other men on the BBS could only help boost her self-esteem and perhaps would increase her own sexual desires.

I don't mean to suggest we weren't affectionate with each other, because we were. We held hands all the time, even lying in bed. We always kissed hello and goodbye, good morning and good night, and Mara loved to snuggle together while we were falling asleep. But between her Crohn's

Disease, her migraines, and her memories of her grandfather, she had no interest in sex. I didn't push her, and when she asked, I assured her I understood and was okay with it. What else could I do? We'd been married only a few months earlier, and I wanted her to be as happy as possible. It wasn't as if we'd never had sex before, but the longer I knew Mara the harder it became for her

It wasn't long before Mara realized that there was a simple way to increase the number of people participating in the forums. At this point we had callers from all over northern New Jersey, as well as a few from New York City and elsewhere. But if I started trading the messages using the daisy-chain method (or echoing, as it was called) between Heart Throb BBS and Zooman's Zoo BBS, we'd suddenly attract a whole group of new users in New York City that didn't want to make long distance calls to New Jersey. It was a simple enough thing to do; I just had to set up the forums on the other BBS, make them private for members only, and get the echo software.

After a few weeks, when I'd gotten that all set up and working properly, Mara had a new brainstorm. As long as I was already echoing messages between the two BBSs, why didn't we allow other BBSs to join and echo the messages as well? She rightly assumed there were plenty of BBSs – large and small – that would love to carry some adult's only forums. For many BBSs, the adult section was how they defrayed their expenses, charging $10 or $20 a year to allow access. These echoed forums would only increase their value, and therefore increase the number of paying members the larger systems would have. The forums originating on Heart Throb BBS became ThrobNet, and within months we had systems all over the nation calling in to echo messages, plus BBSs in Canada, Spain, England, Norway, Australia, and New Zealand. Our little message board to keep Mara busy had turned into a global enterprise.

At this point Mara and I had to discuss whether we wanted to try and turn this into some kind of money-making business. The easiest way would be to charge each BBS that wanted to be a member a flat fee per month, or per year. It wouldn't be a windfall but the money would definitely come in handy. But Mara was against that idea. First of all, she said she had gotten involved with this whole thing as a hobby and wanted it to stay that way. Second, with her health always up in the air, she didn't want to feel a responsibility to the other BBSs if a hospitalization, severe bout with depression, or anything else stopped either or both of us from paying full attention to keeping things running smoothly. And finally, despite disclaimers in the forms we made each BBS operator fill out, Mara didn't think it was a smart idea to be in an adult business when we had no idea what the laws were in each part of the country, or in foreign lands. Mara's points made some sense, so we dropped that subject entirely. This would remain a hobby, and not a business.

But problems did begin to surface. Mara's high profile on ThrobNet continued to draw the attention of many males. A few of them started to correspond with Mara directly, and she was quite secretive about those messages. Again, I didn't pry. I had been hoping Mara would form some new friendships, so I didn't want to interfere. One fellow she flirted with constantly went under the user name "Lover Man," and apparently lived somewhere in northern New Jersey.

One day I came home from work to find Mara quite upset. She proceeded to explain to me that she and Lover Man had been spending time talking on the phone a few times a week, and that "somehow" he had found out our address. I didn't understand how that could easily happen, since we didn't use our real names on the BBS and had a PO Box for incoming mail. But I let Mara continue. It seems Lover Boy had come over to the apartment unannounced, and didn't want to leave. She didn't let him in, and talked to him for about thirty minutes through the door, before he finally gave up and left. I asked if she wanted me to talk to him but she got equally upset about that idea. She said she felt confident he had gotten the message and it wouldn't happen again.

It wasn't until a few weeks later, when restoring some data that Mara had accidentally deleted (she sometimes got a little careless with the "delete *.*" DOS command), that I found a message Lover Man had sent Voluptuous Violet after the incident at the door. He expressed confusion over why she hadn't let him into the apartment "this time" since it hadn't been an issue "the other time." I couldn't be certain what had happened, or when it happened, but I had my suspicions. It was a known fact between Mara and I that she seemed unable to tell any man No when it came to them making sexual advances; in the hospital it had been sort of agreed that this was because through the sexual abuse she suffered, she had learned that accepting sexual advances is what made her "special." I could only assume she and Lover Man had enjoyed an afternoon of sex at some point. The cheating hurt – it always did. But it also hurt because Mara had no sexual appetite at all any longer, especially when it came to me. Yet for this guy she barely knew, she was willing to jump right into bed.

The one thing that really surprised me was she never confessed any of this to me, when in the past she had often felt the need to tell me, even when I had zero idea. I didn't know what to make of that omission. Maybe she wanted this encounter and therefore felt less guilt, or maybe she was just tired of apologizing. Either way, it was around this time that Mara started working on her subconscious solution to avoiding these problems, and any guilt associated with them: since she couldn't successfully avoid all contact with men, she would try to make herself as undesirable as possible and therefore there would be no advances in the first place.

It was time to give up the fight and slowly gain as much weight as possible.

Chapter 26 - I Don't Need Anyone Except You

As the months passed, Mara's mental state was generally stable, although that wasn't such a great level to begin with. The two biggest factors which affected her happiness on a day to day basis were her worsening Crohn's Disease symptoms, and her inability to get the kind of emotional support she wanted from her parents.

Neither one of those issues were directly under her control, but in both cases how she responded to them was partially by choice. When it came to her Crohn's Disease, it was an up and down struggle. Sometimes she would have a few good days in a row, and then at other times the illness would overtake her and she'd need to spend days going from the bathroom to the bed, occasionally ending with a hospital stay for a few days to try and stabilize her.

Part of the problem was there just wasn't much anybody could do for her Crohn's Disease. Sulfa drugs and cortisone steroids were the only medications to take. Besides that, surgery was often an inevitable outcome, but that wasn't some kind of cure-all. More than once Mara cried at her GI appointments, asking the doctor if he would consider doing surgery on her. The doctor would explain that since all her issues were in her large intestine, she would likely need a full colectomy (removal of the colon). There were times Mara decided the pain was too great and she would rather have that surgery done, but there were two barriers. First, no doctor would conduct that surgery unless her Crohn's Disease became worse and didn't respond to other treatment at all, and second there was no guarantee that she wouldn't begin to show symptoms of Crohn's in her small intestine later on. Suffering through the awful days until she found a period of remission was the only option.

Mara continued to search for other answers. There were a few times we drove halfway across the state to see a new GI, in the hopes that they would have some alternative to what she was being treated with. Working against Mara was the fact that she was a difficult and emotional patient. Usually the doctor would simply explain they had nothing else to offer, but in one case when Mara wanted to switch to this new GI regardless of what treatments were currently available, he shook his head and said "I'm not the doctor for you." In other words, he refused to take her on as a patent. That really set her off, and she cried heavily the entire way home. It was almost as if someone had left her at the altar.

Besides new treatments, one of the reasons Mara was interested in finding a new GI was that her current GI was such a good friend of her Dad. It wasn't that she didn't trust him, but just that she didn't like having him put in the position of being in the middle. Mara's relationship with her parents – strained to begin with – was disintegrating to where she didn't want to talk to them. Any communication between them inevitably ended up with Mara crying…or screaming and throwing things.

A large part of Mara's frustration with her parents involved the fact that she was caught in a cycle of hope and disappointment with them. She had somehow tied her forgiveness of her Mom and her parents' acceptance of her experiences with the grandfather in with each of them showing signs that they were becoming the parents she wanted (or the parents she felt she needed) instead of the parents they actually were.

A simple example of what I mean was an exchange she had with her Dad. During a particularly hard period mentally, Mara expressed to her parents that she didn't feel they were giving her the emotional support she needed. Granted, being emotionally available wasn't exactly their strong suit. There were times they could let their walls down, but it didn't happen very often. Even with each other, there was such a lack of visible affection. I couldn't tell if it was just their personality, or if they simply weren't in love with each other any longer.

I can't recall if this was over the phone or in person (although given the time period it was most likely over the phone). Mara was bemoaning the fact that her parents didn't understand what she was going though, and didn't properly understand the impact the sexual abuse had on her.

"Mara," her Dad said, "I love you and I am here to help you. Anything you want or anything you need. Just tell me what I need to do and you know I'll do it."

"Good, Dad. It would mean a lot to me if you read this book *Healing the Shame that Binds You*. It explains a lot about sexual abuse and how it affects the victim."

"Oh, I don't need to read that," her father replied. "I'm a doctor, I already know everything that could be in that book. But if there's anything you want me to do, just name it. I'm here to support you."

It was almost comical the way her parents saw the world, and themselves, completely different than Mara and I did. They truly believed they were supportive and emotionally available. Of course, point of view is very important. Maybe they **were** giving all they were able to give. On one occasion we were over at Mara's parents' place, and watching the film

"Mermaids" with Winona Ryder and Cher. As the film was coming to an end, Mara's mother looked at her and said "You know, I think that's the kind of mother I am."

"What kind of mother?"

"I've always been like Cher in this movie. Loving and understanding. But sort of cool and hip and wacky. Not the normal strait-laced suburban mother."

Mara started laughing, and kept laughing until she was red in the face. "You think you're Cher in Mermaids? **That's** the kind of mother you think you've been?"

Despite her Mom's requests, Mara refused to offer an example of how **she** saw her mother. I think part of it was to avoid an argument, and part was the realization that if her Mom truly thought she was Cher, Mara's opinion would be very hurtful and painful for her to hear.

I already knew what movie character Mara associated with her mother. It was Mary Tyler Moore's character in the film "Ordinary People." Cold, detached, more concerned about what the neighbors and friends thought than what was going on in her own family. In short, a real cold-hearted bitch. I thought that comparison was a bit unfair…but it was still accurate in some ways. When Mara would describe a recent conversation with her Mom to me, and the kind of responses she would get, she frequently would sum it up using one of her favorite lines from that movie: "You can't save French toast." If you've never seen "Ordinary People" that won't make any sense to you, but if you have, you'll understand **exactly** what I mean.

I kept trying to gently push Mara towards the realization that her parents would never change, and that she either had to accept them as they were or not at all. But time and time again she would build up some big project that she thought would finally break through the wall and transform them into the parents she wanted. And time and time again she would be let down. Some of Mara's attempts were doomed to failure before they began simply because they were so outside the norm. Once she spent two weeks making some cassette mix tapes for her mother, filled with songs she felt had special meaning for her. She also included some notes about why each song was important to her.

She gave it to her mother and waited for a response. After a few weeks of waiting she couldn't hold it in any longer and asked her mother outright what she thought of the project she had given her. "I liked some of the songs," her mother said. "But some of them just weren't my kind of music." Mara was heartbroken that her Mom put such little effort into digesting all the material she had provided, but I never expected anything different. As a matter of fact, I always believe her mother had a much better understanding of Mara's mental state than she let on. It wasn't a question of not understanding, it was just that her Mom couldn't, or wouldn't, express emotion in the way Mara wanted her to. That's not who she was.

Mara's Crohn's wasn't improving much, which to her was the worst situation. If she felt better it would be wonderful, and if things deteriorated, she could still dream about the supposed panacea of surgery. As weeks and weeks went by, her temper flared and her patience grew shorter and shorter. Everything anyone in her family did seemed to irritate her or infuriate her. It wasn't long before she stopped answering their calls, and forbade me from answering or speaking to them.

On one occasion Mara's Grandma Gladys (her mother's mother) called and left an upset and angry message on the answering machine, directed at me. She criticized me for not calling the family and keeping them updated on whatever was going on. "So, your wife is tongue tied and can't speak. Does that mean you're tongue tied too?" In an attempt to dissuade Gladys – and her parents – from continuing to bother her, Mara took that message and swapped it as the new outgoing message on the answering machine. So the next time her parents, siblings, or Gladys called and got the answering machine, that's what they heard.

It wasn't long after that when the calls stopped coming. I don't know for certain but I believe Mara finally got to the point where she told someone directly "I don't want to talk to any of you. Stop calling me."

Mara's attempt to isolate herself was now effectively complete. She spent less time on the BBS, talked to nobody on the phone, and refused to see her family. She had already told me that I was her reason for living; now she was putting it into practice. "I don't need anyone but you" she told me.

It was all on me now. Supporting Mara financially, emotionally, mentally, and in every other way was my duty and nobody else's. I knew this was what I had signed up for, and now I was on my own.

Chapter 27 - Spiraling Down

As sick as Mara was, she still found herself having to defend herself from people on occasion. The knee-jerk reaction to her was to feel she didn't "look sick" and that her only apparent issue was being overweight. Whenever she encountered this, Mara became very defensive and hurt. Mixed in somewhere was also a bit of guilt; perhaps she felt that since she didn't "look sick" it was her fault that she was. Whatever the reason, Mara felt guilty about being physically and mentally ill, and about not being able to work and contribute financially. That guilt didn't often motivate her to do much cooking or cleaning, but it was still there, and I recognized it.

After the wedding, our insurance coverage came through my job, in what was known back then as an insurance "association." It was similar to a group policy, except the members of the association didn't necessarily work for the same company, but instead worked for a number of companies too small for their own group but who were indirectly associated in some way (in this case, we were all in the same industry and located in the New York/New Jersey area, and did business with one firm at the center of the association). It wasn't a great policy but it wasn't terrible, with decent coverage for doctor visits, hospital stays, and prescriptions.

At some point after one of her hospitalizations, it was suggested to Mara that she apply for Social Security Disability. She had paid her disability taxes while she was working, and it seemed only natural that since she was not able to work any longer that she should try and become enrolled. At first, she felt a bit guilty about that, until I pointed out that she wasn't given any choice about whether those taxes were taken out of her paycheck, so why should she be denied the right to apply when she needed it?

Of course, she wasn't denied the right to apply. It was simply her application that was denied. Mara was furious. She couldn't understand why Social Security would deny her coverage when she had been hospitalized multiple times, spent half of her day in the bathroom, and was actually fired from her last job for being unable to go to work and perform her duties due to her illnesses. Sadly, this rejection left her feeling not just angry, but also guilty and defensive again. Even the government was telling her she wasn't really sick.

I didn't know how we would pay for it, but we agreed to consult with a lawyer who specialized in this area. He explained to us that the unspoken rule at Social Security was "if you're warm, you can work." In other words, as long as you're alive, you're don't quality for disability, at least not initially. In today's world it doesn't seem to be quite the labyrinth it was back then, at least from a distance. Fortunately, our attorney assured us that he felt he could get Mara approved based on her current condition. Even better, he explained that she would be due back disability starting a specific period from when she last worked, and his fees would be a given percentage of that lump payment. In other words, he felt confident enough in Mara's case (once he had looked at some of her medical records) that he was willing to take the entire job on contingency. That was a great relief to me, as we didn't have the money to pay him up front, and it wasn't as if we could turn to Mara's parents for help with it.

There was one snag: Mara was adamant that she should be approved for disability benefits on her Crohn's Disease alone. She didn't want her mental issues brought into the conversation. It wasn't that she was trying to hide them; the lawyer had been fully briefed on her problems and her mental hospitalization. It was more a matter of pride; Mara saw the use of her mental problems as an admission that she was – in effect – crazy. It was a leap she didn't want to make. She also felt it was insulting that they would continue to deny her coverage when she spent so much time crying in agony in the bathroom.

Our lawyer was very cognizant of Mara's feelings, and had a terrific bedside manner. Little by little he massaged Mara's opinions, helping her to see the entire process as an impersonal bureaucratic dance instead of some kind of judgment of her or her illness. "You're just a number to them, a line on a computer screen." At some point he was politely blunt: with the mental illness combined with her Crohn's Disease, he could get her approved. Without, there was only about a 25% chance of success. She reluctantly gave in, and a few months later she was earning $450 a month in disability income.

Just as important was the Medicare coverage. When you combined that with her regular insurance through my job, most doctor visits or hospital stays would be nearly fully covered. There was a lot of confusion with Medicare about whether they should be the primary or secondary insurer, but either way it was a big help. It also confused the hospitals and doctors, so to be safe they only billed the Medicare-approved amount whether Medicare was primary or secondary. That also cut back on the doctor bills.

We didn't get to enjoy the dual coverage for very long. The vague setup of the Insurance Association suddenly became even stranger. The Association was losing money, or bankrupt, or something else which should have been impossible but was happening. I think they had been purchasing insurance coverage and decided it would be better to self-insure, which fell apart when some members became seriously ill. Conveniently, the law allowed the Association a way out of the problem: they would simply dissolve, and then start a *new* one. But to be admitted into the new one, you had to be healthy. That meant Mara was going to be kicked off the insurance.

As it turned out, there was some legal requirement that forced them to keep Mara covered for six months more before they kicked her off. And at first, we didn't see this situation as a major problem. We would just get a Medicare supplemental policy from Blue Cross and Blue Shield to back up Medicare, and our out of pocket expenses would still be very limited.

Except for one area: prescriptions. In the 1990's there was no such thing as Medicare D; Medicare provided no prescription coverage, and neither would the Medicare supplemental policy. We were going to go from paying between 10% and 20% of the cost of Mara's prescriptions to 100%. And that was going to hurt, in a *big* way.

Mara's psychological problems had gotten worse, and more complex. After switching psychiatrists, she was diagnosed with bipolar disorder and a few other things. This meant she was now on three different psych medications, plus two for Crohn's, and a pile of medications meant for "as needed" use: ones for nausea, diarrhea, intestinal inflammation, intestinal spasms, migraines, anxiety, intestinal pain, and I can't even remember what else.

One of Mara's most recent issues with her Crohn's Disease had been acid reflux. It burned constantly and over the long-term would greatly increase her risk of throat cancer. An endoscopy already showed a few small ulcers in her esophagus. Standard antacids did little to help, no matter how much of them she took. She drank Pepto Bismol like water and ate Tums like candy. Finally, her GI put her on a new drug, Losec. This is a common over-the-counter drug these days, currently known under brand names like Prilosec. (It is my understanding they changed the name from Losec because pharmacists were occasionally confusing it with another drug with a similar name meant for an entirely different medical problem). Mara had to have blood tests to check her liver levels every few months for as long as she was on the medication, and it didn't prove to be much help until she started taking it both in the morning and at night. Our monthly cost for that drug alone was close to $800, and I was only making around $500 a week at that stage (and business was getting slower and slower). The only way we could afford it was to put it on a credit card.

Credit cards became a new survival method for us. Our credit was still good, although starting to become extended, so when we would get an application in the mail for a new card I filled it out without fail. Mara still got some offers in her name, and she'd apply for those as well. Discover was a new card at that time, and we each grabbed one of those when offered. We also picked up cards from department stores if we could make use of them for clothes, appliances, and things like that. It was a slow but vicious cycle, charging our regular purchases and then making minimum monthly payments which barely covered the interest charge. Only the influx of new cards allowed us to spread the financial pain out to as many places as possible, in an effort to keep things manageable.

This new development only added to Mara's depression. Every month we were falling deeper into debt, and her disability benefits only covered a part of the money we were spending on prescriptions. We were only just barely breaking even beforehand. I did my best to reassure her, and to let her know I didn't blame her in any way for the fix we were in. How could I? Her mental illness was not of her doing, and the hours she spent in the bathroom on a bad day were filled with crying and pain. It would have been one thing if I felt there was some way – any way – she could have been working. But there wasn't. Her attempts to help around the house, to clean here and there or to do laundry, were enough to wipe her out physically. And on those rare occasions when she was feeling okay, I preferred we go out and try to enjoy a movie or something. Injecting a few hours of joy into Mara's life was more important than asking her to help clean the bathroom or mop the floor.

Because I was there so often picking up prescriptions – and paying with no insurance coverage – I had many occasions to discuss our situation with Helena, the main pharmacist at the drug store we used. She greatly sympathized with the spiral we were caught in, but there wasn't anything she could do about it. Finally, one day she gave me a pamphlet about a New Jersey state program which had become available called Pharmaceutical Assistance for the Aged and Disabled (PAAD). She didn't have a lot of specific information about the program, but she thought it might offer some hope, and possibly a way out of this mess.

Sadly, after requesting the full details on the program, we found there was nothing it could do for us. I made too much money at work for us to be considered for benefits (the program worked strictly off gross income; it made no allowance for what percentage of that income was going to prescription expenses). In fact, the only way Mara could qualify would be if we divorced and if she then moved in with her grandmother (who she wasn't even speaking to) or found her own place with rent assistance. Just getting divorced and continuing to live together would still disqualify her. It wasn't a major disappointment, because at this stage we never got our hopes up about anything.

There was only one thing about the financial hole we were in that was positive: things had gotten deep enough that they didn't matter any longer. Sometimes I would be at work and Mara would call and ask what we were going to have for dinner. If I didn't know, she'd often suggest I pick up Chinese food…enough for two nights, if possible. Often, we'd be home eating fried dumplings or egg rolls and Mara would ask "I wasn't sure if you would pick up dinner, because I don't think we can afford it."

"We can't afford it," I'd reply. "But at this point, what's the difference? Either things are going to get better – in which case it won't matter – or things are going to get worse…in which case it won't matter."

That was flawed logic, but it was easy to find solace in it.

Chapter 28 - A Moment of Levity

As bad as things could be for us, I don't want to give the impression that Mara and I never had fun. We tried to find humor in everything we did, including poking fun at each other and ourselves. That's something I have always done, and Mara was often the same way. When everything sucks, finding something to laugh at can make you forget for a moment.

I'd gotten involved in the Diplomacy hobby in the late 1980's, and at some point I started publishing a monthly Diplomacy newsletter. If you're not aware, Diplomacy is a seven-player game set at the start of World War I. There are tactics involved, figuring out the best movies to make just as in chess or any other strategy game. But the biggest part of the game involved negotiating with the other players, and trying to get them to do what you want them to do while making them think it is in their best interest.

The Diplomacy hobby was full of personalities, and the newsletters often had a lot of non-Diplomacy material included. Other games, humor, politics, letters, drawings…just about anything you can imagine. While Mara had no interest in the game itself, she did enjoy some of the other games I ran in my newsletter. But most of all she liked having a vehicle for occasionally poking fun at me in public. As with most things, her enthusiasm would come and go, but when she was in the mood she would write up a column about our life and have me include it. She didn't like to write about her illnesses or problems; these columns were a form of escape for her.

One of the more popular columns she contributed appears below. It was a piece she was really proud of. Dark humor, self-deprecating jokes, and a peek into what life with me could be like. At the time, a lot of our readers said it was hilarious. A few said it was like fingernails on a chalkboard. Mara found happiness in both responses. Like a true artist, she just wanted to evoke a reaction…it didn't matter **what** that reaction was.

I really liked the scenario last time (my column on Doug's procrastination) so let's get right into the next scenario – everyday life at the Kent apartment. The following is a nearly 100% accurate and true transcript of a typical conversation between Doug and myself.

The Setting: The dark and depressing Kent kitchen (Doug still hasn't replaced the burned-out bulbs in the overhead light). Doug and Mara are both seated around the table.

Doug: What's for dinner?

Mara: I have no idea.

Doug: What do you mean you have no idea? What are our choices?

Mara: Peanut butter and jelly.

Doug: Again? Wouldn't you rather have pizza?

Mara: Would you?

Doug: I don't care. Which do you prefer?

Mara: Well, I could go for either.

Doug: Pizza is really better, but it's a lot more expensive. What do you think?

Mara: I don't know, I'm not really hungry.

Doug: Okay, we'll have nothing. I have my snacks in the bedroom anyway.

Mara: Well, then, what am I gonna eat?

Doug: You just said you weren't hungry!

Mara: But we have to eat something, otherwise we'll be hungry later.

Doug: No we don't. We'll have nothing. There's nothing to eat, there's nothing to get delivered, so we'll have nothing, okay?

Mara: Alright, fine, we'll have nothing.

Doug: You know, a good wife wouldn't let her husband eat just snacks for dinner. What kind of diet is that? It's not healthy!

Mara: You're the one who said we should have nothing!

Doug: No I'm not, I never said that. So, will it be pizza or peanut butter and jelly?

Mara: I don't want to wait for the pizza. Let's have the peanut butter and jelly and get it over with.

Doug: (walks over to the cabinet and looks for a clean glass. There are plenty of large glasses that just require a quick rinse to use, but Doug settles on a tiny juice glass since it's easier than cleaning one himself). But I don't want that for dinner!

Mara: Why don't you just admit you want pizza then?

Doug: (opens the freezer to get some ice. Sticks hand in the bucket, but there is none in there, so he removes an ice cube tray). I don't want pizza, but you aren't giving me any better choices.

Mara: You know what the choices are, so choose! Why do I always have to make the decision?

Doug: (removes the last two cubes from the tray. Puts the empty tray back into the freezer, under another tray so by the time anyone finds it empty he can deny he put it in that way. He fails to notice that the tray he outs it under is also empty). You're the one who's supposed to make dinner tonight, so you choose.

Mara: (sees **exactly** what Doug is doing with those ice cube trays). So I choose peanut butter and jelly! Get me the stuff and I'll make it.

Doug: (turns on the TV to the news so he has an excuse not to pay much attention). Okay, here's the jelly and the peanut butter.

Mara: Get me the plates and a knife. You make your own this time.

Doug: No! **You** make the **best** peanut butter and jelly sandwiches so you make it.

Mara: No, this time you make your own.

Doug: Fine, then I won't eat.

Mara: Fine, asshole, I'll make it for you.

Doug and Mara: (in unison, as a particularly ugly or decrepit person appears on the TV screen) [both pointing at screen] That's you.

Doug: Here's everything, now make my dinner, woman!

Mara: (opens the bread. As she pulls the first piece out, it tears).

Doug: That's your piece!

Mara: I know. You always stick me with the ripped or burned stuff.

Doug: (examines his bread). This bread feels funny. Kind of mushy and wet. Was there any mold in the bag? I won't eat it.

Mara: No mold, but it's all kind of damp.

Doug: Then I won't eat any of it. I guess it's pizza or nothing.

Mara: It has taken 45 minutes to get to this point, and now it's going to take at least another half-an-hour for the pizza to get here.

Doug: Who cares? I wanted pizza in the first place.

Mara: Fine, let's go to the bedroom and watch TV till it gets here.

(scene shifts to the bedroom)

Doug: (placing the juice glass with three drops of soda left on it on the pier behind us). When we finish this glass of soda, you have to get up and get more. I call it.

Mara: (drinks two of the remaining three drops) You should have filled it when we were in the kitchen.

Doug: While you're up, why don't you get us a bigger glass? There are some by the sink you can rinse out.

Mara: Didn't you check the dishwasher? There are clean glasses in there! (gets up and walks out towards the kitchen).

Doug: Hey, Mara, while you're in there fill up the ice cube trays. I think they're empty.

Mara: (returns with a large glass of soda). Here. What's on TV?

Doug: Nothing. Want to watch a video?

Mara: Which one?

Doug: I don't know, which one do you want to watch?

Mara: Are we going to go through this all over again?

Doug: I guess not. We can just watch TV. (turns the TV to some nature show where wild animals run around and do whatever they do. Something with a big butt of hairy legs comes on the screen).

Doug and Mara: (in unison, pointing) That's you.

I know you might find it hard to believe, but that conversation actually took place over a 45-minute period a few weeks ago. We had to reconstruct what we said, but it's about 95% accurate. Now, some of you may be thinking that this type of fiasco is unusual for us, but it's not. For example, take this "Update on Our Pathetic Lives" column we post on our computer bulletin board every week so the locals know how we're doing:

"7-28-91 - Culinary arts were a major focus this week. Wednesday we made a steak in the toaster oven, but it smelled kinda like liver so we chucked it and had peanut butter and jelly instead. Friday we were GOING to have steak, but Doug complained until we ordered pizza. We had already defrosted the steak so we put it in the fridge. By Saturday it looked a little like cat food, so we chucked it and took another one out. We made that for dinner but when it was done it also smelled a bit like liver, so we threw it away and had peanut butter and jelly again. I almost cried – I had my heart set on a piece of good red dead animal flesh. I'm not sure how many times we'll go through this before we decide not to eat steak again (or stop buying the cheapest thinnest ones they have). That will cut out about 50% of our recipe file. Sunday we had hamburgers, which we ate even though the buns felt a little weird. So far neither of us have gotten sick from them, so that's a good sign. We were thinking about going to a movie this weekend, but by the time we settled on T2 (Saturday) it was too late to make the first showing, so we took a long nap anyway. We ended up wasting the entire day, but since we had nothing to do it wasn't a total loss. Sunday neither of us wanted to admit that we didn't want to see a movie, so we each tried to make the other feel guilty about skipping the movies for another week. In the end we watched football and baseball and took a nap. My sister came by Friday, but we managed to make her feel so unwelcome that she left after 5 minutes. Another success story! P.S. – If we died on a Friday here, due to a gas leak or something, no one would know until Monday when Doug didn't show up for work. If it was a holiday, that would mean it would take until Tuesday. Maybe that's why Doug refuses to take a vacation – he's worried we would die and it would take two weeks for anyone to discover the bodies!"

I think the BBS update was an exaggeration, but the rest of Mara's column was almost entirely accurate. I wish she had found the motivation and energy to write and participate more frequently, but even her occasional appearances were greeted with a warm reception. I think readers loved how she was able to poke fun at me in ways nobody else could. And Mara knew I thought it was hilarious. That was just the way we used humor to get through each day, no matter how sick or miserable she might feel. Laughter kept us going.

Chapter 29 - When is Rock Bottom?

Life just seemed to keep getting worse for Mara, and for us. It was a slow decline at this stage, but a constant one. Mara no longer felt comfortable driving, so even though she had the car at her disposal all day I needed to be available to take her to all of her doctor appointments. It was just as well, because her memory was getting quite bad. Aside from when she had a therapy appointment, she always wanted me to go in with her to see the doctors. Part of that was because she would forget what she said, or forget what medications she was taking. She also didn't have the mental strength to get into discussions with them or to ask a lot of questions, so if there were things she wanted to know we would discuss that beforehand so I could remember to ask for her. And then on the drive home Mara would ask me to repeat – in simpler terms – whatever the doctor had told us while in the examination room.

Mara's bipolar issues were becoming more and more noticeable. For days she wouldn't want to get out of bed at all, and then for nights she wouldn't sleep. There wasn't much I could do but learn to sleep with the television on all night, and try to find things she could enjoy from home. She still liked to play some Nintendo games from time to time, but she didn't want new ones; she just liked playing the same ones we owned over and over. One of the department store credit cards had paid for that luxury, and it was money well spent.

I knew Mara's family had an old pinball machine when she was growing up, so I decided we would spend $150 on one for the apartment. Mara couldn't comfortably stand for too long at the machine, but she found great joy in playing (and hadn't lost any of her skill). I was still trying to bring happiness into her life, no matter how sick or depressed she was.

Sadly, it was around this time that our black cat Ubber developed kidney failure. Ubber was possibly more important to Mara that I was, and losing him was going to rip her heart out. We tried to keep him going for a while by giving him subcutaneous fluids a couple of times a week, and surprisingly his blood tests showed great improvement; our vet hadn't expected it to work. So Ubber was able to stay with us for a few more months. We both knew the end was coming, but I was hopeful Mara was preparing for it.

Ubber's health hadn't been that great for a while, as he had developed a form of epilepsy. Our cats were our children, so we adjusted everything we did to try and keep him comfortable. Any rhythmic tapping or crumpling of a bag of chips would make Ubber's eyes bug out as if he was about to have a fit. The actual epileptic fits were much scarier for us than they were for Ubber. His body would stiffen, he'd fall over, and his tongue would stick out. As we'd been advised, we would never shake him or try to wake him up. Instead we would pet him gently and speak softly to him until he came out of it. He'd be confused and lethargic for the rest of the day but otherwise okay.

Eventually Ubber's treatments were failing to lower his toxin levels. He suffered an especially long and violent epileptic fit, including vomiting, urinating, and defecating while he was unresponsive. There was no fighting it, and we didn't want to selfishly keep him alive and make him suffer. It was time to say goodbye. Putting a beloved pet to sleep is a terrible and very emotional experience. I can still hear the sound of Ubber crying out when they put the line into his arm, through which they would be injecting the drugs needed to end his life. It all seemed so unfair; he was our favorite cat, and yet he was the one we had for less time. I've been through that process many times since, and before or after each one I am reminded of Ubber and get a terrible knot in my stomach over and above the misery I feel already.

Mara was completely shattered. She cried nearly non-stop for two weeks, unable to sleep and getting out of bed only to use the bathroom or go to the kitchen. Every time she'd start to pull herself out of the hole she was in, something would remind her and she'd start crying again. Time to feed the cats? She'd put food out for Ubber by mistake. She'd look to see him in all his favorite places out of habit: watching the birds from the bedroom window, laying on his scratching pad, or sleeping under the table. But the worst for her was when our tabby Tigger would run out in the living room and start crying for Ubber to come out and play. That just broke Mara's heart every time she heard it. Sweet Tigger had always seen Ubber as her best friend, and now he was gone and she couldn't understand why. It was too much to take at times.

Eventually Mara would only cry a few times a day over Ubber, and that's when she started spending her time memorializing him. She took days adding and deleting songs to a list she was going to record on a cassette she could listen to when she wanted to think of him. I understood the motivation behind that, but it seemed to me all the songs she chose – except for one or two – represented her misery at his death rather than the love they shared while he was with us. But it was her project, so I left her to it.

The one thing I chose to do in his memory was for both of us. I took a favorite photo of Ubber – lying on the windowsill with his head tilted upside down and his cute little fangs showing – and had it blown up to poster size, which I then put in a frame and hung on the wall secretly for Mara to find one day when she wandered into the living room. Of course, she had me move it to the bedroom once she saw it, but for a change I could see the photo reminded her more of how much joy she found with him and less of how much sadness she felt now.

Feeling nostalgic over Ubber also had Mara thinking more about her family, and considering opening communications with them. She was still very angry and bitter about everything they had said or done, whether deserved or not. She would search for the smallest thing to take as a personal attack. At one point during their estrangement, Mara's mother had sent her a postcard with a brief message saying that she missed her. It was clearly an attempt to test the waters without violating the privacy Mara had demanded when she cut her family off. But to Mara it was just an example of how little she meant to her Mom. That was because the postcard had part of someone else's name written on it, which had them been crossed out. Obviously her mother had considered sending that postcard to someone else once, and then changed her mind, crossing the name out. But to Mara that crossed out name made the card some kind of second-choice gift, a leftover given to her because it hadn't been needed for its original purpose.

After thinking about it for two or three months, Mara finally got in touch with her mother by phone and suggested a visit at our place to talk about the communications problems and failures which had led to Mara's intentional isolation. I don't remember a lot about that meeting. Both her parents came to our place, where Mara's Dad and I sat quietly most of the time while Mara and her mother argued and tossed blame back and forth. Mara even talked about that postcard and how upset it had made her. When her mother denied any knowledge of what she meant, Mara went off to the bedroom and returned with the offending postcard; she had saved it just for this purpose, to use as evidence of how thoughtless her mother was. I do remember her Mom really teared up about the postcard; it was as if she was suddenly seeing (or remembering) what a tightrope act it could be to deal with Mara when her mental state wasn't at its best. I felt bad for her, in a way. I knew better than anyone how difficult it could be, but I was mostly used to living on the edge of the blade.

Whatever happened, the real purpose of getting together hadn't been to attain apologies or promises of things changing. I knew Mara would never have suggested them coming over if she hadn't intended to open the lines of communication fully. When the accusations and recriminations were done, nothing had been accomplished but perhaps some anger had been released and resolved. There were hugs and handshakes all around, and Mara asked her Mom to call when they got home so she knew they'd made it safely. That request meant a lot to her mother.

In retrospect, I can see this whole period of not speaking to her family was part of a cycle that continued throughout Mara's life, before and after the meeting. Mara would draw a line in the sand, or state that she was willing to do something if she wasn't satisfied. That threat would be waved off, and then Mara would follow through. From that moment onward, the dynamic would always be different, because her parents carried with them the realization that whatever she was talking about was more than an empty threat. Instead, it was a legitimate possibility, one that would always be in the back of their minds. Past experience changes future behavior.

A few months after familial communications had been restored, Mara woke up with a new problem. She didn't know what it was, but she kept telling me it was different than anything she had previously experienced. It started with terrible nausea; she couldn't keep anything down, but she didn't feel like she had the flu or food poisoning. Then the pain started; lower pain, near her side. Mara's immediate assumption was appendicitis but it was on the wrong side for that.

We went to see her GI, who took blood and a stool and urine sample. Within an hour he said he was fairly certain of the diagnosis: Mara had a kidney stone. He explained that these were unfortunately much more common with sufferers of Crohn's Disease, but for reason they didn't fully understand; the best guess was the disease interfered with the absorption of certain minerals. I had no real knowledge of the way kidney stones worked, but I was quick to learn. The GI said that if the pain was as bad as Mara was describing, the stone had already dropped out of her kidney and into her ureter, which connected the kidney to the bladder.

Apparently the ureter acted in the same way as the intestine or the esophagus, contracting rhythmically to push along the fluids released from the kidney. Tiny stones were common, and pass with no notice. It is only when a stone is a bit larger that it can get stuck in the ureter. At that time, like something stuck in your throat, it can become lodged and only moves after a great deal of effort by the ureter (along with excruciating pain and nausea).

There wasn't any immediate treatment he could do. He referred Mara to a urologist who would follow her progress, and under his instruction the GI wrote out prescriptions for stronger pain killers, stronger anti-nausea drugs, and told Mara her job was to drink as much water as possible. The more fluids that passed through the ureter, the better chance the stone would be nudged along.

This went on for more than a week, with no relief. Mara had been given little paper strainers to urinate into so she could catch the stone when it passed. This was both to know the stone had passed, and also so they could test it to see what it was formed of. That would provide the most effective treatments to avoid future stones. The only thing she caught in her filters was blood. Even with the painkillers, she said this was worth than how she imagined childbirth would feel. It wasn't localized pain to the spot of the stone – wherever that was. It radiated all over her front, side, and through to the back. The best Mara could do each day was try to fall asleep now and then, and the rest of the time be groggy enough not to notice how much pain she was in.

A trip to the urologist provided no additional relief. For Mara there were only two options: pass the stone, or go through surgery. A newer treatment was breaking up the stone with sound waves, but Mara wasn't a candidate for that because she was Factor 11 deficient in her blood, which made her a bleeder. The risk of internal bleeding from that procedure was too great. Surgery had its own risks, and Mara's poor overall health, regular use of painkillers, and weight were all obstacles to that option. The best the doctor could do was ask Mara to hang on for another week to ten days. If nothing passed by then, they would go up through her urethra and bladder and into the ureter in an attempt to lodge the stone loose and remove it, or at worst to break it up somehow so it could pass on its own.

Mara had an ongoing joke she used throughout her life: she was "the 1%." Whenever a doctor mentioned that some result or some ailment or some side-effect only occurred with one percent of the people (or any other small amount), she would almost automatically reply "well you've just met the one percent!" Her urologist didn't say only one percent of his patients would require surgery, but he did say is was infrequent. So she expected surgery to be necessary the first time it was mentioned. The prospect of surgery didn't frighten her at all, because she viewed both the removal of the stone or dying asleep on the operating table as equally mixed blessings. Death would be an end to her pain and misery, but also an end to life. Surviving and having the stone removed would eliminate the pain and nausea she had been in for weeks, but as she was quick to remind me, "my body is smarter than I thought. It can only handle one soul-crushing pain at a time; you notice I haven't had any Crohn's problems or migraines while I've had this kidney stone?" She did want to get better, but getting better for Mara only meant she would go back to dealing with her other physical ailments.

Even her mental state had been a bit better through the kidney stone. Perhaps the slew of painkillers kept her too doped up to be depressed, or it was possible she really felt like this could be the final battle she had been expecting for a long time. When she was lucid enough to have a conversation, Mara would offer me all kinds of advice and requests for what I should do if she died from this kidney stone. It was nothing unusual: please take care of the cats, please go on with your life and try to be happy, stay in touch with my family for at least a while to make it easier on all of you. She never talked about funeral arrangements; I assume she knew as well as I that her parents would do whatever they felt was appropriate no matter what she requested. Like the wedding, her wishes would come second. "Funerals are for the living anyway" she reasoned.

And of course, she was right about the outcome. After another week of no improvement, there was no other option than to schedule surgery. Mara had asked that her parents not come and wait during the surgery, which was just as well. I'd be there, and I preferred to be alone. I'd certainly keep them updated if I heard anything, and the doctor had instructions to contact Mara's father when it was over to give him the "medical terminology version" of how things had gone. I have a vague memory of Mara's mother being in the waiting room during all or part of the surgery, but I can't be certain. If she was, it wasn't truly against Mara's wishes; they'd have agreed to it beforehand. Her parents were obviously concerned about the surgery but while it was serious, they didn't view it as life or death. That wasn't minimization in this case, just being realistic.

As always seems to be the case, Mara had to be at the hospital at 6am even though the surgery wouldn't start until maybe 9am. It may have even needed to be pushed back a day or two because of a medical emergency with another patient; again, certain details are hazy. But on the appropriate morning we were there on time and Mara was wheeled off to prep. I met with the urologist who assured me this was not generally a risky procedure, and even given Mara's personal danger factors he felt it should go well. Then he left, and the clock started moving slowly as I waited for some kind of news.

I had brought a few books with me, but I couldn't relax enough to read them. Instead I alternated between shifting uncomfortably in my chair and pacing up and down the hallway. Somehow the old Andy Gibb song "I Just Want to Be Your Everything" popped into my head, and I kept it playing over and over in my head. My obsessive mind began to believe that if I stopped playing it over and over, something terrible would happen during the surgery. I'd often been bothered by racing thoughts or stupid ideas like that, and not always in an attempt to ward off misfortune. As I paced and listened to the song, I remembered how I used to walk home from Junior High School. I would have thoughts and then in my mind I uncontrollably counted the letters in each word as it passed through. "That four breeze six feels five nice four and three brisk five on two my two face four."

The operation was supposed to take about two hours, so of course it took nearly four hours for the doctor to come find me in the waiting room. It wasn't that he was avoiding me or busy tending to another patient; it was just that the procedure took a lot longer than expected. I knew everything was disaster-free because he was smiling as he approached. He explained that they had a terrible time getting the scope up into the ureter; Mara's seemed to be a bit smaller than normal (back to the rule of the 1% again, I thought to myself). He also didn't want to force his way through anything as he wanted to avoid unnecessary bleeding given her Factor 11 deficiency.

He held up a test tube for me to look at. Down at the bottom was a brownish little object, sort of the color of fried chicken skin. "Take a close look" he told me, and I did, holding the tube up to the light. The stone was somewhere between 3/8" and ½" long, and perhaps 3/8" wide. It was sort of in the shape of an infinity symbol or a sideways 8, wider at the ends and thinnest at the center.

"Once we got the scope up there, I saw what the problem was," the doctor said. "This little bastard was stuck in her ureter, sideways. Unless her body managed to snap it in half somehow, there was no **way** she was ever going to pass this thing."

I was able to see Mara in recovery about an hour later. She was pale, as white as a ghost, but happy to learn they had gotten the stone out. The doctor came by again and reminded her about likely side effects from the procedure. There would be blood in the urine, urgency, and continued discomfort or pain while her ureter slowly recovered from the ordeal of having a jagged shard of fried chicken skin stuck in it (and being stretched to the limit by the scope used to find and remove the stone). They would do tests to determine the makeup of the stone itself, and then in a week or two when she had a follow-up visit he would be able to suggest any diet modifications which might lessen the risk of additional stones in the future.

"I should point out," the urologist said, "that once you've had a kidney stone, the odds are much higher that you'll have another at some point in your life. Possibly multiple times. Some people are simply more prone to getting kidney stones, either from genetics, physical makeup, diet, and other reasons. Plus, with your Crohn's Disease, you're already in the at-risk group."

Eventually Mara was allowed to leave, and given a chariot ride to the parking lot (that's what the orderly pushing the wheelchair called it). I loaded her in the car and headed home, glad that she was finally free from that kidney stone. We both knew she'd be in pain for a few more days, but at least the worst was over.

"Big deal," Mara said. "Now I get to spend the rest of my life looking forward to my next kidney stone, and maybe the one after that."

"I wouldn't be so sure about that," I reminded her. "Maybe this will be a case where being in the one percent actually works to your advantage."

Chapter 30 - Everything is Bigger in Texas

Back in 1989, things at the company I worked for had been booming. Some brilliant moves coupled with timely publicity had driven a lot of business there in 1987 and then again in 1989. My boss had long been tired of the high tax rates we had to pay, both individually and as a company. We were both paying Federal income tax, New Jersey state income tax, New York state non-resident income tax, and New York City non-resident income tax. It seemed like everything the company did required a tax; there was even an annual corporate tax the firm had to pay on the rent. Not a tax on rent collected by the company (had it owned real estate); in this case it was an actual corporate rent tax charged as a percentage of the rent the firm paid. It made no sense to me. Anywhere money changed hands, one or more taxing authorities wanted a cut.

With that in mind, and considering how well things were going, my boss made preliminary plans to relocate the entire firm from New York City down south to Dallas, Texas. He even had Mara and me fly down and look at apartments. Despite having a terrible sinus infection while we were there, Mara liked Dallas. The cost of living was amazing compared to New Jersey. The winters were mild, the people were friendly, and the Mexican food was amazing.

Unfortunately, it didn't work out. 1989 was the peak and things at work slowly started pointing downward. There were organizational changes, cutbacks, relocations, and a real slowdown in business. It wasn't drastic or sudden, but just a progression of negative results. Yet all along, Dallas was mentioned as a possibility. If one deal hit, or if this happened or that happened, we'd head to Dallas. That was one reason we stayed in the same apartment in Rahway for so long, instead of trying to find a cheaper place: while we had a yearly lease, we also had a 60-day notice out clause which would allow us to move without penalty if we were relocating out of state, which the landlord had added at my request the first time we came up for renewal.

Eventually the company was relocated to a home office of four people. And then three people. And finally, two people: my boss and myself. We were in the red every month but my boss continued to fund the company, looking for the best alternative to get things moving in a positive direction. I'd look over the want ads in the Sunday paper every week, depressed at what I saw as a lack of opportunity for me if we went out of business.

Then in 1994, when I had given up all hope of the Dallas dream and instead was busy considering how I could pay our growing pile of bills if I had to switch to a new job, a miracle occurred. A Chicago-based company was going to open a branch in Dallas, and they were interested in hiring my boss to come work there. The new CEO was trying to throw money around to attract some industry names and build the company from a regional firm to a more recognized national one. My boss was able to secure a position for me as well.

Moving across the country wasn't going to be easy, but we'd been waiting to do it for over five years. And there were a number of distinct advantages, besides the lower cost of living. One was that I'd be getting a raise. Another was that as this was a larger firm, I'd have more opportunities there. And most importantly, I'd have new insurance through an actual group policy, which meant Mara would be covered too. Our prescription expenses would instantly drop my 75%. We both knew it was probably too late to win the financial battle – bankruptcy might be a necessity if things didn't turn around even more than they were about to – but at least we had a chance.

Mara's family wasn't so thrilled at having her move far away, but it did make Mara even more my responsibility and less theirs. That was an unspoken positive to them. My family was sorry to see me leave too, but we'd already started to scatter across the country. The New York area would remain our home base, but only a few of us were planning to stay there. If opportunity or relationships moved us elsewhere, we'd follow those and see if we could put some roots down in a different part of the country.

As far as the actual move went, we arranged for our belongings and those of my boss to be moved by the same company in the same truck. There really wasn't time to get down to Dallas and hunt around for a place to live. We thought about an extended stay motel, but a friend who was already in Dallas and was planning on joining us at the new firm made a few calls and found us a small house to rent through a leasing company. He looked it over and said it was small but very nice, a good neighborhood, and had a great back yard with trees and a small hot tub jacuzzi. I trusted his judgment; if he said it was good, we were fine with it. And the rent was actually slightly *less* than what we were paying for our one-bedroom apartment!

As to getting from New Jersey to Dallas, flying seemed the obvious answer. These days I hate to fly, but back then it wasn't such a problem for me. However, Mara was completely against flying. The thought of a Crohn's attack while on the plane terrified her; locked up in that tiny bathroom while others kept banging on the door trying to get their turn. Besides, she reasoned, there was no way she was going to trust an airline to take care of our three cats. She had heard far too many horror stories of animal cages thrown around like beach balls, or mysterious deaths in the cargo hold. Nope, Mara said she was willing to move, but it was driving or nothing. "If the cats don't go, I don't go, and I'm not putting those cats on a plane." We did discuss the idea of Mara flying in while I drove, but she didn't care for that idea. She wanted to be there to keep me awake if I got sleepy while driving, and she also didn't want to spend a few days in Dallas alone waiting for me (nor did she want to spend a few days with her parents if she was going to fly in after I'd arrived). It sounded like we'd be driving to Dallas, together.

Our Hyundai Excel wasn't in great shape. It was eight years old now, and I while it was safe to drive to work or the grocery store, I wasn't confident it could survive a trip halfway across the country. Little things were constantly going wrong with it, and the last thing I wanted was to be broken down at the side of a highway in the middle of Arkansas or someplace. So we did some investigation and found we could rent a car at a great rate with no mileage limits or region restrictions. Dallas was growing, and the company was happy to have someone rent a car in New Jersey and return it in Dallas when they were done with it. We figured we'd keep it for a few weeks until we found a new or used car we could buy in Texas. Plus, if something went wrong with the rental on the way, the rental company would either fix it immediately or give us a different car. Breaking down wouldn't strand us, it would just temporarily inconvenience us. One less thing to worry about.

A few days before the move, Mara's mother and I drove to go get the rental car. Mara couldn't do it, because she still had no confidence driving. We went in our Hyundai, and Mara's Mom dropped me off at the Hertz location and headed back to our place. I inspected the car, signed all the paperwork, and drove back to meet Mara and her mother.

There was only one problem: Mara's mother never made it back to our place. The clutch in the Hyundai gave out about five minutes away from the rental place. I must have driven right by her on the way home, but I wasn't watching for the car and never noticed. It was mentioned later by her in an only slightly-joking way that I probably saw her and drove by her on purpose. I think she felt that had at least a 25% chance of being true. But it wasn't. I got home and had to turn around and go right back out to Mara's sister's place. The car had been towed there by AAA, where one of her friends was going to look at it. The original plan was for Mere's sister to sell it for us, and then we'd have that money to go towards our next car. To this day I have no idea what happened with the car; Mara's sister said it needed "work" and it was never mentioned again.

The next day – a Thursday - was "moving day." The movers were going to my Boss's place first to pick up "a few boxes and a TV" and then were coming over to our place to pack and move all our stuff. We'd be leaving the following morning. We expected the movers by 9am, but "a few boxes and a TV" turned out to be closer to forty boxes they had to pack and move, some furniture, and his huge old-style projection TV which was as big as our car.

When the movers finally got to our place it was after 1pm, and there were only two movers. I had given them a detailed list of our belongings in order to make it clear this wasn't a two-hour pack and move job, but I suppose the message never made it all the way down the ranks. Those two guys looked like they wanted to cry when they saw how much stuff we had to pack up (and we already had about 20 boxes packed before they arrived). They quickly called for more help, which arrived in the form of one more person. They were finally finished at about 1am. That wasn't ideal, since we were leaving first thing in the morning, but there was nothing to be done about it. I had to be in the office Monday morning – early – to get things set up. We had Friday, Saturday, and Sunday to make the drive and no more.

We had tossed around the idea of staying at a hotel or motel Thursday night, but in the end we chose to rough it on the floor because it gave us a better chance of leaving on schedule, and also because we didn't want to leave the cats there alone overnight. We knew the trip was going to be stressful enough for them as it was; at least having us for some company would keep them calmer after seeing everything moved out of the apartment. As it turned out, with not getting to bed until after 1am, going to a hotel would have been a waste of time and money anyway.

At 4:30 in the morning the alarm went off. Three hours sleep was a bit less than I had planned on before starting this three-day trip, but there wasn't time for any more. A quick shower later, we packed the car with three cat carriers (Whisper and Tigger were sharing one, while Biff and Bibs each had their own), some clothes and personal items, a small cooler of cold drinks, and a huge bag of medicine for Mara. We also had my briefcase and a strongbox with travelers' checks, credit cards, cash, and important papers. My work computer had been sent by Fed Ex to Dallas so it would be there ready for me when I showed up Monday morning…*if* I showed up Monday morning.

We had mapped out our travel plans long in advance, and had AAA send us a set of maps to follow. Starting in New Jersey, we would cross over into Pennsylvania, down to Maryland for a couple of minutes, head into West Virginia, and then travel southwesterly across Virginia. The first night would be spent in Wytheville, VA (as we had booked both motels in advance as well, both to ensure a room and to secure places that allowed pets). Day two would see us finish our Virginia travels, drive across Tennessee, cross a few miles into Arkansas, and stop in a little town called Heth. Day three was the shortest leg, driving through Little Rock and Texarkana and straight to Dallas.

The plan had positives and negatives. Day 1 was the longest day by design, since we wouldn't be exhausted from driving already. Day 2 was a little bit shorter, but I expected traffic trouble around Memphis because of a huge Elvis Tribute Weekend celebration going on in the area (which I learned about when I discovered most hotels and motels within 100 miles of Memphis near the interstate were already booked up). Day 3 was the shortest day, so we could arrive in Dallas by early afternoon and perhaps find time to go out and buy a futon or a day bed for comfort while we waited a few days for the movers to arrive. The route was marked, the miles measured, and we were ready to go!

As usual, there were a few last-minute delays, like chasing the cats around trying to get them into the cat carriers. But we manage to leave only an hour late, around 6:00 in the morning. We had also given Bibs a mild tranquilizer, because he hated being in the car and without fail would spray in his carrier within ten minutes. Apparently, the pill worked, because he didn't pee. However, he did move into stage two of his car travel routine: loud, obnoxious, non-stop crying. Crying isn't really the right word for it; it was more like howling in anticipation of a terrible, painful death. We decide then and there that for the next two days we'll double the dose (the vet told us we could give it to him up to four times the dose, but we weren't comfortable with that idea). There was nothing more to do than keep going and hope he'd tire himself out in an hour or two.

Around ninety minutes later we have crossed into Pennsylvania. Bibs was quiet, and the other cats seemed to be handling things fine; nothing much for them to do but sleep. But then Mara started to feel nauseous. It isn't her Crohn's, it's some kind of panic attack. Numbness spread all over her body and she started to cry. She was convinced she would get far too sick along the way, and that there was no way she could survive a three-day drive. I talked to her in a steady, quiet tone and after five minutes I managed to calm her down enough that I didn't need to pull over.

Not pulling over wasn't much of a time saver, because five minutes after her panic attack ended, Mara needed to use the bathroom. We pulled off I-78 somewhere in Dutch Country to search for a bathroom. We passed a shabby-looking gas station but Mara said it looked disgusting and wanted to keep searching. We drove around for fifteen minutes, until it became clear she had two choices: use the gas station bathroom or go in a field. She chose the gas station. Mara wandered off to the restroom while I bought $7 worth of gas. She kept in touch with me during her bathroom trip with a walkie-talkie, which she had me buy a set of so she could warn me if she was going to be a while or if she needed help with anything. I was shocked to learn the gas station didn't sell coffee, so when we got back on the highway, I had to pull off at the next exit to get some. Staying awake was high on my priority list.

Twenty minutes later Mara started to feel sick again and needed to use the bathroom. She also decided she might need something in her stomach to cure this odd nausea. We stopped in Midway, PA at the Midway Diner, which seemed to be a popular truck stop as well. While she went to the bathroom, I got her a bagel with tuna fish on it, to go. Out in the car Mara took one bite and declares it is the most disgusting tuna fish she has ever tasted. She did manage to eat the top half of the bagel (the half without tuna), but her stomach was still bothering her afterwards. She said it wasn't normal Crohn's nausea, so I chalked it up to the anxiety.

Speaking of the anxiety, only fifteen minutes further down the highway Mara goes into a much worse anxiety attack. It was so bad I had to pull off to the shoulder and try to calm her down. Nothing I said seemed to mollify her. Finally, I offered to drive her back to her parents' place so that she can fly down instead, and that I would then turn around and drive to Dallas on my own. Truthfully, I had no intention of fulfilling that offer; I just said it because I thought it might calm her down. I don't know **what** I would have said next if she had called my bluff. Fortunately, that didn't happen; having the option presented to her made her feel less pressure, and perhaps she misunderstood and thought the offer was open-ended. We dried her tears, pulled back onto the highway, and continued on our way.

We had been on the road for nearly three hours at this point, and covered a grand total of one hundred miles. At that rate we might not have hit Dallas until a week from Monday. I pushed the speed limit the best I could, and at least once expected to be pulled over. If nothing else, the drive was rural and rather pretty.

A few hours later we crossed into Virginia, where I encountered the first 65-miles-per-hour speed limit I had ever seen in my life. What a relief! I figured this would be a good chance to make up for lost time. Mara was a lot calmer by now, although she was still nauseous and needed to stop to use the bathroom about once an hour. The fall views in the Virginia hills were simply breathtaking, which seemed to keep an extra layer of peace on us. The cats were sleeping quietly, Mara was realizing that she could survive this trip, and traffic was light.

The only real problem was how tired I was. I filled up with more coffee every time we stopped for Mara, but I had become jittery and stressed. I couldn't count on Mara to keep me entertained when I got sleepy, as she was trying to close her eyes whenever she could just to feel a bit better. There was no choice but to fight through it and keep going; I tried to sing along with the cassette tapes of music I had – quietly – to stay mentally aware. At one stop I thought I had broken the car; we pulled up to a rest stop but I could not get the key out of the ignition. I fiddled with it for a few minutes and had just about given up. I was going to call the rental company to have them send out a tow truck or a replacement car, and that's when I realized I had turned off the car while it was still in Drive! I slapped it into Park and out came the key, crisis averted. I felt like an idiot, which was enough to keep me wide awake for…well, for the next two minutes.

By 5:30 we were exhausted and cranky, but our spirits were lifted when we saw a sign: "Wytheville 15." Only fifteen miles to go and we'd have made it through the first day. I knew the motel was right off the highway, so we were minutes away from a warm bed, a real bathroom, and being able to let the cats out of their carriers and feed them. It wouldn't be home, but it would be a wonderful change from spending twelve hours in the car. Mara was still nauseous but she hadn't needed to stop to use the bathroom for over an hour, and felt sure she could wait until we got there. All the restroom stops and a number of construction zones had slowed our progress, but at least we were nearing the finish line of Day One.

As you might expect, there was one last kick in the nuts waiting for us. As we rounded a bend in the road we screeched to a halt. Traffic was at a standstill. We sat, sat, sat...and then inched forward a bit. And then sat some more. Eventually Mara could make out an orange sign up ahead in the shoulder: "Road Construction – Next 7 Miles." Arrrrg! It must have taken us nearly an hour to get through those last fifteen miles. Neither of us spoke, or played any music. We just gritted our teeth and tried to keep calm. My nerves were shot, and I assumed Mara's were too. The less we said to each other, the better the chance we'd avoid an argument.

Eventually we make our way to the motel. We check in, let the cats out (who immediately run and hide), and relax for a little while. It's late and we need dinner, so I decide to go pick something up. It's at about this time that I realize Mara isn't nauseous any longer. Her tummy hurts a bit from her Crohn's, but the strange nausea she fought all day has miraculously disappeared. Somewhere in the back of my mind I am transported to my sixth birthday party, where some friends and I went duck pin bowling. On the way home I was looking at a gift I'd been given – a set of Matchbox-style motorcycles. I remember reading the details on the box, and suddenly feeling like I had to throw up. We pulled the car over but nothing happened. But when we started driving, I felt sick again. I soon learned not to read things in the car, because if I did....

...Mara had been **car sick** the whole time! It wasn't anxiety or Crohn's or anything like that. It was motion sickness. Just stupid motion sickness. Maybe she had a head cold or something to exacerbate the problem, the way she did in college. I felt relieved and angry at myself all at once; if I had thought of this before, we could have avoided a lot of her discomfort.

    I made it a point to stop and get some Bonine and a few other things at a pharmacy when I went to grab dinner. With luck, those would take care of the problem and Mara would be able to survive the next two days with much less misery. I had to laugh at myself as I drove back to the motel: my natural sense of direction was so poor, I found myself going the wrong way on I-81 and had to make a U-turn before I could figure out where I was going. I was navigating us halfway across the country, but I couldn't drive two miles from our motel without getting lost.

    When it was time for bed, I checked around the motel room to make sure everything was okay. That's when I completely lost it; I started to cry uncontrollably, as I couldn't find our grey Persian cat Biff. The only explanation that made sense was that he somehow dashed by me and ran outside when I came back with dinner. Biff was never the smartest cat in the world; if he'd gotten out, odds were good that he was scared by the first person or car he saw and took off somewhere, never to be seen again. I started pulling all the furniture away from the walls and voila, there was Biff, hiding behind the dresser in a space that seemed physically impossible for him to have ever gotten into, let alone to have hid comfortably. It's hard to imagine a 20-pound, fluffy cat fitting into a space less than 12" x 8". I was pretty sure that he never would have made his way out of that spot without moving the furniture. It didn't matter; at least he was safe. I would have been upset at the thought of losing Biff like that regardless of the situation, but after 12 hours in the car, a dozen cups of coffee, and three hours sleep I was in no position to stay calm or think clearly. We finally got to sleep around 11pm, since not even the nightmare of nearly losing one of the cats could fight off the exhaustion.

Six hours later it was time to wake up. We took showers, gave Mara her pile of morning medication, gathered up the cats, packed the cars, and off we went. The moment we get on the highway we are engulfed by horrendous fog, thicker than I had ever encountered. You could see maybe five feet in front of you, and that was it. We were on a schedule, and I was younger and less cautious back then...if I saw that fog today there is **no way** I would try to drive through it. I've seen far too many news reports of massive pileups in the fog, chain reaction accidents with multiple fatalities.

We fought our way through for half an hour, and then pulled off to grab some breakfast (and to see if the fog might burn off as the sun came up). The Country Diner, where we stopped, had no bagels, so Mara got herself eggs and toast to go. I just get a large cup or terrible coffee. Bathroom break #1 for the day takes place, and we hit the road again.

An hour after we left the motel, we'd travelled about thirty miles. It was at this point that I suddenly realized we'd left my briefcase, our strongbox, and Mara's wallet back in our room. Mara had insisted we hide those items safely so nobody would steal them if they broke into the room; I didn't see how anyone could break into the room since we were always going to be inside of it, but I'd agreed as I saw no harm in it. Now this brilliant strategy has completely backfired, and we have to turn around and go back the way we came, hoping they were still in our room and not lost forever.

On the drive back to the motel I tried to explain to Mara how she'd be better off if I left her at the side of a road and drove off a bridge. She wasn't convinced. The return trip was agonizingly slow, as the fog was only slightly improved. When we arrived, the cleaning woman was just unlocking the door. She happily let us in and our things were still hidden where we had left them. More stress but another crisis averted. Mara also took advantage of being back at the motel by using the bathroom again.

Now ninety minutes behind schedule, we started off with the most positive attitude we could muster. Aside from the lost time and the fog (which was still there but not nearly as dangerous at this point), nothing terrible had really happened. Mara wasn't car sick, the cats were just chilling in their carriers (even Bibs, with his double dose of light tranquilizer), and it sounded like we would have sunny skies for most of the day.

Mara needed to make another bathroom stop rather quickly, and by coincidence we pulled off at the Country Diner again. Déjà vu all over again. This time I waited in the car. Mara returned with another cup of coffee for me and a gift which she said was "for not blowing your brains out so far." It was a coffee mug with some verse on it about the name Doug; just the kind of thing you'd find at a country-ish store off the interstate, but sweet nonetheless. As I write this, nearly 25 years later, I still have that mug in the kitchen and use it about once a week. It brings me memories of some of the happier times.

Most of the day's driving was happily uneventful. Mara kept herself on a decent dose of Bonine, Imodium, and some Percocet to avoid nausea, diarrhea, and to let her sleep if at all possible. There was a lot less road construction during this leg of the trip. The scenery wasn't quite as beautiful through Tennessee as it had been in Virginia, but it also has more variety which is helpful in keeping my mind active and my sleepiness at bay. I pass the time with my typically off-key singing to the radio or our mix tapes. I may not be a good singer, but I'm not a shy one.

This was also the day of the trip with the most miles to cover, so a sleeping and happy Mara also meant we made better time. Even so, traffic picked up quite a bit 100 miles out of Memphis, and continued to get worse and worse. I expected as much, due to the huge Elvis celebration going on. The skies were looking a bit foreboding as well, but then the sun went down and it was impossible to tell. Around 8pm we had finally reached the outskirts of Memphis, only 20 miles off, when we hit a major construction zone. Unlike the night before, traffic was still moving at a slow but steady pace, with the entire interstate down to one lane in each direction, divided only by a double yellow line and pylons. There was no shoulder or breakdown lane here; I assumed that we had been rerouted to part of the service road as a detour from the road work. It was just at this moment that the skies opened up and a torrential rainstorm started.

It wasn't a good situation. There was no cover, no lights on the side of the road, and no exit to pull off. All anyone could do was keep driving. The rain was coming so hard and so fast that the windshield wipers couldn't properly keep up. To make matters worse, there's already plenty of free-standing water in the road, and every time an 18-wheeler passes us going the other direction (with traffic on that side moving at twice the speed of the traffic headed towards Memphis) it deposits a tidal wave of rain on the car, completely blinding me for a second or two. But there is truly no escape. The only option was to maintain speed with gentle breaking when necessary, and keep moving. If anyone in this mess started stopping short, we'd have all found ourselves in a massive pile-up.

I just kept gripping the steering wheel, white-knuckled, and moving forward. Eventually we made it out of the construction zone, passed Memphis, and crossed over into Arkansas. The positive at this point was traffic dropped by 80%. The downsides were that the rain was falling twice as hard as it had been in Tennessee, and the Arkansas portion of the interstate was in horrible shape, and as dark as a starless night. Mara was wide awake by now; she'd slept through the worst of the Memphis drive. With no letup in the rain I decided to drive the last 25 miles of the day's journey in the right lane with my hazards on, doing about 30 miles an hour. Less than twenty vehicles passed us in that time. It was almost as if nobody wanted to come to Arkansas.

It was after 9pm when we finally made it to Heth and found the Best Western. It didn't matter to us at this point if the room had rats and three squatters living in it, I just needed some food and a bed. Fortunately, it was clean and dry. We unloaded the car, and then I started checking the yellow pages for some place to get dinner. Heth was a bit smaller than I expected it to be (today is lists a population of 623, and it was probably less in 1994). The only place within miles was a little restaurant down the street, or more accurately across the parking lot. The rain was finally letting up, so I didn't even need to drive there. I'd lived nearly my whole life in the northeast, so when I saw they only had six items on the menu, one of which was "Macaroni and Cheese - $1.50," I didn't feel too confident. But as I said, my experience with the small-town homestyle place was limited. I grabbed a couple of burgers, which were much better than just edible. Warm food, a dry bed, and only one more day of driving left. And that was the shortest leg of the trip, by design. It was safe to figure that if we were able to survive the Memphis monsoon, Sunday would be a much easier day.

We only had 400 miles to cover on that final day, which I hoped we would be able to cover in seven hours, with a minimum of stops. Naturally that didn't happen, as Mara was now paying the price (plus interest) for her Imodium the day before. Pain wasn't a terrible issue, but frequency was, and we probably pulled off for bathroom breaks more than once per hour. Besides that, Mara spent most of her time trying (and failing) to doze off.

Around 3pm we finally crossed into Dallas county, and started making our way towards the house we were renting. We had the keys, which had been sent to us, but we'd still never actually seen the place. We were both curious to discover where we'd be spending the next year or more, both the house itself and the neighborhood in general. I wasn't worried about either being a major issue; we had been assured both by my future associate and by the leasing company that it was a quiet neighborhood and that the house was in decent shape. But Texas was bound to be a big change from New Jersey, and it had been over five years since we'd come down in preparation for the move that never happened.

It was at this point I rediscovered a forgotten skill Mara had: the ability to look at a map and get **everything** wrong. Since she couldn't sleep, she wanted to play navigator and direct us to the house from the interstate. Fortunately, I asked her to give me a few steps in advance, and immediately recognized that to follow her directions would violate the laws of physics, time, and probably seventeen different states. Her feelings were a bit hurt when I got exasperated and demanded she had the map over to me, but tempers were miniscule by now. As always, the closer you get to the end of a bad experience, the slower the clock moves. I couldn't use my energy worrying about sulking or resentment. I only had enough gas left in my personal tank to get us to the house.

Amazingly, we found our way there without a wrong turn. Unlike New Jersey, Dallas is mostly laid out in a grid pattern, and major roads often have three lanes in each direction. There aren't that many long, meandering roads where you have to peer into the trees to find the hidden side street. We drove past a shopping center at a major intersection (making mental note of some of the things we saw, including a few restaurants and a grocery store), made a left, drove slowly along a residential side street, and there it was, exactly where it was supposed to be: our new home.

Things could have gone much worse during that three-day trek, and they certainly could have gone a whole lot better too. But we had survived, against all odds and despite a few speed bumps of our creation. It was time to start a new chapter in our life, as Texans.

Chapter 31 - A Period of Adjustment

The house in Texas was really quite nice. Granted, it was dusty, smelled of a bug bomb (which they must have set off in the days prior to our arrival), and there were plenty of dead bugs showing how effective it had been. But other than that, it was more than satisfactory. The back yard had a tree and a privacy fence, and the above-ground jacuzzi. With a bird feeder or two out there, there was little doubt the cats would spend all day staring out the sliding glass doors. The layout of the house was a bit odd, but it was twice as large as our apartment had been and the neighborhood seemed very quiet. Overall, it was a pleasant surprise.

The plan for that first night was for me to go out and buy an inexpensive futon for us to sleep on, which we would eventually use in the second bedroom for when company came over. I went out in search of a place to buy one, and found a number of stores and then a shopping mall with department stores such as Sears and JC Penny. Unfortunately, none of them had what we were looking for. Both Sears and JC Penny said they could order one, but that wasn't going to be of use for tonight so I skipped that idea entirely. Instead I picked up a few sandwiches and went back to the house. We would just have to spend the next few nights sleeping on the floor in the bedroom; we had our pillows and a comforter with us in the meantime so it shouldn't have been a big deal.

When I got home the cats were cautiously wandering from room to room. Every little sound would make them jump, and I don't think Mara was any different. Different house, different state, different sounds, different smells; there was a lot to get used to. While I was out, I picked up a pair of dress pants and two shirts and ties to wear to the office during the week; I'd forgotten to include those in our personal items in the car. I was exhausted, and after we ate I wanted to get to sleep as early as possible, especially since I had to be at work around 7am the next morning if I was going to get everything set up in time.

Of course, nothing is ever so simple. Mara made certain to moan and sigh and move around for an hour, keeping me awake. Finally, she declared that she couldn't sleep on the floor and we'd have to spend the night in a motel. That was extra money I really didn't want to spend, and I also felt bad about leaving the cats in a new place all by themselves. But there wasn't time to argue; Mara wasn't going to let me get any sleep until I let her have her way, and sleep is what I needed more than anything.

Fortunately, I had seen a motel across the street from the mall when I was out, so that's where I took us. We checked in and went right to bed. I told Mara I would have to bring her back to the house on the way to work (which wasn't really out of the way) so she could be there for when the phone company arrived later in the day, and to keep an eye on the cats. I knew she'd be bored and uncomfortable, but we each had our jobs to do. At least she'd have a bathroom right there if she needed it.

Monday morning I woke Mara up around 5am. I got ready for work, and then dropped her off at the house on my way to the office. The phone company was due to arrive Monday or Tuesday, so until then she would have no way to communicate with me during the day. I was far too busy at the office to spend time chatting anyway. The office space was still generally empty, as new hiring continued to take place, but by the end of the day I had my computers and my printer set up and was back on schedule with things. That felt good, and my new coworkers seemed generally pleasant.

I picked up some dinner after work, plus a few groceries to stock the fridge, and then went home. Mara complained about having to sit and lie on the floor most of the day, although she was able to take a nap. But she also had a funny story to tell about how the house was haunted.

After I had dropped her off in the morning, she'd gone inside and two of the cats had come out to greet her. Tigger was too busy looking out at the back yard. But she heard a strange banging noise as soon as she entered. It wasn't loud, but it had an odd rhythm. Bonk...pause....bonk....pause. She followed the noise into the kitchen, where she almost screamed out in fright.

Two of the small drawers in the kitchen island were opening and closing. The top one would open, and then close, and then the one beneath it would open and close. Mustering whatever bravery she could, Mara went over to investigate. She released the top drawer from its runners and the mystery was instantly solved. Poor Whisper had somehow found her way into one of the drawers, opening it and climbing inside. Then she must have crawled out the back of the drawer to investigate the empty space behind it, and in doing so she closed the drawer behind her. Now she had been going from one drawer to the next, pushing and pulling in an attempt to find her way back to the outside world. Once Mara had removed the drawer, Whisper ran out but then stopped in the kitchen to look back at the trap she had been in. Mara's guess was she couldn't have been stuck in there too long, because she didn't seem panicked; Whisper was pissed off more than anything. Poor little girl.

The phone company hadn't arrived, which meant they were due to show up Tuesday. I did have two other pieces of news for Mara. One was a surprise: at the grocery store I had picked up a cheap lawn chair. Now she had somewhere to sit until our furniture arrived! She was very happy about that. The other news was related: it sounded like the movers wouldn't get to us until Thursday or Friday, despite them promising Monday delivery originally. I had always felt that Monday seemed a little optimistic, but Mara was incensed. She hated when companies didn't keep their word. There was nothing we could do about it though; we'd just sleep at the motel until our belongings arrived.

Overall the transition from New Jersey to Texas wasn't going to be that drastic, but we did have a lot of things we needed to accomplish. We had to get the phone lines installed, set up the BBS again, find a veterinarian for the cats, get a car of some sort (so we could return the rental), and then begin the slow and complicated process of finding new doctors for Mara. That was the part I was least looking forward to. Mara didn't feel secure driving in the first place, and certainly wasn't going to drive in Dallas until she learned her way around. So I'd need to make myself available to take her to every appointment, of which there would be plenty as Mara shopped around between specialists and GPs until she had the combination she wanted.

Prescriptions were not a pressing concern, as we had made sure to either have refills remaining on everything or to have her prior doctors willing to refill by phone for at least a few months. Obviously they didn't want to be refilling prescriptions on an open-ended basis, because somebody needed to be monitoring Mara and how she was doing. But in the same vein, they didn't want to deprive her of the medications she needed, so as long as they felt secure that Mara was actively looking for new doctors, they were ready to accommodate her for the time being.

We dealt with a number of minor snags here and there during the following two weeks, but at least when that time had passed we had a bed to sleep in and all of our belongings with us (although they were still packed in boxes, piled all over the place). The cats were getting used to the house and loved the view to the back yard; Tigger in particular would chase some larger birds back and forth from one side of the glass door to the other, trying to figure out how she could get at them. The birds appeared to understand the situation: this dumb cat doesn't know what a door is. They'd hop back and forth, back and forth, taunting Tigger. Now and then the other cats would join in, but they'd get tired of the game and bash themselves into the glass, scaring the birds off.

It was a great relief to go get Mara's prescriptions filled the first time and have insurance cover most of their cost (especially for the generic drugs). But while that was going to save us a lot of money, Mara was determined to spend nearly as much on our car. Or should I say, our minivan. I don't know why, since we had no children and there was no way Mara was going to have any in the future, but Mara was dead set on us buying a minivan instead of a smaller car. Considering the fact that I'd be the one driving it 99% of the time, I should have put up more of a fight. But there was no real point; Mara would have just complained and argued and cried until she had her way. She also insisted on handling the negotiation when we went to buy the thing, which meant we paid through the nose. She chose a black Plymouth Voyager with grey interior, and even though it was the old model year we barely priced ourselves below sticker price. I was just amazed we were approved for financing at a decent rate, considering how much debt we were carrying. I guess that didn't bother them, as long as we paid our bills on time, which we had somehow managed to do up to this point.

Good or bad, the deal was done. We had our new vehicle, our rental house, and I had a good job with great benefits. We were away from Mara's parents (although they were already talking about coming down to visit), and it looked like things might be looking up for us at last. Or, if not looking up, at least we'd stopped the bleeding and were going to be stable for the time being.

Now it was time to tackle the real project: finding Mara her new doctors.

Chapter 32 - Is there a Doctor in the House?

Mara's search for new doctors was to focus on the two biggest priorities first: gastroenterologist and psychiatrist. With Mara, a physician needed a very tolerant and kind bedside matter above all other skills. Partially because her Dad was a doctor, and partially because she had developed a terribly thin skin, Mara was unable to deal with doctors who challenged her, or who suggested she had habits or behaviors which might be making things worse for her. I understood her point of view; after all, she had already suffered the usual "you don't *look* sick" barbs from friends or family when it came to her mental illness and her Crohn's Disease.

But one factor which made bedside manner even more important - Mara's weight. It had been steadily increasing from just before she was diagnosed with Crohn's, and by now she weighed over 250 pounds. That sounds like a lot, but it's even worse when you realize she was only about 5' 3" tall. But Mara would fight tooth and nail to dispute any suggestion that her weight was affecting her health in any way.

The older I've gotten the more I have understood this opinion of hers too. I can't count how many times I've seen personally or heard indirectly about doctors dismissing health complaints of overweight patients and suggesting losing weight as the one and only course of treatment. Get a lot of sinus infections? Try losing weight and exercise. Think you have the flu? Lose weight and exercise. It's far too often used as a cop-out prescription for lazy medical professionals who don't want to investigate further.

Of course, in many cases being overweight is a contributing factor to disease, and it needs to be addressed. Diabetes, high blood pressure, heart disease, respiratory problems...those are all highly correlated to weight, or at least managing weight can improve the symptoms or decrease the amount of medication that needs to be taken. But Mara had taken the all-or-none stance. She's heard weight used as an excuse or a reason too many times, so now she refused to accept it as a problem whatsoever.

In reality Mara's weight wasn't a primary cause of any of her health problems except two: her snoring, and her back. Mara's snoring had started to get worse, and seemed to grow louder the heavier she became. She wasn't prepared to look at that as a health concern at this stage, and I was able to sleep through most anything once I fell asleep so I wasn't going to put up a huge argument. But it was an issue I was going to keep an eye on.

Mara's back was a whole other matter. While it was true that some of her lower back pain started after she had been rear-ended in a car accident in New Jersey, the correlation with her weight was undeniable. She could still walk without a lot of pain, but only up to a given distance. If we went to the mall, she would need to stop and rest. The movies were not an issue as long as she didn't have a long wait; she could walk to her seat, and once she was sitting things were fine. Standing too long or walking too far were the problems. Again, Mara refused to consider anything but the car accident as the source of her pain, and any suggestion from a doctor that her weight was making things worse would set her off and shut her down.

So when it came to new doctors, Mara needed someone who was going to tolerate her stubbornness and treat sensitive topics with kid gloves. They didn't have to ignore her weight altogether, but it had to be brought up gently. They also had to learn how to avoid suffering her wrath and sending her into an angry tirade. It wasn't that they should be in fear of Mara, but once they lit the fuse not only would they experience a terrible verbal lashing, but she wouldn't properly consider their orders or recommendations. Mara's doctors needed a special level of tolerance.

The other mindsets Mara had about finding a new psychiatrist and a new GI were the opposite of what I thought she needed: she wanted a psychiatrist who would leave things as they were, and a GI who would be aggressive about trying new treatments. Her mental state had clearly been getting worse, while still going through ups and downs. The last thing she needed was to stick with the medications she was on, at the doses she was taking. I didn't want anything outrageous to be attempted, but it seemed to me that a different mix was required. Besides that, with her steady weight gain, I was betting the doses should be adjusted as well. I wasn't certain if or how body weight directly affected the dose requirements for psychiatric drugs, but at the very least different weight meant a different body chemistry which meant her doses needed to be adjusted.

As for the GI, while certainly it would be worthwhile to investigate newly-developed medications, I was fearful all Mara really wanted to do was restart her push for surgery that would do nothing to ensure improvement, but which would still alter her body permanently and give her a more fatalistic attitude towards life. She could get gloomy enough as it was; the last thing we needed was her to lose the little hope she still had. The one thing I did want to try and get her GI to do was figure out a way to get her off of prednisone, or at least get her dose to a very tiny one. We both knew the long-term problems a history of corticosteroids could inflict on her body, and once again I wanted to avoid those long-term "the future will be worse than the present" depressions Mara was prone to. In one sense, being away from her family – but still in contact with them – was going to give Mara a degree of freedom, but living in Dallas also meant intervention was entirely on my shoulders. I was the only line of defense between Mara and self-harm.

The final plan I had, which I hadn't revealed to Mara and didn't plan to until she had successfully located her new GI and psychiatrist, was to find her a skilled general practitioner. I didn't like the way some of her medications from one doctor overlapped with those from another. There were too many painkillers (especially when you included migraine medication), and I really wanted a single doctor to look over the various treatments and medications to see where problems might arise. Also, being in Texas now, she needed someone to go to for her non-Chron's issues. She couldn't just go see her Dad, and with her temper I wanted someone she could trust available for her annual sinus infections and other such problems. My hope was that whoever I found for myself would be a reasonable candidate. Dallas was a much more centralized location than New Jersey had been, and it had a reputation for very good doctors. It was time to take advantage of that, especially as Mara would now have both Medicare and insurance from my employer.

The search for a GI didn't take that long, or at least not as long as I thought it would. But that's because I thought Mara would want to spend time shopping around, looking for the best fit. In fact, her plan was to test drive instead: she would choose a GI, and if she grew tired of him, she would "return" him and go with somebody else. For whatever reason Mara did not want a female GI (although I always felt a female would be easier for her to deal with, and she had no problem with the concept of a female psychiatrist). Maybe it had more to do with her Dad, or perhaps it was just that she felt a male doctor would have a little more pull if and when she needed to be hospitalized again.

The GI that she settled on initially seemed generally pleasant. He wasn't willing to even consider the idea of surgery, but he did say that after a colonoscopy and an endoscopy he might change his mind. He also mentioned that there were two experimental drugs he wanted to look into that Mara might qualify for. Each were meant to replace the sulfa drug she was on. As for her steroid dependence, he said he would speak to colleagues about any possible ideas.

In terms of her medication, for the time being he was fine continuing her with what she had: sulfasalazine, prednisone, Compazine for nausea, Imodium, Prilosec, Darvocet for pain, and also added some other drug which was meant to reduce intestinal spasms. He instructed Mara to put one under her tongue when she was having a bad bout, and said it might help reduce the pain and frequency. He encouraged Mara to eat more fiber, saying that it would help maintain a consistent quality instead of diarrhea followed by constipation. He also said it would improve Mara's intestine stability, helping them to operate more effectively.

On the drive back from the office Mara was generally pleased – and the fact that he didn't mention her weight was like winning at roulette to her – but the remarks about fiber had gotten on her nerves. "What does he want me to do? I can't eat vegetables; they make me sick. I love salad, I miss salad, it was one of my favorite foods. What the hell does he think, that I just want to eat junk all the time?" I decided not to comment. While it was true that she had trouble with vegetables, the fact was she was in the bathroom three out of seven days at a minimum anyway, and was too stubborn to try easing some vegetables into her diet. I did remind her that there were other forms of fiber she could eat, but she wasn't in the mood to listen. I made a mental note to get some Citrucel at the store; it might help a bit, and she couldn't complain about it too much as it just tasted like budget orange drink.

Finding a psychiatrist looked to be a bit more difficult. There was a lot of misunderstanding about whether they needed to accept Medicare or not, because nobody was clear on which insurance would be primary. Until that was straightened out, Mara was forced to limit her search to those psychiatrists that **did** accept Medicare. And unlike other types of medical professionals, there aren't that many who do (or there weren't back then). Once she had built a small list of possibilities, she had to figure out who was accepting new patients. And then she had to determine what their office hours were; since I had to drive her to the appointments, I needed time to get home from work, pick Mara up, and then get to their office. If the last appointment was at 4pm, the odds were small I'd be able to get here there in time.

For the time being there was only one psychiatrist that fit all the necessary requirements. The good news was he had appointments as late as 5pm. The bad news was that he was south of where I worked, and we lived to the north. That meant I would fight rush hour traffic in both directions, driving north to get Mara and all the way back south to take her to the appointment. It wasn't that I considered taking Mara to her appointments to be an imposition. My problem was I hated to be late (to anything), so I heavily stressed every drive, cursing traffic and grinding my teeth as I raced to get her there on time. We never had any accidents going there, but I imagine my heart wasn't too happy with how I was treating it in the process.

The psychiatrist Mara was forced to choose wasn't going to be doing any therapy; he was willing to monitor, prescribe, and change her psychiatric medications but nothing more. That suited Mara just fine, since she was not really interested in focusing on therapy at that time. With the move over, she wanted to unpack the house and start exploring Dallas on the evenings and weekends (when she felt up to it). Therapy would just get in the way. I was rather disappointed, because I never felt medication alone could do anything but attempt to keep Mara stable...or more stable than she would otherwise be. The only way Mara was going to experience real change in her mental state and her thought process was therapy with the *right* therapist, somebody who could show her how to break the cycles she constantly found herself in. For now, Mara wasn't willing to look for the right one, or one at all.

I was comforted with the first appointment, as the psychiatrist said he wanted to consider changes in medication for Mara, starting with upping the dose of what she was already taking, and then look at switching to a new combination of drugs. Since Mara insisted that I accompany her inside during her appointments, I was able to express my concern about Mara's periods of very little sleeping followed by too much sleeping, and her sudden fits of rage. I knew Mara wouldn't have brought those up on her own. Fortunately, after the appointment Mara was too irritated with the idea of changing medications to even remember that I was the one who brought those topics up in the first place. And since she hadn't found another psychiatrist that she could even consider seeing, she had no choice but to at least listen to his recommendations.

I found myself feeling rather upbeat after the first month or two in Dallas. We'd survived the move, Mara had her doctors, and with them came slightly new approaches to treatment. She had been too busy unpacking and getting used to the house to get too depressed, and Mara also really enjoyed having more space than the cramped New Jersey apartment. I knew there would be plenty of bumps in the road ahead, but at least it seemed like life in Dallas gave us both a bit of hope that I thought we'd lost for good.

Chapter 33 - The Days Go Slow, but the Weeks Add Up Quickly

It wasn't long before we had settled into a routine. Weekdays were work for me, while Mara either stayed mostly in bed (if she was sick or depressed) or otherwise watched television and messed around on the BBS. If it wasn't too hot outside, she might make use of the jacuzzi (although the heat on that would go out all the time, and she was afraid to relight the pilot light because it was natural gas, which meant she figured she would blow herself up). Mara had put herself in charge of monitoring the chemical levels in the jacuzzi, so it would fluctuate between overbleached and green, depending on the cycle of her interest and motivation. On weekends we would try to go to a matinee and then have a late lunch or early dinner out, if Mara was up to it. She often chose her entrée based on what she thought the cats would enjoy as leftovers.

Once a week or so Mara would fax me something at work. It would be a drawing of one of the cats doing something funny (Bibs standing by the "big white box" a.k.a. the refrigerator, where he knew all the food came from), or detailed descriptions of the kind of bugs she encountered. Bug life in Texas was very different than the bugs in the New Jersey apartment. Water bugs freaked her out, especially how similar they looked to true roaches. (One fax had a drawing of a water bug and the caption "I screamed at this one").

Things were going okay for us. Mara's Crohn's was up and down, but no worse than before. In fact, she seemed to do better for longer stretches now, with the downside being that when she had a bout with Crohn's it was very severe. The one area of her health I was especially concerned about –

besides her still-increasing weight – was her sleeping. It wasn't just the pattern of hardly any sleep for a few days followed by not wanting to get out of bed at all. What scared me more was that she was waking up choking at least once every night, and sometimes more than once. I knew that if her coughing fits were waking *me* up too, they must be bad.

I had managed to find myself a very nice GP, and sooner than I expected to. What happened was I started waking up with chest pains. They were hard to describe, but they were on both sides of my chest, in the upper left and upper right, and I only had them when I first woke up. Then they would slowly fade as the morning went on. I checked with our insurance and found this GP not far from where I worked. Not only was he on the insurance plan, but he also had a lot of equipment in his office. That meant I could just pay the co-pay cost ($30 or something) and insurance would cover blood work, x-rays, or whatever else they could do on site.

The doctor couldn't find anything initially wrong, so he suggested I undergo a stress EKG test the following week. I had no idea what that was, but it wasn't long before I found out. He had me walk quickly (or was it jog?) on a treadmill, as the treadmill slowly increased its pitch until it hit about 45 degrees. The whole time I had sensors on my chest and elsewhere, monitoring my heart. Then they had me sit down and they kept monitoring as my heart slowed its pace, until it was beating normally again.

He told me that the entire test looked normal, and cursed at me for still being young and able to quickly return to a normal pulse. I laughed, but he half-jokingly mentioned that some patient he had given a test like this to a year ago had come out with perfect results, but still had a heart attack and died a month later. At any rate, there appeared to be nothing wrong with me.

His best guess was that somehow I was bruising my chest wall. It might hurt, but it wasn't serious. He advised me I could take a small dose of ibuprofen for the pain, and said I should keep an eye out in case I was able to discover how I was hurting myself.

It must have been less than two weeks before I figured it out. I often slept on my back. I woke up in the middle of the night and found our Persian cat Biff sitting on my chest. This 20-pound monster fuzzball was sitting there on his butt, with his two front paws stuck out like tripod supports. All of his weight was being supported by those legs, and they were placed *exactly* on the two spots the pain radiated from. This dumb cat was bruising my chest wall while I was sleeping. I bet he got a big laugh hearing me tell Mara about the test results. They understand English, believe me - I speak from experience.

Anyway, I convinced Mara to go see my doctor so he could figure out what was going on with her waking up choking. He listened to her explanation, took one look at her weight, and diagnosed her with sleep apnea. I'd never even heard of sleep apnea, so he had to explain to us what it meant, how it worked, and the long-term dangers it carried; as usual, Mara was ahead of the curve, experiencing medical problem before they became common knowledge or "popular." He told Mara she would need to have a CPAP machine and wear a mask while she slept, which would maintain a positive airway and allow her to sleep without her breathing stopping again and again.

As usual, Mara was not happy with this diagnosis, especially since it was based in part on her weight. Would she be able to sleep with this mask on her face, and with all the noise the machine was going to make? She was also concerned about how expensive this CPAP machine was going to be.

That's when she discovered that between the two insurances, there wasn't any out-of-pocket cost for that kind of durable medical equipment.

That information gave birth to her next idea, or at least a contingency plan. "If my back keeps getting worse and walking gets harder, I'm going to have him prescribe me a wheelchair." That was not exactly a goal I was looking forward to her accomplishing. There was simply no question in my mind that her back would improve if she would try to eat better and lose some weight. As always, I was conflicted, because I knew some dietary limitations and some of her medications made losing weight difficult. But it hurt to know she was using those obstacles as the confirmation that she should throw in the towel.

Still, while I would try to bring up the subject in a positive way, I didn't fight nearly as hard as I should have. Mara was unhappy and sick too often already, I reasoned; why should I push her and argue with her? Just to take away some of her otherwise happy moments? Besides, when Mara became stubborn there was no changing her mind, so I had to tread carefully just to keep the small possibility open. I was forever second-guessing myself, trying to figure out of I was doing more harm than good, or if I was enabling her.

Mara's fears about the bulky, loud CPAP machine were well-founded, but both of us got used to it rather quickly. It also helped me learn to sleep in even louder environments than before. That would come in handy a decade later when I was in Federal Prison. There was some trouble finding a mask Mara could wear that fit properly and didn't immediately break in some way, but overall at least I knew she wasn't going to wake up choking any more, and she'd be getting enough oxygen while she slept.

Although it came close once or twice, we got through our first year in Texas without Mara being hospitalized. Work was an up and down affair, and I feared losing my job and suddenly finding myself without prescription coverage for Mara again. But things weren't too bad. Unfortunately, the owners of the house decided they wanted to come back to Dallas and re-occupy it, so after ten months we had to move again. The leasing company found us another house to rent, as Mara refused to go back to an apartment after having the extra space the house gave us. This new house was approximately the same size, and the identical rent, but in a less desirable area and without the wonderful back yard we had been spoiled with. Rent prices were rising in Dallas, so we had to take what we could get at this point.

As we prepared to move, Mara and I discussed the BBS and Throbnet. We decided it was time to give them both up. The people we had been unofficially partners with were interested in trying to turn it into a revenue source, which we didn't want to be bothered with (especially as Mara was barely spending any time on the forums any longer). Plus, we both saw the writing on the wall: CompuServe and Usenet were starting to spread, and America On-Line was about to begin. The days of the local BBS were doomed, despite how busy Throbnet was at the moment. So we said goodbye to both the house and the BBS at the same time.

Packing turned out to be very stressful, and much of the time we found ourselves arguing bitterly. It was almost as if we both knew the honeymoon in Dallas was over, and we were about the find ourselves back in our old lives but in a different place.

If we both felt that way, we were right.

Chapter 34 – Circular Patterns

Our move to the new house was stressful but otherwise uneventful. The cats weren't as freaked out about it as the move to Texas. The house had a few issues, as rental homes often do, but nothing awful. Mara was pleased to learn one of our neighbors had a group of stray cats they fed and watered, all of whom had been fixed. They would wander into our small back yard and once in a while Mara would be able to pet them.

Soon after the move, Mara's parents decided to come for a weekend visit. They stayed at a local motel, which all of us were happier with then the alternative. It was easy to see the disapproval in their eyes when it came both to Mara's housekeeping and her interior design skills. Everything they saw resulted in some kind of criticism. Why is the litter box in the kitchen? Why haven't you bought a new couch? Why are you using that area as a messy craft area for Mara? One would think they were being asked to olive there instead of me.

The second evening they were in town, they decided they wanted to go to the Fort Worth Stockyards to have dinner. The stockyards are fun if you live in Fort Worth, and are a favorite with tourists who think that all of Texas is cowboy hats and country line dancing. But we'd never been there, nor did we have an interest in going. Still, they insisted, and Mara's Dad wanted to go in our van, with him driving. It was raining, dark, and traffic was terrible. It was almost amusing sitting in the back with Mara as her parents bickered back and forth.

It took over 90 minutes to get to the stockyards, not the 40 minutes Mara's Dad has insanely expected. Her mother was getting hungry and extremely cranky, and for a change was inflicting her criticism on her husband instead of us.

We drove around for ten or fifteen minutes while he looked for a place to eat. It was this moment that – to me – perfectly encapsulated their entire relationship. Mara's mother was getting louder and shriller, saying if she didn't eat soon, she would get a migraine.

"Just find someplace for us to eat. I don't care where, anywhere!"

So Mara's Dad started to pull into a steakhouse we were about to pass.

"No, not **HERE**! Somewhere **ELSE!**"

I almost felt sorry for him at that moment.

Monday while I was at work Mara's parents took her out to buy a new couch. The one we had was perfectly fine for us, and was a sleeper sofa. But it was old and not stylish; they wanted to buy Mara a leather sofa. When I heard about it later, I thought it was the craziest idea I'd ever heard. We had five cats, and they were guaranteed to scratch up and rip the leather no matter how often we clipped their nails. It was unnecessary and a waste of money. But they badgered Mara until she agreed.

Still, that wasn't enough. They then "bargained" with Mara and explained that since *they* were buying the sofa, *we* had to contribute by buying ourselves an ottoman. And not just any ottoman, but one where Mara custom-chose the design and fabric (in other words, unnecessarily expensive and something that didn't fit with the rest of our belongings). Of course, when it came time to make the purchase, Mara's mother vetoed Mara's choices and made the decisions herself. We still had to pay for it…$350 for what amounted to a low stool covered in carpeting, that we had no use for. Lovely.

I didn't spend much time talking to them during the visit, but Mara's parents did corner me at one point when Mara was in the bathroom. "You have got to force her to lose weight" they implored me. "She's getting way too fat." They said it in a way that suggested I hadn't noticed. How was I supposed to accomplish that? I wasn't about to go into all the reasons for the weight gain, which were both physical and psychological. And it wasn't as if they'd done a good job making Mara feel positive about losing weight. These were the parents who publicly told Mara she was fat when she had been only five- or ten-pounds overweight. This was the loving mother who used to sit across from Mara and puff her cheeks out like a squirrel filling its mouth with nuts whenever she thought Mara was eating too much at a meal. If the sexual abuse and her mental desire to make herself unattractive to men – so she wouldn't have to try and rebuff their sexual advances – hadn't been enough to screw her up, their lack of parenting skills hadn't done a bit of good.

It wasn't long before Mara asked her doctor to prescribe a wheelchair as a medical necessity. He approved that request, mainly because walking really had become more of a challenge for her. When we'd first moved to Dallas, we'd walk through the mall together holding hands. That had changed to dropping Mara off right in front of the movie theater so she could make her way to the seat without having to stop and sit, and forgetting the mall (and the grocery store) entirely. In one respect the wheelchair was sort of admitting Mara wasn't going to lose the weight needed to make her back less of an issue, at least not at any time in the near future. On the other hand, with the wheelchair Mara would be able to go out and do things instead of being stuck at home.

A supply company delivered Mara her wheelchair a few weeks later. It was a manual wide-carriage model, so even if she continued to gain weight, she would be able to sit in it comfortably. The two sides folded together to allow for easier transport, which meant we could put it in the rear of our van with no problem. It was a bit heavy but I could deal with that. The only part of the design I hated were the front wheels. While the large side wheels were the standard metal-spoke wheels you think of, the two front wheels were made of rather cheap plastic with rubber treads. I feared that going over bumps or small obstructions would be an issue, and sure enough we sometimes encountered problems. I started having to keep a few screwdrivers in the rear pouch of the wheelchair so I could pry the tread back over the tires if they bent and slipped off suddenly. It was always a sudden, surprising stop when it happened, and it seemed to really piss me off. My temper would go through the roof. I didn't want to get so angry about it, because I wasn't mad at Mara for being in the wheelchair or for having to push her around in it. I was just pissed off because those wheels seemed to be such a poor design. Far too much weight was distributed forward in this wheelchair, so why would they support try to support that weight with such cheap, breakable wheels?

Mara was happy to be able to go to the mall again. And movies became more fun for her; she seemed to love having us arrive just before a movie started so that she could force people sitting in the seats meant for those accompanying people in wheelchairs to relocate. Sometimes I thought that was a factor in when she chose just-released movies for us to go to: she thought they'd be crowded and somebody who arrived long before us but grabbed those seats would find themselves stuck sitting in the front row. Unfortunately, we often didn't get to stay for the whole movie, as her Crohn's would send her to the bathroom multiple times and suddenly she was in too much discomfort to watch any more. I know she felt bad about it, and I never gave her any grief. I could always come see the movie later by myself if it was really important to me.

Mara found two other "joys" in using her wheelchair. The first was when we'd go out to eat. Often if there was a line, the restaurant would seat us sooner than many others depending on how many tables could be made wheelchair accessible. She never asked for that sort of treatment, but she wasn't about to refuse it. The other thing she enjoyed was on occasion where we went to the mall or somewhere else with multiple exit points. If she started feeling ill or uncomfortable, she would have me leave her in one area and go get the car myself; it was faster than wheeling her all the way back, as I could navigate the crowds much easier. Then I would pull up into a handicap parking space and get out of the van. More often than not, someone would come over and start yelling in my direction about how I wasn't handicapped and it wrong for me to take that space (even though I would hang the placard from the rear-view mirror). I'd ignore them and walk into the mall. A minute or two later we'd see the complaining individual writing down our license plate number or something, a determined look on their face. Then they'd look up and see me wheeling Mara towards the van, and they'd sheepishly back away. I never used the placard unless Mara was with me, or unless I was dropping her off or picking her up; I understood how important those spots were for people who needed them. But it still felt like a victory to be falsely accused and then vindicated.

Mara's Crohn's had been getting progressively worse. Her GI had switched her from the sulfa drug to a new one which was still in clinical trials (which meant she got the medicine for free; that would have been a bigger deal before she had prescription coverage, but it was still nice). The new medication seemed to work as well or better, but it was only effective in lengthening the time between her really bad attacks. When one of those hit, she could tell she'd be in the hospital soon. Even if she didn't tell me it was coming, I knew too, just by the fact that she'd shave her armpits and legs suddenly out of the blue.

There wasn't much the hospital could do for her but give her stronger pain medication and a much stronger dose of steroids, both intravenously. Sometimes they would try and play around with something else, but Mara and I both understood that hospitalization was a three- or four-day process which was meant to stabilize her and keep her hydrated. When these bad attacks arrived, she couldn't even keep water down.

From past experience, Mara had built a routine of sorts for when she went to the hospital. She would let her GI's office know a major flare up was coming, and then when the day came that she couldn't wait any longer we'd call the GI before going to the emergency room. That way he could alert them to what was going on, and there wasn't as big a fuss about getting her admitted.

On occasion we'd be unable to reach her doctor first. That always made Mara angry and nervous, because she knew the ER doctor was bound to try their own treatments or want to run tests. Aside from blood work, there was no test that needed to be run. But since they didn't have immediate access to her medical file, they wanted to play the game and diagnose her problem.

Once in a while they'd quickly back off when a doctor or nurse asked for a list of her medical problems and what medications Mara was taking. We always made it a point to keep an updated computer file of all that information, and Mara carried two or three printed copies of the latest version in her purse. When you handed the ER doctor a full page of problems and medications (including all her "prn" medication, a.k.a. "as needed"), they usually saw there wasn't much they could do and would go back to trying to contact Mara's GI.

Mara also learned it was important to pay attention to what the doctors and nurses were doing, even if she knew she would be admitted. On a few occasions someone would give her an injection of Compazine, which is an anti-nausea drug which Mara took orally. It rarely – if ever – did anything for her in either form. But once they'd given her the injection, hospital policy would be that she would need to wait six to eight hours for any kind of pain relief. That was guaranteed to send her into a rage.

There are two emergency room visits I remember in particular where we were unable to get in touch with her GI before going to the hospital. For the first one, Mara was in terrible pain and very nauseas, but hadn't thrown up. She told me she'd eaten about an entire box of macaroni and cheese for lunch, so we knew she was loaded for bear if it came to that. The ER doctor and nurses in this case were very understanding; they just wanted to talk to her GI before doing anything. A nurse had tried to slip Mara a Compazine injection but she'd been aware enough to refuse it. Overall Mara was not in an angry mood; she was mostly out of it, and almost a little child-like.

While we sat around the exam room waiting for word, she jumped up from the exam table and ran over to the sink. There was a steady two-minute eruption of macaroni and cheese, and then she just stood there looking faint.

A custodian came in and yelled at Mara for throwing up in there. "Next time just do it on the floor, that's a lot easier to clean up than this!" I didn't get into any kind of argument with him; Mara had simply acted instinctively and she didn't really know what was going on.

I tried to gently lead her back to the exam table to sit or lie down again but she whispered in my ear "I messed myself." I guess in the midst of all that vomiting, she had defecated too. Fortunately, we had brought some clothes with us, as we tried to do when she was expecting to be admitted. I suppose my experience was similar to what parents go through. I didn't get mad, and I didn't even get grossed out. I closed the door for privacy, and peeled her underwear off. They were filled with a muddy substance, with trails on her legs and elsewhere. I Threw that pair of underwear away, spent a good five minutes gently cleaning her up. She even got some on the bottom of her feet somehow.

Finally, it all looked good, waist to feet, and I got another pair of underwear and pulled them up her legs. As she teetered her way towards the exam table, she halted and started to sob quietly. "I'm sorry," Mara said. "I'm so sorry."

"It's okay my love, it wasn't your fault. It happens."

"No, I mean I'm sorry, it just happened again."

There was nothing else to do. She had one pair left, so I repeated the procedure, talking calmly to her and reassuring her that it was okay. And really it was. She was sick, and there was nothing intentional about this. I promised to bring her more underwear the next day so she had a supply with her. Soon after, she fell asleep on the exam table and was eventually admitted.

The other ER visit I remember in particular was another where we were unable to get in touch with Mara's GI. Her Crohn's had hit her hard for about three days, and she had been unable to keep anything down in the meantime, with her nausea growing progressively worse over the three days. Even water or popsicles would get thrown up.

The ER doctor that took charge of Mara was young, opinionated, and seemed insulted at the idea that he should contact Mara's GI to get a consultation. No, he wanted to handle this on his own. Perhaps he thought Mara was overdramatic, or being a hypochondriac. Or maybe he believed that Mara was only interested in painkillers, especially since she refused a Compazine shot (as always) with the explanation that if she took that they wouldn't give her anything stronger for hours and hours. I'm not suggesting this doctor always acted this way – we all have bad days – but he was clearly arrogant and had no interest in listening to Mara, me, or her GI.

At one point during his examination (or cross examination, take your pick) Mara had started to move to get off the exam table where she had been sitting. The doctor had come back with some kind of snide remark, something like "Oh no, if you're feeling that sick, I don't want you wandering around the exam room. Please stay seated there."

"It's just that I feel like throwing up again" Mara replied.

His solution was to give Mara a very small kidney-shaped dish. "If you need to throw up you can do it in there."

The doctor explained that there was really nothing they could do for Mara, especially since she refused to accept the Compazine injection. He told us to wait while he tended to another patient, and that he'd be back with a prescription for Mara (some kind of supposedly stronger nausea drug). His inclination was to give her that and send her home.

Perhaps ten minutes later, I knocked on the open door of the room where the doctor was taking someone's blood pressure. "Excuse me," I politely said. "Could I get some help?"

"I'm busy taking care of this patient," the doctor replied. "I'll be back in to see your wife in a little while."

"Okay, thank you, whenever you have a minute" I politely and quietly said, and turned to leave.

As an afterthought, the doctor looked up again as I was walking out the door and asked "Why? What's the problem now?"

"Umm...Mara threw up a bunch of yellow bile, and then fainted a minute later. She fell off the exam table and I can't wake her up, so I need help bring her 'round and getting her onto the table again. She might be bleeding too, I'm not sure if she broke any teeth or her nose or anything when she collapsed."

Two nurses rushed past me and into the room where Mara had been. I turned and followed them. They were slapping Mara's hands gently and talking sweetly to her. It looked like she had a cut on her head but no other major injury. The kidney dish they'd given her sat on a small table next to the exam table, overflowing with bile and little things that looked like bits of bird seed. They helped Mara up and sat her in a chair, and told her to stay put. One nurse began to take Mara's blood pressure, while the other left the room.

A new doctor came in minutes later, and told us Mara had been admitted and would be moved to a room shortly. We didn't see the other ER doctor again.

Chapter 35 - The Knife

[[This incident is also described in my first memoir, "It's Their House; I'm Just a Guest," but I wanted to include it here as well.]]

I've been asked many times what the worst moment in my relationship with Mara was. Sometimes they mean what was the saddest moment, or the most disturbing, or the craziest. There are many ways to answer the question, but in general I choose to relate that one moment when I had given up on everything: the marriage, the future, and my own life.

Mara's Crohn's was stable at that moment, despite the occasional hospitalization. But her mental state continued to deteriorate. Her weight was also still a problem, as she steadily gained a few pounds every month. Day to day you wouldn't see a difference, but a pound a week adds up. She complained of missing her family in one moment, and the next hoping she would never speak to or see them again. She was angry, erratic, and miserable. Mara was tired of living, and tired of hoping for the relief that never came. Every step forward was somehow followed by two steps back. Aside from work, I spent all my time by Mara's side, awake or asleep. But nothing I did could ease her misery.

My brother Andrew had owned a Bowie knife years earlier, and when I was a teenager, he had given it to me. I never had any use for it, but we kept it in a bedside drawer as a form of protection. We didn't have any guns; not even I was crazy enough to keep guns around Mara. There was no telling who she might use them on, including herself.

One night we were lying in bed watching television. As a general rule at this stage, I would fall asleep hours before Mara would. She'd stay up until 2am or later watching television, unable to sleep, and instead would sleep until 10am or later in the morning, waking up only for a moment to take the handful of pills I'd give her before leaving for work.

Mara had been strangely quiet all evening, neither laughing at the TV nor complaining of any discomfort. I rolled over, gave her a kiss goodnight, and started to settle in to fall asleep. At that point, Mara reached back and opened her own bedside drawer, pulling out the Bowie knife and showing it to me.

"Tonight, when you are sleeping," she said in an emotionless monotone, "I am going to stab you to death."

"Okay," I replied calmly. "And why would you want to do that? Did I do something wrong?"

"No, but I'm tired of living. And if I kill you, I won't have a reason to live anymore. So I will be free to kill myself. And that's what I am going to do. I'm sorry, but I just can't take it anymore. And I don't want to kill myself and leave you behind to deal with the guilt and the mess."

I could actually see the warped logic of what she was telling me. But I didn't know what to do, or what to say. Life had been dragging us both down, and for a long time I'd had no hope of things getting any better. At any rate, I was tired too, physically, mentally, and emotionally. And I felt completely helpless in my life. I didn't see how anything would ever really get better. Sure, there would be better days and worse days, but the trend was set: downwards.

I rolled over on my side and faced away from Mara. I didn't want to look at her. I just put my head down on the pillow, said "I love you," and closed my eyes. Death has always been a huge fear for me; trying to fathom the concept of nonexistence makes me shake all over, and when that happens I have to snap out of that quickly. I knew Mara was serious, and I felt fairly certain she would follow through with her plan. But in my state of misery, it didn't matter. The fear of death, and the thought of that knife plunging in and out of my body, barely moved the needle. I simply didn't care any longer. In only a few minutes I was asleep.

The next morning my alarm went off around 5am, as usual. Mara was still awake, sitting up, holding the knife. Her eyes were bloodshot and red, and I could see she had been crying on and off.

"I couldn't do it," she said quietly. "You looked so peaceful and innocent; I couldn't kill you." I gathered her morning pills, which she swallowed with some water before rolling on her side to pet one of the cats and put on her CPAP mask. As I walked to the bathroom to take a shower and get ready for work, she looked up at me.

"I hate you, you bastard. Why can't you just let me die?"

And she turned on the CPAP machine, and went to sleep.

While I showered and my brain began to wake up a bit, I thought about what had happened. I thought about how I just rolled over and went to sleep, accepting my fate. The more I thought about, the more I realized I had woken up disappointed. In my own way, I was sorry Mara hadn't killed me.

And that was about when I knew I had to make some changes in my life. Maybe not that day, or that week, or even that month. But I needed to start thinking about the present, and the future, and how to make one tolerable and the other possible.

Chapter 36 - The More Things Change...

When we moved to Dallas, we came with my boss from New Jersey, and he and I went to work for the same firm. In less than a year, he had quit and moved on, while I stayed. He had asked me to join him in a new venture but there was no way I could follow him, since now that I had decent health insurance for Mara that had to be my primary focus when it came to a job. Even if he had been able to pay me more than I was earning (which he wasn't) I couldn't leave.

My duties at the company changed in the time after he left, but the manager there was never unclear: he wanted me to keep working there, and he would find me a position if there was nothing else for me to do. At first, I assisted some of the big money-makers, and then as they slowly left, I moved to a position dealing with our New York and Chicago offices, handing all the orders in the office instead of each person calling in their own.

It felt good to have a little job security, and to have impressed people at that firm enough that they had my back and were insistent that I stay around. Unemployment was a big fear for me. I figured I could find a new job if I had to, but again, the insurance was more important than the salary. I couldn't really afford to make much less than I was earning, as we had accumulated so much debt that everything seemed to go to bills and credit card payments. But if worse came to worse we could always consider bankruptcy. The one thing I **couldn't** consider was losing Mara's health insurance (especially the prescription coverage).

Unfortunately, everybody at my firm could see that business was getting worse and worse. The bigger producers left one by one, and rumors of the entire firm's demise started to run rampant. We were owned by a big Mexican bank, and that company's fortunes were faltering. There were reports of corruption at the bank, which was a problem for the Mexican authorities but had no day to day effect on our dealings, although it also meant that financially our firm could find itself cut off at any moment. And sure enough, a few of us got a warning call one evening that the following morning the firm would be seized and after a week or so to straighten out moving all the client accounts to somewhere safe, the entire firm would be shut down.

My coworker Betty and I went back to the office that night to collect our personal items, my computer and printer, and client books for each salesman that they wouldn't be allowed to remove later. And then the race was on. She and I would be paid for another week or two, along with one or two other administrative personnel in the Dallas office, but nobody else in our location. And I knew I couldn't afford to live without a paycheck, so I had maybe ten days to find another job.

While the commissioned salespeople were scattering to many firms, it seemed overall there were two companies most people were going to. One was a competitor of ours, and another a small collection of independent salespeople. This second firm was also where all the unclaimed accounts of clients would be sent temporarily, so there would be no interruption in those clients being able to access their money or anything else. Those two firms seemed to be my only immediate options.

I preferred the former, but only the latter was willing to give me a salaried position. I would take over their IT department, but at a sizable cut in pay from what I had been making. The ability to earn a little money in sales would allow me to compensate part of the difference, but no matter what it was going to make finances very tight for the time being. All I really cared about was the health insurance, which wasn't quite as good as what I'd had before but was still a very decent policy.

Through that whole mess I had been a complete emotional wreck, and stressed out day and night. But I didn't have any real outlet for the stress. Mara either didn't care at all, or was simply convinced that I would figure out a way to make it all work. She had no interest in discussing it. She just wanted to go on with life as it had been. She told me "Money and work are your responsibility. Figure it out yourself." It sounds very cold, but in reality I believe she was hoping I'd be unemployed, because it would give her further reason to kill herself.

My friend Betty was one of the people who had also gone to this new company, so at least I didn't feel completely alone there. The new position was a change, and a challenge; they were very behind in some aspects of technology, and hardly anyone knew how to operate their computers. I found myself getting in early, leaving late, and coming in on Saturdays to get a head start on Monday. Mara was a bit bothered by the extra hours, but she spent most of that time sleeping anyway. In a way, having to handle so many things at once was an escape from the misery of life at home.

As if I wasn't unhappy enough, my Mom was in crisis. After years of living off of alimony and child support, with an occasional part time job, my Dad had finally gone to court to have those payments ended. He had been on disability for a while, suffering from Parkinson's and unpredictable diabetes among other things. My stepmother Barbara had been the one who was working so they could afford to pay my mother her alimony, and I'm sure she just got tired of it. There was no reason the alimony should have gone on that long in the first place, and certainly no reason my mother couldn't have been making a living somehow.

In her typical fashion, my mother had no money saved, tons of debt, and was about to have nowhere to live. Out of myself and my five siblings, only four of us still spoke to my mother at all, and from that group Mara and I were the only ones with a spare bedroom. We agreed she could come live with us for a while, until she figured something else out. One of my brothers drove a truck full of boxes across the country, filled with her belongings. And the next thing we knew, the garage was overflowing with old boxes while the guest room was swamped by my mother and her immediate necessities. I now had two crazy women living with me, albeit crazy in very different ways.

At first, having my mother around wasn't that bad. She spent most of her time in her room, except for when she joined us for meals. She enjoyed the company of the cats, which surprised me since she had told me from as far back as I can remember she was allergic to cats. That was probably one of those convenient parental lies, as years later I found childhood photos of her holding cats over and over again.

If I was going to the grocery store, or taking Mara there, we'd ask my mother if she needed anything special. Once in a while there would be a specific request for an ingredient needed for a recipe she found in a magazine she'd kept for ten years, but more often than not the only think she asked for was Heineken. And not just any Heineken, but the bigger and more expensive Heineken tallboy bottles. I found a liquor store that carried them, and I became known to them as the Heineken guy since I was in there at least twice a week buying beer for my mother.

Despite the drain on our problematic finances, we tried to include her in things what we did. On one occasion Mara wanted to go to a baseball game. She didn't have any heavy interest in the Texas Rangers; Mara just liked to go on "Dollar Hot Dog" night. She invited my mother and I invited Betty to join us. For years later, Betty loved to tell whoever would listen the story of what a fiasco going to the ball game was. We sat in a specific location because it included a "seat" (an open space) for Mara's wheelchair. My mother demanded two programs, one to keep and one so she could fill out the scorecard. Every time Betty or I got up for any reason, Mara would ask for a few more hot dogs and my mother would ask for a few more beers. Betty and I spent the entire evening rolling our eyes at each other, especially since Mara seemed to get angry whenever I tried to engage Betty in conversation. When we were home that night, Mara was very angry about how I had "ignored" her by trying to talk to Betty now and then. I explained I didn't think I was supposed to invite a friend to the ball game and then refuse to speak to them. Betty was one of the few outsiders to ever see me have to deal with my mother and Mara at the same time. She now wears that badge with honor.

As it had when my brother lived with us in New Jersey, Mara's attitude towards my mother gradually went from friendly to tolerant to hostile. She was suspicious of my mother; she had no income and said she had no money, but she would take the city bus and disappear for the entire day, and when she returned tell unsolicited stories about having lunch at one restaurant or another. Another day she returned from an excursion with an air cast on one of her ankles, explaining that she fell stepping off a curb somewhere and had to be taken to the emergency room.

Mara's mood swings were violent enough already, but when the topic of my Mom came up, she went into overdrive. One day the two of us had gone to a shopping club store to get some items; things we went through quickly we tried to buy there in bulk. Mara would always fill our cart with extra snacks and treats for herself, and it was her practice to eat one of them (or start to) on the way home. On this occasion it was a big plastic jar of "fake brand" Peppermint Patties. Mara was on a tear about my Mom; she'd found a garbage bag in the garage with about 30 empty beer bottles in it, and knew that had to include some she got on her own.

"I don't understand where she is getting this money? We buy all her food, we pay for everything, and she still goes out to eat and buys extra beer? She's not old enough for Social Security. Could she be stealing it from us somehow?"

I didn't really have any answers, so I focused on the road. Then Mara started to cough and choke. I looked over and asked if she was okay, and she nodded yes. Her mouth was stuffed with the candies and she was trying to swallow way too much at once. I went back to driving and she went back to complaining, but she was still stopping every few seconds to cough or choke. Finally stopping at a red light, I looked over again; even as she yelled and nearly choked to death on her mouth full of mints, she was unwrapping more and cramming them in as quickly as she could. It was a frightening sight. I knew part of this was her anger, but a big part was just a glaring example of how Mara still used food as a means of comfort, and to soothe any strong negative emotions. I grabbed the jar out of her hand and put it behind my seat. Mara looked over at it longingly, and spent the rest of the ride home chewing and swallowing what she had already stuffed in her mouth.

It was around this time that I had a mini-breakdown. I confessed to Mara that I was utterly suffocated and I needed to start making a few friends and spending some time out of the house on my own, even if it was just going to happy hour after work or something. In the preceding decade we had gone from a small circle of friends to barely any, and on the rare occasion someone from out of town came by the house (or I invited a coworker along to something) it was in the company of Mara. I knew it wasn't healthy for the two of us to have nothing but each other. Right or wrong, I couldn't really talk to Mara in full detail about the problems in my life, both because she was the cause of some of my unhappiness and because she had so many issues she was dealing with already I was forced to play the strong supportive role 99% of the time.

The only area Mara had encouraged me to make connections outside of our constant twosome was in the area of sex. The sicker, more depressed, and heavier she got, the lower her sex drive became. Eventually she had zero interest in anything physical whatsoever, with me or with anybody else. That, of course, was part of the reason she ate the way she did: gaining weight was self-defense against her sexual problems, and if she could kill off her sex drive and make herself unattractive, she wouldn't need to concern herself with being propositioned. Unfortunately, there was no way she could do that while maintaining a sex life within the marriage. I suppose she could have pretended to still be interested, but I didn't want that. I wanted her to be honest with me whenever she could. Likewise, I did not take her up on her offers to go find a lover or a one-night stand because that's not the way I was wired. I have never been one who was interested in having sex with someone just to have sex. I need an emotional and intellectual attachment with a woman before I desire them physically. So instead I just forgot about sex as well. No sex, no masturbation, no nothing. If you turn your sex drive off completely it is easier than dealing with the lack of intimacy. It was difficult at first, but after the first year it all becomes routine.

Over the summer I found myself with zero appetite for about a week. It wasn't that I chose not to eat; I just didn't have any need to. I was surviving on my daily vitamins, black coffee, and fruit juice. I probably lost fifteen pounds, but I didn't know what to do about it and didn't really care. Mara expressed concern, and even my usually oblivious mother noticed. After perhaps ten days, I cooked dinner one night and ate a small portion, and little by little I got most of my appetite back. I didn't know if it had been a strange heavy depression, or my body's way or rebelling at my life, or something else entirely. It came, and it went, and then I found my self-awareness of my emotional state newly heightened. I couldn't bury emotions any longer, even if I didn't express them openly. I felt everything, all the time.

Now with this new job I was starting to make more friends, and longing for some personal time. This was also the first job I'd had where I was able to go out of the office for lunch a few times a week. Socializing was like a drug: once I started doing a bit of it, I realized how much more of it I wanted. I'd go to lunch with a few people from the office (which also gave me the opportunity to pick up the check and have them pay me in cash for their share, which I could use to make some of our other credit card payments), and I finally had an opportunity to talk about my life from my perspective and not from a combined point of view (or even solely from Mara's position, which is what often happened). It had been so long since anyone wanted to know how *I* was doing, and how *I* was handling things.

Me being me, there was a terrible sense of guilt tied in to anything I ever wanted to do outside of work hours. There was the constant thought that Mara needed me; she might be in the bathroom, crying in agony. Or she could just be lonely, and depressed, and considering her time without me as an opportunity to finally end it all without any interference. Those fears made it difficult to enjoy that time away, or to relax and live in the moment. That's something I had problems with already, so the combination made it much worse.

This really left me with a no-win scenario. I could spend all my time at home with Mara and feel suffocated and hopeless. Or, I could try to spend a few nights a week out of the house and feel guilty and anxious. The only thing that sometimes alleviated the guilt made me feel guilty in an enabling way: Mara would often ask that if on the way home from wherever I was going I could stop and get her something to eat. More often than not "something to eat" meant something sweet and fattening, or an entire second dinner from a restaurant or fast food place. It felt like a bribe for allowing me to leave the house, or a reward for not killing herself in my absence.

Part of the problem was that food was just about the only thing that could put a smile on Mara's face. It was like her birthday; there was the happiness at the surprise of what I brought, and then the joy as she devoured it. There just wasn't a lot that made Mara happy any longer. Going to the movies did, but only if she was able to make it through the whole thing without having to leave and come home. Even then, she inevitably spent ten minutes or more of every movie in the bathroom, and I'd have to try and explain what was going on and what she missed. She also found happiness with the cats, but not the way she did when Ubber was still around.

Bibs was her favorite now, and he had developed a real needy and emotional streak. When it was time to eat a meal, Bibs demanded a small plate of his own. Of course you could ignore that, but then he would sit next to you, reach up with his paws, dig his claws into your hand, and physically force the fork down to his mouth. He was big (but not fat) and **very** strong. He knew how to get what he wanted, or make you wish you'd given it to him.

He was also very cognizant of when I left the house. When I went out the front door in the morning, Mara said he would sit and stare out the window for ten minutes making sure I was gone. But if I left the house later in the day – on a weekend or perhaps after coming home from work – he would park himself by the window and howl. Mara described it as both cute and heartbreaking. Eventually she made a few audio recordings of it so I could hear what I was missing. I didn't know whether to laugh or cry when I heard it.

But it wasn't just me Bibs wanted to keep around him. Mara and I went out to the movies one day, and even managed to go to dinner afterwards. When we came home, we discovered one of the cats had pissed and shit on the bed while we were out. There was no way to know for certain who had done it, but we kept an eye on all of them for days to make sure their trips to the litter box were normal and uneventful. There seemed to be no physical problem with any of the cats. It was behavioral, not medical.

Sure enough, the next time we left the house together for more than a simple doctor appointment, we came back to the same disgusting mess on the bed. We both knew who it was. It had to be Bibs; he was pissed off that we were leaving him home alone, and was expressing his great displeasure. I guess it was more directed at Mara, since he had gone on her side of the bed both times. The message seemed to be: I hate when Dad leaves, but when Mom leaves too, I get **very** angry.

There wasn't an easy solution to the problem. We didn't want to have to sedate him every time we went out. The best we could do was buy a bunch of cheap plastic shower curtain liners and spread one out over the bed if we tried to go out to enjoy ourselves together. It was a workable if unpleasant solution; half the time Bibs would skip the display altogether, and the other half of the time I was able to clean up the mess without washing all the sheets and chemically treating the mattress to get the odor out.

There were still a few happier moments mixed in with the dark cloud that hung over us. Mara discovered she really liked to go to Dave & Busters to play a particular "kill the zombies" game, which she could do fine from her wheelchair. When she felt up to it, we'd go do that and often eat dinner there as well. I was very familiar with the location, since it was across the street from my office, and their bar often was where I would spend happy hour with a coworker or two. I was drinking more than I should be, but it was one of my few escapes from everything pushing me into the ground.

There was also a little video game place in the same building as our favorite movie theater. In there was a pinball machine Mara loved, so we'd go there and sometimes decide to skip the movie entirely. Soon after we became addicted to it, we discovered that this particular pinball machine had a minor short in it, which could allow you to earn free games by flipping the flippers as quickly as you could when a certain sequence unfolded. Frequently we'd leave the machine with over 25 free games piled up, offering them to some random kid to enjoy. I even looked into getting that game at home, but it was very expensive, not like our old worn machine.

Things between Mara and my mother came to a head around this time. Mara's older sister came to visit for a few days, and while I was at work the three of them had a heated argument. I never learned what started it, but it put my mother into one of her old-style crazy modes (or perhaps she was in it already). She screamed at Mara, telling her that we weren't taking care of her properly, and that there was nobody in the house smart enough to have a conversation with. She also said the house stank and was filthy (which was not true, but not entirely false either). She even came up with a story, out of the blue, that her injured ankle wasn't from tripping off a curb but was from "jumping off a bridge trying to kill myself."

As much as moments in the past can continue to haunt me in the present, I am thankful I wasn't present for this shouting match. If I were, it would be something I could never forget. The upshot was that when I came home Mara and her sister gave me a few of the details, and also explained that in the midst of her criticism my Mom had sort of backed herself into a corner. With all her complaints, she was challenged about why she stayed, and in response she swore she would be out by the end of the year. Describing that, Mara was firm: that was one promise she was going to be forced to keep. She had to be out by the end of the year, by December 31st 1998, as promised. That gave her only a few months to leave.

The stress in the household was only getting worse. Just walking past my mother's room made my stomach hurt. Mara was nearly always angry, and was spending more and more nights awake until 3am, watching TV over my sleeping body. My attempts to get a break were still filled with guilt and misery, and now I was finding myself growing more and more attracted physically and emotionally to one of my coworkers. I jumped at any opportunity to spend an hour with her after work. I was starting an odd winning streak at my favorite radio station, winning tickets to concerts by being the correct caller (or through trivia games; "reverse trivia" was my best, where you asked the hosts a question and if they can't answer it, you won). I won 10th row seats to a Depeche Mode concert, which was this coworker's favorite band. And I won front row seats to the radio station's annual music festival. At least at the concerts I could lose myself in the scene and the music for ten or fifteen minutes at a time.

I could tell I was slowing falling apart, and I didn't know how much longer I could hold things together before I had some kind of a collapse. And Mara was reminding me more and more of my mother. I didn't know what to do, or who to turn to. Mara refused to go to another mental hospital, either convinced nothing was wrong or simply not caring. I couldn't tell which. All I knew was it felt like there was no hope for the future, for either of us. Not that I ever really believed there was, but now the end felt ominously close.

It was time to do something I dreaded doing, both because of how Mara would react and because of how I knew all blame would fall on me, as it always did. It was time to call Mara's parents and ask for help, or advice, or **something**. Long ago I had given myself the impossible task of giving Mara reasons to keep going, and I could feel the failure growing.

Chapter 37 - Both Shoes Drop

There was no question Mara was slipping. I could tell things were really getting bad after Thanksgiving. I'd had the flu over the holiday, but still cooked us a small turkey and other dishes. Mara wasn't showering much, or doing anything really. She'd lie in bed, dressed in underwear and maybe a flannel nightgown, watching TV and sleeping, although sleeping was something she usually did during the day now, unless her Crohn's was acting up. In that case she'd spend most of her time in the bathroom in terrible pain, and then take two pain pills every few hours until she was doped up enough to pass out. She refused to call her psychiatrist for additional help, and I wasn't sure if her weekly therapy appointments were doing any good at all.

I'd made up my mind one morning to call Mara's mother in New Jersey and suggest she come down, or at least give me some direction on how to handle things. Mara, in uncharacteristic fashion, had called her mother, sister, and brother to talk to them in the preceding days. It had become more common for her to avoid them at all costs, refusing to answer the phone or speak to them, even when I picked it up and held it to her ear. I took this as a sign that she might be making the rounds to say goodbye or something. She hadn't said anything specific about suicide around me, but to be honest that in itself was a sign of bad things, since usually the subject would come up in passing multiple times a week. The fact that she wasn't mentioning it made me suspicious.

When I arrived at work that morning, there was some sort of computer system problem that had to be dealt with immediately, so I lost myself in that headache for a few hours. Once everything was up and running again, I went to my little office (more of a windowless closet really, but that's another story) with a cup of coffee. I returned two or three urgent calls from out-of-town customers who had their own system issues, and then took a long sip of coffee and a deep breath, preparing to call Mara's mother.

Just then a call was transferred to my phone, and I found to my complete surprise that it was Mara's mother calling me instead of the other way around.

"I was just going to call you" I said. "I need to talk to you about Mara. She isn't doing well."

"I know," her mother replied in a very odd voice. "I'm here in Dallas, at the emergency room. Mara tried to kill herself."

I didn't really know what to say or what to do when I heard Mara had actually tried to kill herself, after all those years of talking about it and thinking about it. I think my initial response was a monotone "You're kidding me." I didn't even bother to ask what method she had used. I just grabbed my coat, told two friends at work where I was going (without leaving any chance for them to do anything in response but have their mouths drop open) and dashed out. The hospital where they had taken her was right down the street from my office, so it only took about two minutes to pull into the Emergency Room parking area and get inside.

It wasn't until I'd had a moment to collect my thoughts in the ER that I began to wonder how it came to pass that Mara's mother (and her sister) were waiting for me at the hospital. After all, they lived in New Jersey, and they hadn't said anything about coming to town. Once we'd hugged and I'd been updated on Mara's immediate condition (stable, and busy getting her stomach pumped), they filled in all the missing details for me.

As it turned out, Mara's mother and sister had been operating under the same suspicions that I had: that Mara's behavior over the past week, especially calling her family members and talking to them without being prodded to do so, was both completely out of character and alarming. So, the two of them decided the best way to handle the situation was to fly down without warning Mara that they were coming, in order to confront her and possibly get her into some kind of mental hospital. I suppose there was a chance of that working; my attempts to get Mara to go back into the hospital had been summarily rejected, but often Mara could be swayed by her parents or sister; partially out of guilt, and partially because she so desperately craved a more meaningful and understanding relationship with her family, and to have them take a selfless interest in her well-being like this was sure to mean a lot to her. Whether it would have meant enough to act on their wishes, or whether she would have simply waited a few days for them to leave and then proceed with her plan anyway, we will never know.

For whatever reason, they chose not to tell me about the visit in advance either. I can't really blame them, as I have no way of knowing now whether back then I would have allowed my sense of loyalty to Mara (especially when it came to her family) to reveal their plans so she could mentally prepare herself. Arriving at the airport, the two of them rented a car and drove out to our house. Knocking on the door, they were greeted by my mother. Actually, "greeted" is a polite way to put it. When my mother opened the door, they said hello and asked how she was.

"Alive" was the only word my mother said. Then she turned and walked back into her bedroom, closing the door behind her. She never reappeared.

Left alone, the two of them went into our bedroom, where they found Mara asleep on the bed. They tried to wake her and discovered she was terribly groggy. Noticing an empty bottle on pills on the bed next to her, they asked Mara if she had taken anything. She admitted that she'd taken the entire bottle of Xanax (maybe 20 pills), and had planned on taking a full bottle of 90 Darvocet as well, but passed out before she'd had time. Four suicide notes were left on the other side of the bed: one to her parents, one to her brother, one to her sister, and one to me.

They frantically called an ambulance. When the paramedics arrived, Mara was still able to walk (or stumble) to the stretcher under her own power. They raced to the hospital, where they took Mara in to pump her stomach, and Mara's mother called me at work. It was a tremendous stroke of luck (or fate) that they'd happened to choose that particular day to fly down, because otherwise there was little or no chance that she would have been found until I came home from work that afternoon. By that time, it would have been too late.

As we sat in the waiting room, the inevitable questions and recriminations started. I had learned to expect and deal with these sorts of conversations from Mara's family. Of course, I already felt guilty enough as it was. After all, the woman I had basically devoted my entire life to caring for and making happy was lying in the other room having a bottle of pills pumped out of her stomach. What better illustration could there be of my complete and utter failure in every regard? But I still didn't need the third degree from these people, especially when in my opinion they'd never done anything to help the situation. When we were married (or before) Mara had become *my* problem.

The family's place was to sit back and offer criticism whenever they felt it was necessary.

"Why haven't you done anything to help her?" "Why wasn't she in the hospital?" "Why did you let it come to this?" "Why didn't you see this coming?" "Why hasn't she lost any weight?" "Why why why why why why why why why why?" Pretty soon that's all I could hear. A never-ending barrage of whys, each one pointed directly at me, the guilty one, the worthless one, the useless one, the failure, the one who was never good enough for their daughter and sister. All those titles slapped on my back, with a new one added for the occasion, in flashing neon - attempted murderer. Because I knew there had to be a drop of suspicion that I **did** see this coming and didn't care. That hurt most of all. Of course I saw it coming, and of course I cared. That's why I was going to call Mara's Mom to ask her to come down and intervene.

And as if things weren't bad enough for me, the worst was yet to come. I was about to discover that, just like with every other physical ailment she'd suffered through, the process of pumping Mara's stomach and cleaning her system out was going to be far more complicated than anyone imagined. It was time for Mara to be the "one percent" again.

My years with Mara had given me quite a bit of experience with medical matters. I was now an expert in the uses and side effects of many prescription drugs, as well as fully knowledgeable in how they interacted with each other. Chronic headaches, migraines, blood disorders, and mental problems (both psychological and chemical in nature) were as commonplace topics to me as the weather or football scores. And, not to be left out, intestinal problems and bowel habits had for years been an involuntary subject of focus in my amateur studies. But now I was about to get an education in a number of other medical areas.

After having her stomach pumped, Mara was admitted to the ICU. Her lungs were not operating at full strength. The doctors were not exactly sure why, although they suspected it was the sedative properties of the pills she had taken. In fact, alarmingly, that lung function seemed to be getting worse, not better, over time. Mara would not completely come around from her drugged state. Receiving her nourishment through an IV, we were allowed to give her ice chips, which was the only word she seemed able to speak on those occasions when she opened her eyes. "Chips, chips" she would whisper like a mantra, but the staff would only allow us to give her a few at a time. Otherwise, we tried to keep her lips moist with a sponge-like tip on a plastic stick, kept in a glass of cold water. The whole scene felt surreal to me, a nightmare or a bad acid trip. I do have clear visions of the three of us (and Mara's brother and father, who flew down to join us when they were told the news) giving her ice chips and wetting her lips.

The initial problem, aside from how unresponsive Mara was, was her temperature. Mara started with a low-grade fever and it rose until it hovered around 102, sometimes higher. They hospital was giving her fever reducers, but she wasn't having any reaction to them.

The doctors suspected Mara would need to stay in the ICU for four or five days, while they got her lungs working better and her fever under control. It was decided that Mara's mother would stay in town, at a Residence Inn near our house. Her Dad and siblings would fly home for the time being. There wasn't anything else they could do, and the immediate danger had passed. After fifteen years of talking about it, thinking about it, and planning it, Mara had finally done it. I knew Mara; she wasn't going to take her survival as a sign that she shouldn't have tried, or that she had a whole wonderful life ahead of her. When she got a bit better and had her mental faculties, she was going to be angry. And she was going to see this whole suicide attempt as just another failure in her life. I could actually hear her voice in my head already, saying "I am such a fuck up, I couldn't even kill myself properly."

Mara's mother and I spent most of the day at the hospital for the next few days, taking turns leaving to run errands or do whatever else we needed to do. I had to keep an eye on the cats, stay in touch with work so they knew when I'd be returning, and think about things to help Mara. I brought a portable CD player in so she could hear some of her favorite music, because I hoped it might make her more responsive. She was still pretty out of it, waking up groggily for a bit and then lapsing back into semi-consciousness.

The doctors were growing concerned about Mara's lack of improvement. She was still burning up, her lungs were weak, and she wasn't really moving anything except her head when she opened her eyes for a minute. Besides that, she was effectively immobile. Until she started to communicate there were no real answers about how she was or her prognosis.

With just her Mom and I there, we didn't talk much. We just looked at each other, sad and miserable. Mara's condition was too much to carry alone, so I was grateful to have her mother there with me, especially as the recriminations had stopped for the moment. We were thinking about what was happening now, and what was going to happen, not what led up to it.

It wasn't until a few days after Mara had tried to kill herself that her Mom gave me the suicide note she had left for me. I don't think she was hiding it from me; I just think she wasn't thinking it was of immediate importance. The note itself was hard to read; it made me feel empty and sad. But a lot of it was much more matter-of-fact than I had expected. It even included a few reminders and suggestions, such as lean on her family for support, don't forget to tell the lawn people not to come, things like that. Mara also made a specific point on the rear of the note, mentioning that my Mom was supposed to be out by the end of the year, and that she expected me to follow through on that even though she had committed suicide. "Kick your Mom out by December 31st" was the clear instruction.

As a matter of fact, my mother had been a complete non-factor. I was told she never left her room when the ambulance was there, and didn't come out until everyone had left (if she came out at all). When I got back home that night around 10pm she wouldn't have had any idea if Mara was alive or dead, but she never asked. She didn't come out of her room. She didn't speak a word to me, not one. Not that day, or the day after, or the day after that. It was as if we didn't exist to each other. If I weren't so physically and emotionally exhausted, I would have pounded on her bedroom door and said something, but I didn't see the point and I wasn't willing to use the little power I had left on my mother when I knew I'd need it for more important things.

Dear Doug,

Thank you for giving me some happiness in my horrible world. I will always love you no matter where I am.

I'm sorry that you can't see that this is the best thing for me. I think it's because you are afraid of dying like me.

I love you so much that I am considering postponing until you come to grips with this. The last thing I want to do is hurt you. However I realize that you will probably never want me to die. For this I am sorry. I love you darling Doug. I hope you see a therapist and get help for your anger and guilt etc. Please don't hate me for being selfish. It's just something I need to do. Please lean on your friends in your time of need. And remember, you don't have to go to my funeral. It's how you treated me before I died that counts. And you treated me with nothing but love and kindness throughout the years.

Love,
Mara

With Mara's weak lungs came lower-than-ideal oxygen levels. The doctors decided they needed to insert a breathing tube to try and increase the air flow. This didn't sound like such a terrible thing to me, until it was explained that the longer she received assistance with her breathing, the weaker her lungs would actually become. Like any other part of the body, having someone else move them for you wasn't nearly as effective as being able to move them yourself. I tried my best not to worry about the long-term aspects of this, since there was so much to be concerned about right on front of us. There wasn't any better option to consider.

The problems with Mara's fever went on for about a week or longer. The doctors tried two different types of antibiotics in case the problem was an undetected internal infection, and neither showed any result. Finally, a young doctor came up with the unorthodox idea of giving Mara some nitroglycerine medication (the type they give to heart patients). His theory was this would open her system up and allow her body to expel the fever through her skin, since he believed the reason the fever would not come down was Mara's skin not properly opening its pores (or something like that). Miraculously, this seemed to work, and Mara's fever finally dropped. Things were starting to improve.

With the stabilization of her fever, Mara was become more conscious and was able to react to us when she was awake. It was at this point that the doctors gave us some more news we didn't want to hear. Mara's lungs were still not able to breathe properly on their own, but the breathing tube was only meant to be a temporary measure. In order to minimize any internal damage, and to make it easier to wean her off the breathing assistance, it was necessary to remove the tube and replace it with a tracheotomy. The issue was they were not sure if this tracheotomy could be reversed at a later date. In other words, Mara might have to have a tracheotomy tube (or hole) for a long period, or perhaps for the rest of her life.

While this was not the worst moment in the entire nightmare for me, it was one of them. I don't remember Mara's mother, who was alone with me when we got this news, ever let her guard down and her emotions show more completely then right then. Crying, choking, and looking utterly lost and helpless, she fell apart. Obviously she had been trying to build hope within herself that Mara could recover from this not just physically, but mentally, and learn to enjoy life. "How can we look at Mara and tell her that things are going to be worse for her now than they ever were?" she asked rhetorically. "She'll just want to kill herself all over again."

I didn't have an answer. Deep down I suspected Mara's only long-term response to this whole experience – whether or not she recovered fully – would be to plan even more carefully next time. She may have failed at her first true suicide attempt, but she'd learn from this and make sure she didn't fail the next time, no matter how many years in the future that might be.

We were determined that regardless of how we really felt, everyone around Mara would make an attempt to act positive once she started coming around. Now that her fever was under control, and her breathing was better (for the time being) because of the tracheotomy, we felt she was finally stabilized and ready to move forward. By this time, she had spent a good week or longer in ICU. Whether it was simply due to my utterly hopeless mental state, or simply because I had learned the hard way that life could always get worse, I tried to prepare myself for the next disaster. There had to be one coming; there always was. I started going to work again, and going to the hospital afterwards.

While I waited to see what bomb fell next, I came home about ten days into the ordeal to a surprise: my mother had moved out. She never said a word to me; I just came home and found her and some of her belongings gone, with a note on a box in the bedroom asking if I could save her other things until she arranged to have someone collect them someday. I didn't know what time she left, where she went, or if she had any concrete plan about how she was going to live. She hadn't spoken to me since Mara attempted suicide, she left without a word, and while some letters or cards would be exchanged over the years we never spoke directly (or by phone) again.

Mara's mother had been staying at a nearby Residence Inn, and now she checked out of there and moved into my mother's old room for the time being. I didn't care – I was rarely home. If I wasn't at work (where I'd be six days a week, for a total of sixty hours) or at the hospital, I was getting drunk, spending time with the friends who could tolerate my presence considering what I was going through, or leaning on the woman who I had started feeling more than friendship for. She didn't have a real understanding of the nature of my marriage of convenience, and that always made me feel worse even when I was trying to feel better. It just seemed way too complicated to explain, so during those periods when the relationship was more than friendship, I played it off as if we were sneaking around behind Mara's back, when in fact Mara was the one who had long demanded I find companionship elsewhere. During the time Mara was in the hospital, though, it was all she or anyone else could do to keep me from killing myself or someone else. How I got through this time without a complete nervous breakdown in beyond me. Instead I survived, and beat myself up with guilt for doing so whenever I get a chance.

The horrible financial mess we were in was bubbling over at about this time as well. Just making the minimum payments on our debt was all I could do, and between that and rent and household bills there was nothing left. Mara and I had talked about bankruptcy a number of times in the years prior, but we'd never thrown in the towel and done it, and now I couldn't face that nightmare while I was busy with the immediate one. So I tried to ignore the problem, and when I couldn't I'd drink it away.

I was an emotional, mental, financial, and professional wreck. I swung between feeling overwhelmed and numb, between hopeless and uncaring. As I fell asleep at night I'd lie there and think about the present, and try to imagine what paths might make the future better. Usually, I couldn't think of any. And some of the time I couldn't see a future at all.

Chapter 38 - Merry Christmas

Now that Mara's fever had been resolved and she was spending more time awake each day, doctors were confronted with a new riddle: her immobility. She seemed barely able to move anything on her own except her head and neck. Somehow, they determined that during the "gastric lavage" – a fancy term for pumping somebody's stomach – Mara must have had a rare reaction to the paralytic drug she was given. It is common to give such drugs to avoid damage to the esophagus and stomach during the procedure, but Mara's reaction to that drug was – as usual – the "1%." They now expected her to require quite a bit of physical therapy before she'd be able to use her arms and legs properly again. Walking was going to be difficult, but would eventually come back. In addition, her muscle tone was worse than ever simply from being bedridden so long, so that would need to be addressed before the physical therapy became effective.

We didn't tell Mara any of these specifics. Instead, we simply told her that she'd get her strength back over time. At least she was talking and communicating. Not surprisingly, she was very unhappy that she woke up at all, much less in a hospital ICU with an IV and a tracheotomy. She seemed particularly bitter that I hadn't somehow stopped her family from saving her; it seemed a betrayal to her. In fact, I think she suspected I'd told them to come to Texas in the first place (which I **planned** to do when I called her mother, but circumstances and fate intervened before I had the chance). And, as usual, she cursed her "terrible luck." When we were alone in the ICU, she would rattle off a number of other recent times she had considered killing herself. "Why did I have to choose the one day my mother and sister came to rescue me?" Mara didn't view it as a sign that she was meant to live. To her, it was a sign – one among many - that she had been cursed. Obviously, this suicide attempt was not one to be referred to as a "cry for help."

After another few weeks, Mara's physical state had improved enough that the hospital wanted to move her out of the ICU and onto the floor which focused on respiratory issues. The main problem the doctors needed to deal with at this point was the state of Mara's lungs. It would take time and treatment for them to build up proper strength. Once they'd done that, they could focus on more aggressive physical therapy to enable her to walk again and move properly; that would likely take place at a different facility entirely. In the meantime, it was felt that after more than three weeks in ICU, it was safe to transfer Mara upstairs.

Mara's mother and I were very anxious about this move. The nurses in the ICU had been tremendous, not just in terms of Mara's medical needs, but also the incredible emotional support they'd given all of us. A suicide attempt, a *real* one, is such a traumatic experience. When someone gives up on life, the guilt which is spread around can make you consider – in a warped way – that making the same choice could end your emotional pain as well. For me, it was all I could do to face myself in the mirror each morning. Between my own self-loathing, and the guilt which I saw heaped upon me by Mara's family and the faces of others, this was my fault, 100%. I had failed Mara in every way possible, and I had driven her to this. Wipe away her mental illness, her years of sexual abuse, her physical suffering through Crohn's Disease and horrific migraines; in my mind, I had willed this to happen, I had failed to stop it, I was at best an accomplice and at worst I was guilty of attempted murder. At the same time, I had to carry the guilt from

Mara's side, of not being able to somehow allow her to die, condemning her to continue her miserable life. I was at fault for allowing her to attempt suicide, and I was to blame for her still being alive.

If I hadn't been so terrified of the idea of death and non-existence, I likely would have tried to kill myself as well during the weeks after Mara swallowed the pills. But there was also the gnawing realization that in doing so, I might inflict on my family the same thing which was being inflicted on me. That was the last thing I wanted to do. Besides, I was too damn tired to kill myself, and in my convoluted thinking, suicide would be akin to letting me off the hook. If I was as terrible a person as I now believed myself to be, the act of living would be much more painful than silent nothingness. Death was too easy. I deserved to live, and suffer, and be miserable, and face the blame for all my failures and wrongs.

Despite the objections and fears of Mara's mother and me, Mara was transferred up to the respiratory floor. She was still on a feeding tube, and she had an oxygen monitor clipped to her finger at all times to make sure her oxygen level was adequate. The trachea tube was still present, staring me in the face every time I looked at her. And now that her lungs had begun to be used, they were slowly emptying themselves of the mucous and debris which had collected there. Coughing fits would be followed by globs of mucous clogging the trachea opening. There was a suction machine next to Mara's bed, with a long wand attached, and we were encouraged to assist by suctioning out mucous if we saw it collected there.

In the meantime, there were other physical and cosmetic issues which I didn't want to deal with. Mara was developing some minor bedsores on the back of her head, where clumps of hair were falling out. I would try to remove the hair as cleverly as possible, but Mara would sometimes notice and get terribly upset. I tried to reassure her, but in the meantime all I could wonder was what sort of terrible bedsores she might be developing elsewhere, such as her back and her butt. Since she was still basically immobile, barely able to lift her hands or wiggle her feet, there was no way for her to lie on one side or the other. With all her weight on her back, 24 hours a day, I knew it couldn't be a pretty sight.

    I don't envy the jobs of nurses. They do a ton of thankless work. They deal with sick, miserable, cranky people all day long, and are usually shorthanded and understaffed. Unable to make necessary medical decisions without a doctor present, they are usually treated as second class citizens. Despite years of training, they spend a good deal of their time emptying bedpans or completing other disgusting and non-technical functions. Mara's father was a doctor, which meant that for some unclear reason, doctors who had met her father would act more naturally around us then they would other patients. This included yelling or berating nurses without hesitation, which only reinforced my belief that many doctors are simply assholes with God complexes.

    On the other hand, there is good and bad in every profession. In numerous cases, I've had to witness how those nurses who develop a negative attitude, or who numb themselves to the chaos around them, simply become uncaring or lazy – or both. Mara's sister had done work as a blood tech, and would horrify us with stories of nurses refusing to check on patients who were buzzing their nurse call buttons because "he is rude" or "she buzzes too much" or even "she won't turn off the TV when I am talking to her." Once, when Mara was a patient in one of the New Jersey hospitals where her father was on staff, she became seriously ill because a nurse hadn't given her any of a critical medication for over twelve hours. The nurse simply was too careless to look at Mara's chart and see that the medication list continued on the second page. If the error hadn't been caught when a doctor wanted to change the dosage, Mara might have died.

December 23rd was Mara's first full day out of the ICU. It was because of my history with poor nursing that I wasn't very surprised to find Mara's oxygen monitor alarm screeching when I walked into her room to visit her after work. I could see immediately that the sensor clip had simply slipped from Mara's finger, and when I reattached it the machine registered normal oxygen levels and quieted down. Mara explained that the thing had been going off like that for nearly an hour, but nobody had been in to check on her. Meanwhile, the nurse call button, which had been clipped to her dressing gown, has slipped as well and was now dangling off the bed. Unable to push the button, and incapable of yelling, Mara had been forced to lie there and listen to the machine scream bloody murder until I showed up.

In some ways, the relationship between patient and nurse can be similar to that of inmate and prison staff. As a patient (or inmate), you are not free to take care of yourself. You rely on the staff to do certain things for you, and when problems arise you have to decide if it is important enough to bring to their attention. If you complain or "cause trouble" too often, you're generally ignored and suffer for it. Likewise, because they have all the power, you cannot afford to make enemies of them even when you are being mistreated. Basically, you have to suck up to them and thank them for doing their jobs. Sure, there are some who treat you better, who care about your well-being, and make up for those who don't. But when you get stuck with a hard-ass, there isn't a lot you can do. If you make an issue of their job performance, even if you are in the right, you'll likely earn the disdain of their co-workers...and suffer for it in the end. And I already knew what a difficult patient Mara could be in the best of circumstances.

With all of that in mind, I went and found a nurse and I could discuss the oxygen monitor with. In my mind, the doctor would not have ordered its use if he hadn't thought it was important. In response, the nurse complained about how the clip kept falling off of Mara's finger, and what a hassle it was to go back in the room to replace it. She'd even tried to find a way to silence the alarm so it would stop "bothering her," but no to avail. I tried to sound understanding, while at the same time expressing my concern for Mara's well-being. I think I did a decent job, since I wasn't overly critical and I did not try to lay blame or complain. Since I didn't receive any eye-rolling or arguing or muttering under her breath, I figured I had done the best I could, and returned to Mara's room.

Walking in, I found Mara undergoing a "breathing treatment." This was something which was both necessary and crucial to her improvement, but which Mara found very unpleasant and uncomfortable. Basically, the respiratory therapist would use a huge football-shaped instrument to force air into Mara's lungs, expanding them as much as possible, and then Mara would be instructed to hold that air (if she could) before exhaling. It was sort of a weightlifting session for her withered lungs. Mara did not want to cooperate, and she'd cry and complain and plead, but at the same time she'd comply because she knew she needed to. I suppose, sentenced to still being alive, Mara knew she'd be happier if she tried to make the best of it...at least until she could attempt another escape from the prison. And breathing is a rather necessary ability.

The therapist finished the breathing treatment, packed up his stuff, and left. I sat beside Mara's bed, wiping away her tears and holding her hand. She was a bit disoriented, as she always was after a treatment, so I didn't say anything. She had told me the effect was the same as breathing in and out rapidly, where you feel dizzy. I just sat there and wondered how life had gotten off track so terribly, and if things would somehow turn around after this nightmare and begin to improve.

About ten minutes after the breathing treatment had ended, Mara began to vomit. It wasn't a projectile Exorcist-type explosion. It was more of a gentle burping, filling her mouth with greenish slop (which was the nourishment provided by her feeding tube).

I immediately realized there was a problem: Mara wasn't emptying her mouth; the mush was dribbling out onto her chin and chest, but she couldn't expel it and breathe by herself. She seemed to have fainted or something. I shouted for help and pushed the call button. Sticking my fingers in Mara's mouth, I tried to clear the airway, but as soon as I would, she'd burp again and more glop would come out. Instead I started to use the suction apparatus to clear things more fully, which allowed Mara to get a breath or two before a new serving of vomit would appear.

The oxygen monitor began to scream again, as the flinger clip had fallen off. I couldn't get up and find a nurse or a doctor because I feared that if I left her side, Mara would choke to death. Instead I sat there, suctioning out the green slop and calling for help in vain, trying to have my voice heard over the oxygen monitor's alarm. The alarm was screeching, I was yelling, the call button was pushed, and Mara was vomiting over and over.

And nobody was coming.

If felt like forever - hours and hours - before someone finally arrived, although it was actually somewhere between 30 and 45 minutes. Time and time again Mara would vomit, and I would suction the food from her mouth and trachea hole. I couldn't be sure if she was conscious or not, so in between calling for help I tried to soothingly talk to her, letting her know it was going to be okay. Her eyes would open occasionally and stare vacantly into space. I noticed her skin was becoming clammy, and her forehead was hot. I could only assume her fever was returning.

Finally, one of the duty nurses came into the room. Surprisingly, her initial reaction was one of annoyance, as if she assumed that I had been doing something I wasn't supposed to. But once she surveyed the situation and realized what was going on, she called for a few other nurses to assist her and took charge of the chaos.

I stood to the side, while the nurses tried to keep me out of the way. As numb as I felt and as dreamlike the whole thing seemed, I was still incredibly pissed off. I found myself with the attitude of "I'm the one who kept her alive for the last 45 minutes, and *now* you're going to tell me that you know what you're doing?" But I watched as they pulled the feeding tube out (at last), kept her airway clear, lowered her head until her body was level, and tried to get an IV into her arm.

The one thing I *didn't* see them doing was calling a doctor, and that really made me angry. Obviously, they were trying to protect themselves and hoped to rectify the situation before I (or anyone else) was able to draw attention to their complete failure to do their job properly. Not that I was likely to forget, but if "no harm was done," they wouldn't be open to much criticism…and I'd be regarded as an overprotective, overemotional husband.

The immediate problem was Mara's vomiting: it hadn't stopped. I could see the nurses were still trying to get the IV in. They couldn't give Mara any useful medication to stop her vomiting until they had a line into her veins. Unfortunately, Mara's veins had always been deep and elusive. They jabbed a number of times, and even thought they had succeeded, but the nurses were unable to get Mara stabilized. I continued to ask that a doctor be called, until finally one of the nurses on the sidelines took it upon herself to quietly slip from the room and ask for additional assistance.

When the resident finally arrived in the room a few minutes later, he had a look of complete shock on his face. I am sure he realized that he should have been called in much sooner, as the whole room had been turned upside down, vomit was all over the place, there were close to ten nurses running around like circus clowns, and there I was backed up near the windows looking white as a ghost and terrified of what I'd been watching.

Immediately he took command, getting her vitals and realizing the situation was not good. He grabbed the IV needle from the nurse, screaming "We don't have **time** to find a vein there" before inserting it into a vein in Mara's foot. I never would have thought of that, and obviously the nurses hadn't either. Within a couple of minutes the vomiting stopped, and the doctor had been joined by another doctor and two orderlies as they transferred Mara to a stretcher and wheeled her out of the room, on the way back to the ICU.

The transfer to the respiratory unit had not gone well, and lasted only about 24 hours. It was a long 24 hours that I would never forget.

Chapter 39 - I Quit

In the weeks that followed, Mara showed slow but steady improvement. Eventually she was moved back to the respiratory ward, and this time there was no disaster. I'd visit her after work and on weekends, usually when her mother wasn't there. Most nights I'd go out afterwards rather than sit at home, unless I was too tired and simply needed to collapse. Sometimes I'd go to a bar with my new female obsession, or I'd just drive around. I was in a bad place; Mara's suicide attempt had failed, which was a good thing. But it also made me realize that when she quit on life, I had quit on the marriage. I hadn't made the decision to leave her or anything, but emotionally I was lost. I had failed at my mission to give Mara reasons to live. Now I was wallowing in that failure, but the failure also meant that mission was over. The only relief was that she had survived; everything else was suddenly worse because of this.

The only good news was that the doctors had determined Mara's trachea tube would eventually come out and the hole would be allowed to heal over. Her lungs were responsive enough that she'd be able to breathe normally. Her physical movement was coming back also, although there was a lot more therapy needed to gain strength and rebuild necessary muscles. Walking without assistance was still next to impossible; she couldn't get up and go to the bathroom, and had to use a bed pan or wear diapers depending on the latest doctor's preference.

About two months after the suicide attempt, Mara was transferred up the street to a rehabilitation facility. They could provide a more focused physical and respiratory treatment plan there, without the need for as intensive medical monitoring. Mara's mother took the opportunity to head back home for the time being, while I did my best to keep an eye on Mara locally. Mara's patience was starting to wear thin; she just wanted to lie in her own bed again, eat what she wanted, have the cats for company…she may not have been happy with life the way it was, but suddenly it appeared to be an attractive substitute for all this time in hospitals.

There were two other developments since her suicide attempt that Mara was happy about. One was small but still notable (and unexplained): the soles of her feet were not healthy and soft. For years her feet had been dried, cracked, and in bad shape. The callused heels would crack open and require super glue to close them up in order to protect the soft flesh underneath. But after two months of being in hospitals – mostly bedridden for all intents and purposes – they had healed and were now the exact opposite. A small victory but Mara was happy about it.

The other involved her Crohn's. While hospitalized a new doctor had taken over her treatment, one who was on staff at the hospital. He had managed to slowly get her steroid levels down to as low as they had been since her diagnosis. And when she was in her worst state after the suicide attempt, he had taken her off all the Crohn's pain medication and switched her to paregoric, which was an old licorice-tasting syrup that children had taken decades ago (despite its opioid ingredients). It had useful antidiarrheal properties and even had a function as an expectorant, so it was helping her lungs and her intestines. It wasn't used much anymore, but he felt it would be perfect for her case, and his instincts were correct. Not only was her pain much better, but the Crohn's itself was suddenly under control.

It only took a week or two before Mara was causing a stink. She had all her mental faculties back, and she wanted out. It didn't seem to matter to her that she couldn't walk properly yet, or even take care of herself fully. She just wanted to leave. I was working sixty hours a week, six days a week, but that didn't matter. Her mother had gone back to New Jersey, but that didn't matter. Mara wanted to come home.

I did everything I could over the next two weeks to convince her otherwise. I wasn't worried about me, or not going out, or anything of that sort. I was worried about how vulnerable and miserable I knew she was going to be. None of her plans made any sense. "I'll just use the bathroom before you leave for work, and then wait for you to get home. If I can't hold it, I can use the bedpan." She knew she would be effectively bedridden. I'd have to leave her food and water and anything she might need by the bed.

The doctors, nurses, and her parents worked on Mara too. The doctors were the ones who really put the pressure on. "Once you leave, you can't just come back. If you go home against medical advice, you're discharged and your treatment is finished." There wouldn't even be any home-based therapy from the clinic. Mara was sure she could get something arranged through a service in a week or two, but I wasn't convinced it would be that easy. With no doctors to refer the care to her, they'd probably need to get copies of her records from the hospital and the rehab clinic. The whole crazy scheme smelled like disaster.

Still Mara persisted. As she always had, once she had made up her mind, she refused to change it. So, one day after work I went to the clinic, wheeled her chair in, and out she came. She had a huge bag of medical supplies to go with her: prescriptions, creams and gauze and tapes for her bed sores, adult diapers if she chose to wear them, a tool to help her build up strength in her lungs, a bed pan, and many other things. With some difficulty she was able to stand up and sit in the van, and soon we were on the way home. By pulling the wheelchair backwards I managed to get it up the steps into the house, and eventually she was back in bed where she wanted to be. The cats seemed very happy to see her.

Twice that evening I had to help her make her way to the bathroom. Just getting there took about four minutes, as her steps were very slow and unsure. She also needed some assistance wiping. Later she took a shower, sitting on a shower stool we'd had for some time that she used to use when her back was particularly bad. I helped her dry off and get into one of her flannel nightgowns, and off to sleep we went.

Even when Mara had made the final decision to come home, I had tried to convince her to wait for a Friday so that we'd have the weekend for me to keep an eye on her while she got used to everything. But Mara wouldn't even budge that inch. So the following morning I gave Mara her morning medicine, and then piled things all around her so she could reach them: medications, food, water, snacks, and anything else she could conceivably need. Mara decided she wasn't going to wear a diaper, and instead would just hold off from going to the bathroom until I got home. If she couldn't make it that long she would use the bed pan. I left for work with a very uneasy feeling, but there was nothing I could do. This is what Mara wanted, and now we had to live with the consequences.

It didn't take long. Late in my work day Mara called me crying. "Please come home, as soon as you can." She sounded like she had been crying for an hour. I managed to sneak out of work a few minutes early, although I knew I'd have to be all the earlier the following morning to catch up. I drove straight home and came inside.

I went into the bedroom and there was Mara in the bed. She just looked up with a sad, red face and said "I think I made a big mistake."

As I wiped her tears and rectified all the immediate problems, Mara explained what had happened. She needed to go to the bathroom and decided she would be able to walk there on her own power, even though she hadn't even been close to doing that yet. But she couldn't even stand from the bed. Finally, she decided she would just have to use the bedpan. Just getting her underwear down her legs was a major endeavor, but she managed to do that and pull herself onto the bed pan. But when she was done, she didn't have the strength to get back off. She was stuck, and there was nothing she could do.

After about thirty minutes of trying to move, she gave up and reached the phone and called me. Now she was sobbing and crying. "I can't do this, I thought I could. What am I supposed to do?"

I knew what I wanted to say. I was so frustrated and emotional and exhausted, I wanted to just explode and yell. I wanted to scream at Mara, "I told you this was going to happen. I begged you to stay at the clinic. Everybody begged you. But you just had to do things your way, and now everything is fucked. Why couldn't you just listen?"

...but I didn't. I couldn't. I had to fight to stay calm, composed, sane, and to be the stabilizing force comforting Mara and letting her know we'd find a way to work this out. This was my life, the one I was stuck with and the one I felt I deserved. And my failure to "save" Mara only reinforced those beliefs.

Besides, what good would yelling at Mara do for her? It might make me feel better, but I'd only feel guilty about it later anyway.

The only idea I had was to start making phone calls. I called the clinic, and spoke to one of the nurses and one of the doctors. No go, and I knew that's what they would say. You need to be referred there anyway, and she'd left, so she would have to start over at square one even if she was going to find her way back in their care. And that wasn't likely to happen anyway; if you leave, they'd prefer you go elsewhere for treatment.

I spoke to Mara's GI, the one who had gotten her Crohn's under control in the hospital. He sympathized with my predicament but he didn't have any useful ideas. He had a really thick skin, and had been subjected to a few of Mara's mood swings in the hospital. He knew how difficult she was, and I think that while he was sorry that I was in this mess, in the end he was just relieved she was someone else's problem and not his at the moment. He was willing to continue treating for as her gastroenterologist. But he knew where to draw the line.

Finally, Mara's psychiatrist had a suggestion. It sounded drastic but it was the only idea that seemed to make any sense. He said we should call 911 and say that Mara was suicidal again. That wasn't really a stretch, because in her current state if she thought she could kill herself successfully it would be near the top of her choices. His argument was that if she was declared a danger to herself, she would be admitted to a psych ward at the hospital for 72 hours where she would at least have some medical care. And then medical professionals could decide the best course of action from that point forward.

Mara didn't even balk at the idea. Anything to get herself back into a hospital was fine with her. She called 911, and a police officer came by soon after. The whole thing was kind of confusing, but he said I should just drive Mara to the hospital myself and he wouldn't bother filing a report or calling paramedics. I called Mara's psychiatrist back and he said he would phone ahead and let the hospital know to admit her under his order on a 72-hour hold. We packed up her small suitcase, I wheeled her out to the car, and back to the hospital she went.

In terms of complications, this was the smoothest hospital interaction I had been a part of. They had us wait in a room, and then a doctor came in and I was asked to leave. He talked to her for three of four minutes and that was that. They put her in a hospital wheelchair, took her suitcase, and sent her on to the psychiatric ward. The doctor told me I shouldn't expect to hear from Mara for at least 24 hours and possibly as long as 72, depending on what they wanted to do with her for treatment and when (or if) she was granted phone privileges. They had her medical records from her recent stay, and they understood her physical limitations and needs. I shook his hand and wheeled the empty wheelchair back to the car. The house seemed very quiet when I got there.

Being cut off from Mara, but knowing she had adequate care and supervision, gave me the opportunity to collapse physically and emotionally. After calling Mara's parents so they knew what was going on, I lay in bed with the cats, silently crying. My face was soaked with tears, but I didn't make a sound, except for the occasional sniffle. I just pet the cats and eventually rolled over and fell asleep. I didn't want to move, I didn't want to talk, I didn't to think. I didn't want to have to make any decisions or worry about anyone else. I just wanted to forget everything.

I had just had it. Being able to not worry for five minutes made me so miserable, but also so relieved. For the first time in a decade I was trying to think about myself. I'd failed at my grand task...and now it seemed I had quit.

Chapter 40 - Back to New Jersey

Things were rather stable for a while. Mara was no longer interested in running away from the hospital, and the time there was helping her physically and mentally. I didn't have any false hopes, but at least she wasn't planning on killing herself again in the near term. Mara was able to get walking again after only a week, although her back problems hadn't gone anywhere. Still, it was a big win for her to be able to get to the bathroom without assistance, and to clean up afterwards.

It was decided that when Mara left the hospital, she would go to New Jersey to recuperate with her family. I think there were two purposes to this idea, which I wasn't really consulted on. The first was that Mara wouldn't be relying on me so much, since everyone could see we were drifting apart, and my support couldn't be counted on indefinitely. The second – and most important – purpose was to have multiple sets of eyes on Mara. At home she'd be alone all day, every day. But up in New Jersey she'd have her mother, father, brother, and sister keeping her busy and constantly interacting with her.

Mara was generally in favor of the plan, except I could tell she didn't like the idea of being apart from me. There was the fact that I understood her much better, and that she wasn't embarrassed around me if she needed help or wanted to discuss personal things. And there was also the unspoken thought that if she stayed close by, she could keep a tighter grip on me and maybe I'd go back to our two-person world. Neither of us thought that was going to happen, but I knew that was Mara's preference.

I felt like shit. It was like I was abandoning Mara and not giving her a chance to prove life could be better for us. The thing was, I knew that she would do better for a while if the heat was on. But I also had to believe that it wouldn't take long to slip into old ways, with her not trying and with me enabling her poor choices. For a long time, I had been the primary force keeping her going, but I just didn't have the strength for that now. And I had no confidence in my ability to succeed a second time around, and if failure was going to be how it end, I did **not** want to go through this kind of suffering all over again. It was lose-lose for me: stick it out and watch it fall apart eventually or keep drifting away and feel like a failure and a piece of shit for giving up.

The plane ride to New Jersey was a problem in itself. Mara wore a diaper in case she didn't make it to the bathroom, and her parents had booked her two seats next to each other so she could be extra comfortable and have plenty of room (and also so there wasn't a passenger stuck next to her with no room of their own). Since this was pre-9/11, I was allowed to wheel her on board and kiss her goodbye. Her carry-on bag had all of her necessary medications, so they wouldn't be lost of her luggage was. I promised to take care of the kitties, and then I walked off the plane. I tried to be strong but it was depressing as hell. I felt like I was saying goodbye to her forever, and goodbye to the marriage. Besides, airports make me nauseous.

I didn't get much of a break, because within an hour of landing Mara was calling me, venting about how they had screwed her over on the trip. Despite having two seats booked in her name, they had someone sitting next to her. These days she probably would have been thrown off the flight considering how bad her attitude about that was. I can only imagine the fuss she stirred up. I don't recall what she said the airline's defense was for this decision; it was probably overbooked and refunded one ticket to Mara's parents rather than bump someone from the flight. Then she complained about where she was going to be staying – her sister had turned her basement into a bedroom – and how hard going up and down the stairs was going to be for her.

And finally, Mara asked the same thing she would ask every time we spoke on the phone: "When can I come home?"

I didn't know what I was supposed to feel. Should I be relieved that Mara was half way across the country? Should I be hoping things somehow worked out and she came back, and our marriage survived? I regretted the past, I loathed the present, and I couldn't even see what the future might hold for me, if anything at all. So I just spent my time working and trying to forget who I was.

As Mara slowly improved physically in New Jersey, my life was one mess after another. I quit my job to go work for a different company, because with what I was making it was becoming impossible to keep the bills covered. I made certain that insurance coverage was good before I made the move. I was still spending a lot of time with my new flame but it was a roller coaster, on again and off again. Together she made me miserable half the time, complaining about everything. Apart she just wanted to get together again. As you might expect her biggest complaint was "when are you going to get a divorce?" I had never said I planned to, but explaining the situation our marriage was in and the tacit approval I had to spend time with her was far too complicated. Besides, I figured it was better to be asked "when are you going to get a divorce" than "when are we going to get married?"

And the fact was, asking about divorce was perfectly reasonable. Mara and I had talked about it many times, but she always asked me to give her more time, another chance, or to wait for our financial situation to get worked out. And there was the guilt of knowing that if we did divorce, Mara would lose her prescription coverage. We'd learned how to work our way through the labyrinth of Medicare pretty well by now, but there was still no prescription coverage available for her.

It only took a few months before Mara was making everyone around her in New Jersey miserable, and causing a fuss whenever she could. I suppose the stairs had actually helped her regain some muscle tone and she was close to as mobile as she had been before the suicide attempt. Back pain remained a major problem, and her weight continued to move higher a few pounds at a time (approaching 400 pounds now), but physically she was ready to come back to Texas. Apparently, it only took a few weeks before she remembered how miserable she was around her family.

For their part, they were torn. Every day felt like a battle to them, fighting with Mara over something. But they were left with the choice of sending her back to Texas to be someone else's problem (but into a failing marriage and away from eyes that could watch over her), or keeping her a reluctant prisoner in the cage she was living in. In the end they decided it was easier to let Mara have her own way. Mara would come back to Texas, and we'd all see how the movie played out.

Chapter 41 - Tying Up Loose Ends

It didn't take long after Mara's return for things to go back into a routine. Unfortunately, it was much the same routine as we had shared before. Mara would spend a lot of the day in bed, and often was up most of the night watching TV. But there were three new developments. The first was that Texas revoked Mara's driver's license. When we had to go in and have a new photo taken for a renewal, she used her wheelchair as she usually did. Someone at the location decided that she may not be capable of driving. So, they sent Mara a notice that it was suspended pending her coming in to take a driving test.

Mara hadn't taken one since she was 16. When we moved to Texas, we both just surrendered our New Jersey licenses and were granted Texas ones, as normally happens when you move from state to state. We looked into the situation, and by law the state had the right to question her ability to drive. The problem with this situation is Mara had been holding on to this idea that she could drive herself around when she wanted to, even though she had only driven the van twice in over four years. We tried a few attempts at practice driving, in empty parking lots and such, but it was far too stressful for her. Mara was not going to be getting her license back any time soon.

This led to the second development: I was finally able to convince Mara to make use of the Dallas Transit Handi-Ride system. Because she used a wheelchair, Mara could schedule rides in advance and get out of the house a bit on her own. There were various rules and limitations she had to get used to, but now she could schedule the occasional doctor's appointment or trip to the mall and go by herself during the day. She was hesitant to schedule anything unnecessary, out of fear that her Crohn's would flare up and she'd have no way out of wherever she was; she'd be stuck waiting for the scheduled return trip. But at least now she didn't feel so completely reliant on me; I thought the freedom would be good for her frame of mind and her self-esteem. Mara even took herself to lunch one day.

The third development seemed to be a precursor to the inevitable end of the marriage: we finally decided to get our financial affairs in order, throw in the towel, and declare bankruptcy. We had accumulated over $130,000 in debt, a large percentage of it from her medical and prescription expenses which we'd never managed to do more than make minimum payments on. We had no assets whatsoever, only the van (on which we owed about what it was worth). No stocks, no real estate, nothing. My father had been trying to convince us for five years to do this, but to me it had always felt like cheating or quitting. But just as I knew I couldn't keep Mara alive against her will, I finally agreed that there was no way (other than a lottery ticket) that we would ever get the debt paid off.

The process really wasn't that difficult. We hadn't made any large or suspicious purchases, and we weren't hiding any assets. My Dad told me the one key was to get a lawyer to help who was licensed by the Board of Legal Specialization. "A lawyer who makes his living doing this, and is specialized enough to be designated by the board, is not only qualified but respected by his peers and the courts" he told me. "When the lawyer representing you is respected, the court knows he isn't going to tolerate any game playing or suspicious moves by his clients. It's sort of a seal of approval for you as the client, that you really need to do this and there is no other way to resolve it."

Mara and I met with one lawyer and immediately hired him. It wasn't particularly expensive, and once we started the process, we would no longer be making any payments on any of our debt. We could even surrender the van, but Mara vetoed that idea. I wanted to get rid of it and get something cheap and small for the time being, but Mara wanted the van, despite the fact that it had many mechanical issues. So – as usual – I gave in on that front.

I felt really guilty about declaring bankruptcy, until our lawyer put some figures together to show me that we had already paid almost double our actual purchase debt in the last five years. The rest was just the compounding finance charges and occasional annual or late fees. "They made their money on you already, and believe me, they don't take this stuff personally." It was intensely personal to me, so it took a while for my mind to adjust to their point of view.

One advantage we had was that we didn't own a house. If we had, we'd have wanted to file in Texas court, because at that time Texas courts protected your home ownership but took away anything else of value (money in the bank, etc.). Since we had no real estate to protect, we were able to file in Federal court, which didn't protect your home but was less concerned with the small amount of money we had (or the money we might accumulate during the process, since once you file you no longer charge on or pay to your credit cards).

In fact, both the lawyer and my Dad told me that of all the credit cards we owed money to, plus the few other creditors like doctors or medical companies, only one creditor would even comment on the bankruptcy, or show up for the hearing: Sears. And when the day came, they were correct; Sears had a representative who apparently showed up at every hearing. It seems

Sears sales receipts had some special language which state that Sears retains ownership of anything you bought there until you've paid off the purchase. Prior to the bankruptcy hearing, the agent sat down with me and had a list of items we still owed money on; Mara had asked not to attend the hearing because it would be too stressful for her and might set off a Crohn's attack, and there had been no objection from the court. For each item on his list he asked if it had been a gift for someone or a purchase for us, and if it was something we bought for ourselves he would then ask if we still had possession of the item. It was all rather straightforward. He totaled up a few numbers and explained that we had two choices: we could return those items to Sears, or we could maintain a balance on our Sears card (the dollar amount being lower than what we currently owed, as it was adjusted for what we had or hadn't paid for and what we did or did not still have in our possession). If we chose to keep the items, we'd just continue to make payments as before until the balance went to zero. We'd effectively still have a Sears card, but with a $0 credit limit. The only things we still owned were a washer, dryer, and refrigerator, so we wanted to keep them. Problem solved.

    The rest of the hearing was much less of a big deal than I had expected, or as Mara had feared. As our lawyer told us, this wasn't personal to any of the creditors. They'd made money on us for some time, and once we started paying only the minimum payments for a number of months, their accounting models had already moved our debt into the higher risk category and adjusted their income and expenses accordingly. He said each of the major creditors made a million calculations like that every day, and we were just numbers in huge computer models to them. There were questions for me to answer under oath, but they were general and non-accusatory. I just had to state for the record that the information we supplied was complete, that we weren't hiding any assets, and that I understood the penalties if we were lying. The rest was legal boilerplate, and the it was over.

We were now broke with ruined credit, but we were starting over with a clean slate, as we were in so many other areas of our lives. In time we could repair **this** financial damage, but it didn't appear we would be able to repair anything else.

With the bankruptcy accomplished, we slowly tried to figure out what was going to happen next. I was staying home a lot more than I had before the suicide attempt, but that seemed to anger Mara more than comfort her. At the same time, she was resentful that I had found any solace in my outside relationship during that period. It was as if she wanted me to give her space, and to take time for myself, but now she no longer wanted me to enjoy it...or to even pretend to. Mara was so bitter about still being alive, even though she swore she wasn't about to try killing herself again anytime soon because she didn't want to wind up in the hospital all over again.

We had discussions about divorce, and we took turns each time being the one who was against it. Even though I had no hope for the marriage, I sometimes left like divorcing would be admitting failure when perhaps, somehow, some way, everything would turn around and we'd find happiness we never had. When it was Mara's turn to object, it was mainly because she was comfortable at home with me and the cats, and because she didn't want to go back to New Jersey. Actually, it was more than she didn't feel welcome in New Jersey. As far as she could tell, her family only wanted her there if it meant stopping her from an imminent suicide attempt. If she wasn't at that stage, they wanted her to be my problem (or her own problem).

Everything was stuck in a Catch-22 standstill. We both wanted a divorce, but neither one of us wanted to end the marriage. Mara had zero interest in anything sexual or physical, and wanted me to fill those needs elsewhere so she didn't feel guilty, but she preferred I had no feelings for anyone (including her) than to carry an emotional attachment for someone. Mara couldn't live on her own, but she didn't want to live with her family. And if she did decide to live with her family, she didn't think they'd accept her back, at least not beyond a few weeks.

There was one strategy we had discussed that might solve that problem. I suggested that if Mara told her family that I was cheating on her, leaving out any of the details or history or extenuating circumstances, they might rally around her and welcome her back while she recovered from the heartbreak and tried to put her life back together; the key was making it appear to be a surprise and a betrayal. But Mara didn't like that idea. For one thing, she knew how much her family had always looked down on me, and she didn't want to give them more reasons to do so. She also didn't want to put me in a position of having to keep my mouth shut and play along, when neither of us knew just how nasty her family might make things between us; Mara wanted us to remain close friends no matter what happened, and she was certain her family would pressure her to cut all contact off. And, from a practical point of view, divorce would mean Mara would lose her prescription coverage just as we were starting to be in the black financially every month.

Thanksgiving and Christmas passed, and while we were getting along okay, we both knew we were just going through the motions. When you've known each other for over fifteen years and been each other's world for much of that time, habits are hard to break. I felt like I really should be coming up with some sort of firm and final strategy for the end of our marriage, but I couldn't bear the thought of Mara being stuck in a situation she didn't choose if I made a move or a decision on my own. I couldn't do that to her.

Work at this new company was not going the way I'd hoped. Despite assurances from the owners, there was absolutely no real business and there didn't appear to be any prospects either. I spent most of the day counting the hours until I could leave, or hearing whispered conversations in the executive office. I didn't know what to do about Mara, and now I didn't know what to do about my job.

And then one day early in the year, Mara called me at work. She was crying, and sounded both angry and disappointed. "You better do whatever you need to do, I just called my parents and told them I found out you've been seeing someone and that I want a divorce." I guess she finally decided that plan was the only way out. I called a few friends, and then I called my female interest and told her "Mara found out about us, I won't be able to talk to you until she and I figure out what to do." I really felt shitty on both fronts; I'd never been especially happy about the arrangement Mara and I had, and now I felt like a heel continuing the false pretense. I don't like to play with other people's feelings. But since she had no idea about Mara's previous knowledge, I guess she always thought this would happen someday anyway.

I was hoping I wasn't going to need to have a confrontation with Mara's parents, but when I got home Mara told me she doubted that would happen. In fact, Mara was rather unhappy about the reaction she'd gotten. Sure, her family was happy to shit all over me, but they weren't being especially forthcoming about suggestions that they were going to help her in any way. Most of what they had told her – aside from "I knew you couldn't trust him" and things like that – was nothing but sneaky tips to protect herself from the evil I was probably planning. "Hide the silver you got at your wedding, so you can make sure you get it and not him." "Don't let him clean out the bank account, he's liable to hide all the money in his girlfriend's name." That one made me laugh; there wasn't any money to hide, and Mara's individual bank account (where her disability money was deposited) was the only account we had with a balance over $1,000. And that was her money as far as I was concerned.

Now that the "news" was out, Mara was trying to figure out the best way to have her sister (or her parents) open their arms and homes to her again. There had been constant arguments when she was living up there before, and that wasn't likely to get any better if she went back. But Mara wasn't ready physically or emotionally to live on her own, so she wanted to live with them for a while, at least until she saved up enough money for a small apartment or something. We both agreed there was no specific hurry for her to move; it could take months if necessary. Mara wanted us to still share the bedroom, but I told her I may as well move into the room my mother had been staying in. If we were going to split up, it was better to get used to the whole idea now rather than later.

For the time being we'd just continue the way we had been: I'd pay all the bills and the rent, and she could save what she could in her account. Even with the bankruptcy, we weren't saving a lot in the joint account, but that was okay since I was still getting a paycheck. We also talked about the concept of filing for divorce. Mara thought her parents might force her to do that right away, but I felt there was no reason to do it at all, unless one of us wanted to consider marriage to someone else down the road. As long as we were still married, I could keep her on my health insurance and she would have prescription coverage. It didn't matter if we were living in the same state or not, we were still legally married and if we had no formal separation agreement there was the "hope of reconciliation."

Mara's parents came down for a weekend and had Mara stay in a hotel with them. We talked a lot beforehand about what things to focus on when it came to talking about the future. There really wasn't an alternative to letting Mara move back to New Jersey unless they wanted to cover all her living expenses, so the battle was more emotional than anything else. We both knew it wasn't going to be particularly fun up there for her, but at least this time they wouldn't be able to push Mara towards moving back to Dallas. Things went well over that weekend; she and her family went around, ate out, bonded, and by the time they left arrangements were being made to move Mara and whatever belongings she wanted back to her sister's house.

There wasn't much arguing over things. I let Mara have what she wanted. She couldn't take the cats, so that wasn't a discussion. Any furniture, DVDs, CDs, or anything else she liked was packed in boxes for movers. It was actually a very sad time for both of us. I've always said that divorce is the death not just of the marriage, but of all the hopes and dreams you built around it. Mara seemed despondent and wanted to spend as much time together as we could. On more than one occasion she broke down crying and asked me to hold her, wanting reassurance that we would still be friends after she left. She also apologized for blindsiding me with the revelation to her parents, but explained she was scared and didn't want them to turn her away. I had to remind her that I was the one who suggested that avenue in the first place; the only way she blindsided me was by not telling me she was going to do it. We'd been everything to each other for fifteen years or more, I wasn't about to cut her entirely out of my life once she moved. We'd still talk on the phone and trade emails, and chat on Yahoo Messenger.

In fact, after the movers had picked up Mara's things and I had brought her to the airport, it was Mara who was silent. I left her a message on her cell phone a few times, but it was over three weeks before she ever contacted me (outside of an initial friendly-sounding message that she had arrived safely). When she finally did contact me, she was very angry. Whether on her own or with prodding encouragement from her family, Mara had gone through the drawer full of credit card bills and receipts that was in the armoire she'd taken with her. They went back five years or so, and she'd come to the conclusion that I was "living a party" while she was in pain at home or in the hospital.

I was a bit hurt but I didn't try to be too overly aggressive in my defense. I decided to let time and slow reasoning instead of emotion help me through her attack. We talked about some of the charges on the credit cards, and I showed Mara how her timelines were off, or which ones were me picking up the tab and getting cash from other people so we could afford to meet the growing minimum payments that eventually drove us into bankruptcy.

And of course, I talked to her about how I had sought solace during the time she was in the hospital, especially when she was still in the ICU and not very coherent. I wasn't about to seek comfort from her family; they didn't like me and we didn't communicate on the same wavelength at all. So naturally I had spent money at bars and family restaurants, alone or in the company of others, including my on-again-off-again girlfriend. I even reminded her of some things I had told her about as they happened, which I was surprised she'd be angry about after the fact when she knew about them from the beginning; a dinner at some particular place and things like that. I didn't try to deny the truth of anything that I had done, but only to explain the circumstances and to show her what fell into one category and what fell into another. After a few days she let that blow over, which led me to believe that it had been a combination of family meddling and her own fear that she'd been blind to something long before. I had to laugh to myself at that, as aside from work we spent every waking and sleeping hour together until a few months before her suicide attempt.

In retrospect, I think the process of splitting up went about as smoothly as could be hoped for. Mara was going to have to start building a life of her own, but she knew she could count on me for support along the way. Her mood was still erratic, happy and friendly one day, lonely and wanting to reconcile at some point the next, angry at her family and at me the next. On my side, I felt miserable and lonely as well some of the time, and a failure nearly every day. My goal had been to give Mara reasons to live and to stand by her no matter what. At some point I started to slip, and when she finally quit on life, I quit on everything. We were both starting over with nothing, and with no clear path to any kind of future. It seemed that my whole life had been building up to this: the one great, apocalyptic disappointment. I'd failed, as I always believed I would. And now I didn't know what I was supposed to do.

Chapter 42 - At Least Things Can't Get Worse

With Mara living in New Jersey in her sister's basement, I was left living in the house we had rented until the lease ran out. I certainly didn't need the space – or the high rent – but breaking a lease in Dallas was like a death sentence. Once you have a record as a "bad renter" it is nearly impossible to find a landlord to rent to you again. It wasn't long after Mara left that Biff had to be put to sleep with congestive heart failure. I called Mara to let her know about it and she asked that I mail her a few of his whiskers to remember him by, after the procedure. As a Persian, I didn't know if heart failure was common. I asked the vet and he said "No, something else usually gets them before this." I took some solace in that, knowing he'd had a very long life.

It felt as if I had two lives now: my daily life of my own, and my long-distance life with Mara. We mostly talked through emails or instant messenger, but we also spoke on the phone every week or so. She always wanted to know how the cats were doing, and she relied on me to be a supportive voice for her in her struggles dealing with her family. I opened an individual checking account, but we kept the joint account open as well because it was an easy way for me to give her some money every month; I'd transfer it to the joint account, and she would then transfer it to her account. She wasn't paying any rent but she still had prescriptions to cover and anything else she wanted.

Things at work had not improved, so I talked to some people I had worked with before and made a move to their day-trading firm. They seemed to be doing well, and I was given the same salary with promises of a big bonus at the end of the year. It would be a lot more work, and very stressful, but at least they weren't about to go out of business the way my previous employer seemed to be heading. And, as always, keeping the health insurance going was a main priority. The coverage was about the same, and Mara was still legally my wife so she would be able to keep using it.

For a few months my communication with Mara was regular but brief. Work was a lot more physically and emotionally exhausting than I had expected, so I was frequently going home after work and just collapsing in bed. I couldn't talk to her on the phone at the office any longer unless it was an emergency, so there weren't a lot of conversations except for the weekends. I did make an attempt to show her I wasn't drifting away, mostly by sending a few used CDs or DVDs I thought she would enjoy (or that she hadn't taken with her but might be particular favorites). At first those gifts confused Mara, and she wondered if there was more to them than simple friendship. But we seemed to be at a stage where we felt free to ask anything and not avoid topics, so she told me about the mixed signals the gifts were sending and I explained that they weren't meant to be more than friendly and caring.

Soon after, my attention was focused on my own health. I found an odd-looking freckle on my left leg, and showed it to my doctor. It didn't look like anything bad – certainly not similar to the photos you see in warning photos about skin diseases – and he said we should just keep an eye on it. A month later it had doubled in size, and despite both of us being sure it was a waste of time, he removed it and sent it for a biopsy. The only thing that made me a bit nervous was this was a family doctor practice where you didn't often see the head man. But for this, he did the excision personally.

A few days later my doctor called me to let me know I had skin cancer: malignant melanoma. I didn't have any experience with such things, so I wasn't worried in the slightest. "Well, we cut it off so I guess we got it in time. Do I just need to keep an eye on the area to make sure it doesn't come back?"

"Uh, no, it doesn't exactly work like that," he told me.

I suppose that I was lucky in a number of respects. First of all, I'd caught it very early, so despite it being very aggressive it hadn't spread to my lymph nodes (although this wasn't determined until after I had surgery). Likewise, that meant surgical excision was all I would need, no chemotherapy or anything else. And finally, I wasn't alone when it came to ignorance of how skin cancer worked or how dangerous it was. So, there was no real panic from Mara or from my girlfriend. Everybody sort of treated this like a routine procedure (which the surgery probably was) and that it would take care of the entire problem (which it did, but we had no way to know that at the time).

The surgery went well overall. The procedure was basically to cut open my calf where the cancer had been found, scoop out as much flesh as they could to make sure they got further than the cancer had spread, and sew me up. There was a secondary procedure done at the same time, removing a lymph node in my groin area to see if it had been affected yet. The only complication they encountered was when they tried to sew my leg back up: even though they had removed stuff, they could barely stretch the skin back over the area. My surgeon said it took two of them to get the job done. I would learn later that the lymph node was cancer free and that they'd gotten all of the cancer from my leg, so all that was left for me to do was heal.

I'd scheduled to take three or four days off from work recuperating, and my goal was to spend that time lying in bed. I was in a lot of pain, and the pain medication they gave me was making me nauseas. I could walk with crutches but not easily, so the less movement I did the better, and leaving my leg elevated was important for healing, limiting swelling, and pain management. My girlfriend brought me home from the hospital, and we settled down to watch Braveheart and take a nap. Everything was in a sort of nightmarish daze from the painkillers and the anesthesia. But at least, for the first time in decades, I was going to be able to just forget my responsibilities and be taken care of. It was my turn to be the one that others worried about.

Sadly (in multiple ways), that dream lasted about an hour. Her cell phone rang, and my girlfriend started screaming. Her mother, who had been fighting a number of health problems, had been killed in a car crash. I quickly shifted from sick invalid to the strong, supportive one. I grabbed a few personal items and we drove to her place, where she packed some clothes. Then we drove down to the small town where her parents lived, about an hour south of Dallas.

I let Mara know how I was doing and what had happened, so she knew not to bother calling me at home for a few days. I left enough food and water out for the cats to be on their own for a day and a half; I figured I could get back home at least once by then. This was the first time I had been personally present around a full family in mourning like this, so I wasn't exactly sure what to do or what was going to happen. I just tried to be a strong, supportive rock for anyone who was upset. The huge "shark bite" in my leg was an easy distraction for most people, and gave them something to worry about where they could actually do something and feel useful; that was a nice change from how helpless they felt about the accident and unexpected death.

After the funeral I returned to work, and my leg slowly healed. With the death of her mother, my girlfriend was thinking about moving back to their small town when her apartment lease ran out, and she wanted me to move down there with her. The commute would be longer but not awful; only the last few miles would be heavy traffic. Rent was cheaper down there, and she really wanted to be closer to her Dad for both of their sakes. I told her I'd be willing to give living together a try, and she should keep her eyes out for a place.

Mara was surprisingly fine with the idea of the two of us moving in together when I mentioned it to her. Perhaps it just didn't make any difference to her any longer, but I suspected it was more because she was focused on her own problems. Mara was finding the stairs up and down from her basement room harder and harder to use, as her back was hurting worse than it ever had. Not surprisingly, her weight had a lot of influence on that; she had started gaining weight even faster than when she lived in Texas. I knew that if Mara was going to try and lose weight, she would need support and positive reinforcement. Instead, her family seemed to give her just the opposite, shaming her for being so fat instead of encouraging her to do something about it.

Mara called me crying after a family get-together she'd attended. One of her aunts, who had always been a bit strange, came up to Mara and opened their conversation with "I just wanted to tell you that you repulse me to even look at you." I had always tended more to the enabling side when it came to Mara, but I also knew that it was her emotional and psychological scars which drove her to eat so poorly (aside from her Crohn's Disease and her lack of any exercise). This became the main topic of conversation between the two of us, whether we were speaking by phone or electronically. I encouraged Mara to reconsider having some sort of gastric bypass surgery. She hadn't been a good candidate for it the one time we investigated it, mostly due to her Crohn's and her tendency to be a bleeder. But with her Crohn's doing a lot better, and there being advances in the options and technology available, we agreed that perhaps it wouldn't be as dangerous for her as it once was. As usual, it wasn't that Mara was afraid of dying during the procedure. Rather, she was fearful of things going wrong and her life winding up even worse than before.

While she looked into it - now convinced that she could find a doctor who would approve the procedure – Mara set up a little web site to America On Line so that friends and family could follow her progress. When she gave me the link and I first looked at it, I was absolutely shocked. In six months, she must have put on over 100 pounds. Her face was not easily recognizable, being all puffy and with a huge, hanging chin. I'd seen her get quite puffy before when her prednisone dose was very high, but never like this. And she was only on a small dose of steroids at this point. It was no wonder that she was having such a hard time getting up and down the stairs; the strain she was putting on her bad back must have been terrible.

In the meantime, a new argument was erupting with Mara. She and her sister were at odds about the lack of air conditioning in the basement where Mara stayed. Her sister felt that with a fan or two it was never especially hot down there, but Mara disagreed. I knew she often had a low-grade temperature to begin with, and her weight likely made that even worse.

Unfortunately, there was no simple solution; the basement only had tiny New England-style half windows, just below ground level. There was no standard air conditioning unit built that would fit in one of those windows, and there were scant options otherwise. The house did not have central air, so it wasn't just a matter of installing some vents.

Mara eventually found some sort of stand-alone air conditioner that either didn't need to vent to the outside, or could vent through a metal expanding tube the way a dryer might. It would take a bit of work to adapt the vent to one of the windows, but it could be accomplished, and the vent could be removed when the weather turned colder in the fall. I had been giving Mara some money every month, but this was going to cost over $1,000 to purchase, and she didn't feel like she could handle that kind of expense all at once. Her parents refused to contribute to the cause at all. Despite being very short on cash, I agreed to give her half the money. I don't know how much was guilt, how much was caring, and how much was a feeling of responsibility, but it seemed like the right (and necessary) thing to do. I never heard much about it after that, so I guess it all worked out.

It wasn't that long before Mara found a surgeon who agreed that she was a candidate for weight-loss surgery. As we'd thought, the technology had progressed to where they could do this procedure faster, more easily, and safer than was possible years before. Even with Mara's tendency to not clot well, the minor incisions that he would need to do make shouldn't be a real problem. It wasn't stated openly, but it seemed to me that the other reason she was now a candidate when she hadn't been before was her physical size was that much larger, which meant not doing something about her weight was a bigger risk than any complications the surgery might involve. She had been gaining at an alarming rate, and was effectively immobile. Disability had even upgraded her old wheelchair to an electric model, as pushing her around was becoming more and more difficult. It was down to a choice now: do something or do nothing, and doing nothing wasn't a realistic option.

I was a little frightened for Mara about the procedure, but it sounded as if the medical risks were pretty low all things considered. I tried to be hopeful that she had finally hit rock bottom with her life, and that this would be the beginning of a true turning point for her. She might be able to see some of this weight melt away, and begin to build a much better, more fulfilling life for herself. Perhaps once things started getting better for a change, she'd ride that wave and start believing in a fulfilling future.

But there was one thing I had major reservations about, and when I tried to talk to Mara about it, she would quickly change the subject. We both knew that a large factor in her gaining weight had been to make herself as unattractive and undesirable as possible, so that she would not have to deal with all the sexual issues she had not yet overcome. Despite years of therapy, Mara had truly made zero progress. And that scared me. I knew if she didn't lose weight, she was destined to live a miserable – and shortened – life. But if those pounds started to melt away, there was no telling how her mental state might spiral out of control. In order to enjoy life, she was going to need to end her isolation in the basement and become mobile, but if she did that, she'd start to encounter men again. I doubted she had developed the skills to say no to their advances, or to limit the misery and self-loathing she felt after the fact.

One way or the other, big changes were coming for Mara. I could only hope those changes were more positive than negative.

Chapter 43 - Bits and Pieces

Because we now lived halfway across the country from each other – and because nobody else in Mara's family was on speaking terms with me – my interaction with her and my knowledge of her life was severely limited. There was never any opportunity for Mara to explain a more accurate version of our relationship, and really there was no purpose. Mara did tell me that when I sent her a CD or movie, or when she casually mentioned talking to me or emailing me, she received a lot of flak. "Why are you even still talking to him? He ruined your life." That sort of thing. I knew I wouldn't get any update on Mara's surgery for a few days at the very least. And the longer we lived apart, the more distant my interaction with Mara became. We had our own lives, and lived in different worlds.

After about a week Mara let me know that everything went okay. She'd asked her sister to pass along word to me but gave up as soon as her sister started to argue about it. Mara didn't have any real estimates for how fast weight would come off, but she said she was going to need a lot of adjusting when it came to eating. There were some things she needed to avoid for the time being, and she had to learn how to recognize when she was full. That had never been something she cared about before; she would eat until she felt emotionally satisfied. Now Mara would need to limit what she ate and would be unable to use food to suffocate unwanted emotions. The doctor had said that, in time, if she ate too much too often, her stomach would expand and she could one day start gaining weight again before she had lost all she needed to.

Once I moved in with my girlfriend, it became harder to find privacy where I could talk to Mara about whatever was going on. There was jealousy and resentment there, and not from Mara's side. Plus, work was becoming so stressful that I needed to go see my doctor about my eyes constantly twitching. He prescribed some antidepressants that helped a little, but they also made me feel like a zombie. I found myself unable to react to anything with natural emotion.

It was around this time that Mara revealed that her sexual issues were already returning. She had lost about 60 pounds, but her back was still a problem. When she had doctor's appointments she would go in her wheelchair and get transported by a New Jersey Transit handicapped system. One day I called her to see how things were going and she was strangely silent and evasive. After a bit she went ahead and told me that on her way to an appointment she had been the only passenger in the vehicle. The driver started complimenting her and within a few minutes Mara was giving him oral sex. As usual, she hated herself for doing it, but had done it again the next time he drove her.

She didn't want to get the driver in trouble since as far as he knew she was a willing participant, but she also didn't want to get stuck with him as a driver any longer, because he would continue to expect oral sex. If she gave it to him, she'd be miserable. And if she found the strength to tell him no, she didn't know what he would do. Even if he was just hurt or disappointed that would be a major blow to Mara, in her confused state of mind. As usual, she didn't think she could discuss this with anyone in her family; they'd either want the guy arrested somehow, or they'd look at her as if she was a whore. I was still the only support system she had for problems like this. In a way that still felt like a burden on my shoulders, except I was even more powerless to influence things than I had been before. All I could do now was listen and offer encouragement and understanding.

The periods of silence from Mara grew longer and longer, while things in my world continued to spiral out of control in their own way. The relationship with my girlfriend was strained, work was slowly driving me to a nervous breakdown, and I was drinking heavily. Mara was only dropping hints about the things she was doing and the problems she was encountering; I got the feeling she worried that I might alert her family to whatever was going on. Eventually things came to a head, and she let me know that she was going to be hospitalized in a mental ward for a few weeks to "get her medication under control." However, her parents were moving to Florida at the time, and Mara and her sister were barely speaking. So, Mara was going to Florida to be hospitalized there instead, and then she would hopefully be able to get a small place of her own when she got out. Living with her parents was an option, but to Mara that was out of the question. For her that was a fate far worse than death.

While Mara dealt with her nightmare, I built a new one of my own. As I described in my first memoir "It's Their House; I'm Just a Guest," just after 9/11 I financially blew up the day-trading company I was working for in a misguided effort to be a hero, and lost my job (and my health insurance). I couldn't get a job in that industry, and with only a little money in the bank I had to sell everything I could to pay the rent and the bills; I was putting my girlfriend through Cosmetology School and she wasn't contributing to household finances at that time. I was able to secure a job driving leased cars around the southwest with a company two of my brothers were working for. It wasn't steady income but it was better than nothing. My girlfriend and I moved into a tiny house that her Dad bought as an investment for $25,000, with no heat or air conditioning. It was cramped but cozy, and the rent was perfect (free).

At first, work had me away from home for a few days at a time. My girlfriend got her cosmetology license and started working, doing hair at a salon in a Wal-Mart while she built a client book and looked for something better. She didn't like me travelling as much as I did, but we needed the money. I knew Mara had made it to Florida but nothing else; I assumed she'd get in touch with me once she was able, whether it was in the hospital or when she was released.

Only a month or two after we moved into the tiny house, I was informed by my girlfriend that it was "wrong" for us to be living together, as in morally wrong. The whole situation pissed me off terribly. There was nothing "wrong" when I was the one paying all the bills, buying her presents, paying for her to go to New York City for a few weeks…but now that I wasn't making as much money, and **she** was finally earning something (and had no rent to pay), the rules had changed. I told her I needed a month or two to save up some money so I could move, and moved into the spare bedroom. When I was home, I rarely left my bedroom, except to go to the kitchen to heat up a can of soup for dinner.

My boss at the transportation company was having some personal issues of her own, and had to fire one of her local drivers. So, she offered to have me work in the office instead of travelling on the road. I'd still be able to pick up some odd trips on weekends, but most of my time would be spent dispatching drivers, helping on the road drivers get to or from their pickup or drop-off locations, or staging vehicles at the office to save the other drivers time. I was making almost as much in the office as I did on the road, and with some weekend trips I was doing much better with a lower stress level. In short order I was being assigned more and more responsibility. A block from the office I found some cheap but generally clean apartments and rented a one-bedroom unit for myself. I could actually walk to work if I wanted to, and walk to see the Texas Rangers play. It felt good to get out of the situation with my girlfriend and focus on work and being on my own (despite that relationship remaining in a constant on-again, off-again cycle for another year; I never seemed to find the nerve to cut the cord permanently).

Eventually I heard from Mara, and discovered she was going to get an apartment of her own in West Palm Beach. It seems she had met a guy in the mental hospital and the two of them had hit it off. Between their disability payments they felt they could swing the rent in the low-end neighborhood. She sounded really happy about this relationship, and was unconcerned about his health problems or that he was a recovering addict. Somehow it felt more like she just wanted to be with someone she cared about, and less that she was using the first available exit to avoid her parents. It was wonderful to hear Mara so enthused about someone, and I kept my reservations to myself. He had a medical issue which made sex between them a health risk, but even that didn't dampen her enthusiasm. She said that when they felt amorous, they just "got the toys out."

Since I no longer had health insurance, and Mara was in this new relationship, we agreed it was time to make the divorce official. This would allow Mara to get state prescription assistance, and it would also protect her from any lawsuits I might face from my former employer. She didn't have anything worth taking at that time, but I was more concerned that she might inherit some money from her grandmother and have to fight to keep it. The divorce would eliminate all of those issues.

I was surprised how simple the process was. First, I made an initial filing with the court. Next, I got some forms online and filled them out. I sent them to Mara and she had them signed and notarized and returned to me in the envelope I provided. The forms waived her need for proper "legal service" of the divorce documents (although she had a copy), waived her desire to appear in court, and agreed to the terms: whatever we each had in our possession would be our personal property.

I had to wait a few months for a court date (I think that was more because of a mandatory period between filing and having your hearing, in case people change their minds or whatever might come up), and then I went down to the small courthouse by myself. The judge asked me a question or two, making sure we had no children and owned no real estate, and then declared it accepted. Just like that, the marriage was legally ended.

I cried a bit in the car out in the parking lot, before heading back to work. It wasn't as if I didn't know this day was going to come. It was just the emotional acceptance that this entire portion of my life was officially over. In ways it felt like we never had a chance from Day 1. And that was something I recognized, but I had moved ahead step after step anyway. I wondered if we would have ever split up if Mara hadn't finally given up on life and tried to kill herself. The relationship had been nearly twenty years of ups and downs (with a lot more downs that ups), but there had been a lot of laughs and a lot of love in between the misery. And now it was done.

But we'd still be friends, even if distance and life was limiting our communication. After all, aside from family members, we'd known each other longer than almost anybody else we knew. We still had our private language, our shared experiences, our inside jokes; things that you can't replicate with anyone else. I knew that would keep us tied together in some fashion.

Chapter 44 - Slipping Away

Things in my life continued to slide downhill, or at best sat in a holding pattern waiting for the next move lower. I was potentially facing criminal charges for what I had done at work after 9/11, I was struggling to end the relationship I seemed stuck in, I was working as many hours as humanly possible to earn enough money to pay my bills and have a bit left over, and all my focus had to be on the present. I was too exhausted to think a lot about the past, and all my regrets and mistakes, and trying to think about the future just made me ill. So, I lived day to day and tried not to allow my mind to stray anywhere else.

Mara's life in Florida, which at least had a bit of hope attached to it at one point, didn't sound a lot better. She and her boyfriend got engaged, and she was very happy about it. But there wasn't much else she was happy about. There were at least one or two tearful, desperate conversations over the phone where she tried to convince me to let her move back "just as a roommate." There was no way I could agree. As I kept explaining to her, I could barely handle my own life at that stage, so the thought of being at least somewhat responsible for her as well was unfathomable. Not to mention, in a week or a month or a year I could be moving anywhere in the county, or going to Federal prison. It wasn't a workable idea, and it wasn't a plan I was willing to even consider. If nothing else, I had gotten better at saying "no" and not being an enabler.

Money always seemed to be the root source of Mara's unhappiness. One day she called to tell me that someone had stolen all their electronics and anything else of value from their apartment. By the next day she had gotten the courage to reveal that it wasn't as much a robbery as a collection for drug debts her fiancé had. He was using again, and had gotten some drugs on credit which he then failed to pay for.

Mara knew she could still talk to me about anything, and as she had nobody else who would listen without judging her, I remained her only outlet for those conversations. The two of them were struggling with money already, to the point that Mara would occasionally have sex with various men in their building or neighborhood to get the rent money. In theory they received enough from disability between the two of them to pay the rent, bills, and for food (with not much left), but drug use was where too much seemed to go. Mara explained it like this: her fiancé would beg and plead for Mara to let him spend $20 on drugs (I think crack was his drug of choice). Eventually Mara would want to "make him happy" and would agree, but on the condition that if he got to spend $20 on crack, she got to spend $20 on marijuana. She hadn't smoked pot since High School so this came as a surprise to me. I guess it was just another way she had found to make life easier to cope with.

Spending $40 on drugs was enough to make the household budget stretch thin for the month, but it never stopped there. Because once he had used up the crack, he would want more, and Mara would be too high to care. There would be three or four trips to the ATM to take out $20 or $40, and by the time they both came out of their haze $100 or more would be gone. And then the two of them would be at each other's throats for the rest of the month, worried about how they would be able to afford food until the next disability payments arrived.

It wasn't long before one of them – or both of them – discovered a convenient loophole they could use at the ATM. Technology has eliminated this trick by now, but back then if you wanted to make a deposit of checks or cash you put it in an envelope and fed it into the ATM. It wouldn't be processed until someone serviced the ATM in the next day or two. But as a courtesy, if you were a customer in good standing you would be allowed to make use of part of the deposit immediately, usually $100 plus a small credit in case the ATM wasn't one owned by your bank and you had been charged a fee.

If it was near the end of the month and they were out of money, occasionally Mara would make a deposit at the ATM and withdraw $100 in cash. Except the deposit envelope was empty, because she must have "forgotten" to put the check or cash into the envelope. The bank would charge her an overdraft fee, and her account would be in the red, but once her disability arrived it would cover all that and she'd Have some money again. It was a sort of interest-free loan with a $25 fee.

I didn't learn about this little trick until one day when Mara asked me if she could start having her disability sent directly into our joint account. The bank had finally grown tired of her sneaky game, and had closed her individual account for good. She had to explain the whole sordid mess to me, and I agreed she could change the deposit as long as she promised she wasn't going to do that again. I didn't want an account with my name on it having that sort of nonsense attached to it.

Mara and her fiancé got married at some point, in what I believe was a courthouse ceremony. From what she told me I got the impression her parents were very unhappy about the whole thing but had given up trying to influence what Mara did. His parents, on the other hand, were very fond of

Mara and hoped that the two of them could get their lives turned around with each other to lean on.

In some ways it sounded as if there were some positive signs. Mara was going to be allowed to work again without losing her benefits, although the details were never made clear to me; it's possible this was a side arrangement being made without the blessing of disability. I didn't get to hear that much about her life because of some level of jealousy her new husband had when it came to me. "I'm your husband now" he would declare, in an attempt to keep her from communicating with me. Mara wasn't going to be controlled in that way, but she kept it low key and to a minimum in order to make life more pleasant for everyone.

My life was anything but, as I soon knew I was going to prison. I was trying to arrange things and save money the best I could so my new girlfriend Heather would have some cash to help her out when I was gone. We managed to upgrade her car to a used Mitsubishi, and soon I had moved in with her so I'd have no lease to break when I left. Heather had pushed for us to get married before I was sentenced, but as I had explained to her, I thought that was a terrible idea. If she wanted to wait for me while I was incarcerated – which I told her I saw she was under no obligation to do – than she could do so. And if while I was gone she changed her mind about our relationship, being married would only make things more complicated.

While I waited to learn what my sentence would be, I went online one day to check my bank account and saw a negative balance in the joint account. A quick investigation revealed that Mara and her husband had decided to play their ATM game again. I was livid. Here I was, awaiting sentencing for Federal prison, and she had decided it was a good time to commit minor bank fraud in an account that had my name on it? I called Mara and read her the riot act. She was very emotional about it; I could tell her remorse was genuine, but I didn't know if she was more remorseful about how this could endanger me or about how nearly $200 had been spent on drugs over a weekend. "You just don't understand," she told me. "Once he gets his first hit of crack, he can't think about anything else. I don't even realize what's gone until it's too late to do anything about it."

I still didn't want to get too openly angry at Mara, if only because it made no difference. Or at least I didn't want to yell and shout at her; she could tell I was very displeased and keeping my emotions in check. I told her she needed to contact disability immediately and go back to having her payments sent to her by check in the mail. The next morning after I went to work, I found a few minutes to go next door to the bank. There I vaguely explained my cause for concern, covered the negative balance in the joint account, and had it closed for good. Since this had only happened once the bank wasn't overly concerned, especially as I made good on the debit and they still got their overdrawn fee as well. Losing this account eliminated any easy way for me to send Mara money other than through the mail, but as I was about to be a guest of the Federal prison system that didn't make a difference. I figured I could find a new way when I was eventually released, depending on what the future held for each of us.

I made it a point to give Mara what I understood was to be my mailing address in prison, and promised to write her with confirmation as soon as I could. I had no idea how the mail or phone systems worked in there, but I told her I would also try to call if possible. That was a bit of a complication with

Mara, as their phone service was often disconnected, so letters would be the best way to go.

One of the last things I did before leaving for my trip to prison was cancel my cell phone service. It was an amusing conversation. As you'd expect, I was transferred to someone in customer retention whose job it was to try and talk me out of cancelling. The fellow started his sales pitch and I had to interrupt him. "Your company has given me good service, and I plan to use you again. But I'm going to prison for a few years, and they don't let me take my cell phone with me."

There was a long silence before he responded. "They've never trained me on a retention strategy for that one. I'll go ahead and terminate your service. I guess all I can say is good luck?"

I made a mental note to use that excuse for the rest of my life if I wanted to cancel a service without argument. Too bad that in this case I was telling the truth.

Chapter 45 - Return to Sender

As soon as I got to prison, I made it a point to write a few people with confirmation of my proper mailing address. I was anxious to stay in touch with as many people as I could while I was a guest of the Federal government, both so I didn't feel so alone and so I could stay up-to-date on whatever was going on in their lives. Mara was on that list, and she was also one of the first people to write me back. It was a comfort to see her recognizable handwriting, although it had grown shakier over the years.

The letter was filled with updates about her life, and questions for me about prison. It struck me how much of our inside jokes Mara still used when talking to me. We had our own private language that nobody else could understand, built out of movie and TV quotes, experiences, and other memories. I could tell she missed having that kind of closeness with her new husband, but they hadn't known each other more than a year or so, and it takes a lot of time to build up such a strong connection. And besides, we'd been through hell together, and that was something we would always share.

I responded within a day or so, and Mara wrote me back a few weeks later. She and her husband had a kitten, which I knew much have been a wonderful change for her considering how much she missed the cats. Mostly she talked about the hassles of going to pick up her paycheck and then having to cash it at the grocery store. The two of them had opened a new bank account at a different bank, but direct deposit hadn't been properly set up yet so neither her disability nor her paychecks were going in there automatically. All things considered, Mara sounded pretty upbeat and alive.

Nov 6, 2003

Doug,
   Got your letter yesterday. I'm at work now. Pretending to be working. I got another lecture yesterday about how I should slow down. I'm working too fast. It's just too damn boring when I'm not working. I know, you have bigger problems. I was thinking about you all last night. How you must be feeling. Are you scared? Are you nervous? I mean, whats going on there in that brain of yours? I'm also wondering if you want to share with me how the first day went? If not, I understand. I'm just curious. I always

2

was. "What's this button for? It says push. I think I'll push it!"

So, right now I have no phone. We turned off the home phone. We were gonna pay the cell phones with my disability check, BUT they didn't direct deposit it. SO I had to deposit the check. Since we are a new account all checks are held at least 6 days. So it'll be 6 days before we can pay the cell phones. They were due on the 3rd. On 4th. they turned them off. SO we have no phone for a week.
(It's 8:15 AM, I haven't worked for 45 mins.)

OH! Get this! goes outside to get cig.s from a friend up the street (we were out). So he

3

comes back in the apartment with a KITTEN! What the fuck is he thinking. He goes outside and yada yada yada comes back with a kitten. He's orange and white and has orange eyes. said on his way to his friend's house the kitten came up to him and purred. He said to himself if he was still there on the way home, he'd get him. & guess he was still there. He looks as though he's 5 mos. or so. He has a LOT of energy. I've seen fleas on him, but he looks pretty clean. He wants to play with our other cat, Baby, but she doesn't like him just yet. We named him Charlie. (Okay, I got to work at 7:30 AM, it's 8:30 AM and I

4

haven't done anything yet) Should I take a break? Haha! They told me to take lots of breaks. Go to the bathroom, or just go up front and sit and talk with the receptionist for a while. They said they have a lot of filing to do, but I don't want to do filing. Filing sucks. I happen to agree.

It's raining really heavily here today. I guess its kinda nice for a change. It's always sunny and hot.

You know, it's kinda funny, I think ___ was kinda jealous when I got your letter. I was reading it, and he was hitting it outta my hands and saying "that's enough, I'm your husband now!"

I'll try and take some pictures

5

of both kitties and maybe even us to send to you.
(Okay, I broke down and did 8 mins. of work.) Maybe I'll eat something now. Some pretyels sound okay. I have 3 hours left to waste. Then I have to take the bus to Boca Raton (45 min drive) to pick up my pay check. Then ride back (45 min again) to the super market to cash the check and pick up a few things. Then home. I won't get home until like 6:30 tonight. Even though I leave here at 1:00 pm. So much waiting for the bus and stuff. Once they set up my direct deposit I won't have to go to Boca to pick up my check.
  Okay, I just spent 1/2 hour

cleaning my fingernails with a paper clip. I have about 2 hours left in here. What have I accomplished? Not much!

Just called here. I gave him the number yesterday. He didn't have much to say. More waste of time. If the temp agency is paying me $8/hr. I wonder what they are paying them. $12/hr? Boy, are they wasting their money.

You know that rubber thing you put on your finger to turn pages. Remember how Beef loved to play with it? I use it everyday. Well, when I work. I think of him playing with it every time I use it. I have film of him batting around a cosmetic applicator. He was so cute.

7

Even though he was big and Beefy, he was still playfull. Waterdrop. Love blinks. Triangle. Remember when he wanted to go in the garage or out in the hall for a walk? What a Beefer!

Alright, I just got done day-dreaming for ½ hour. Lets see, that leaves about 1½ hours left. Can I make it?

Alright, I did a little work. I have 40 mins. to go.

Okay, I'm signing off. Gonna do some work to pass the remaining amount of time and then get the hell outta here.

Love,
Mara

But in that second letter, Mara mentioned how her parents wanted them to go to their house for Thanksgiving, and how she didn't want to, but she felt it was necessary or else her parents would think she was going to kill herself or something. She then proceeded to spend a page explaining that she still thought about it all the time, and had told her husband she was ready whenever he was, as long as they could be certain it would succeed this time. How nonchalantly she talked about it was sort of a punch in the stomach for me, as I'd been hoping her outlook on life had improved since getting married and working part time. I suppose it was wishful thinking. Mara did promise that she'd write me a goodbye note first, so I knew I had some time to work on her mood through letters and – perhaps – phone calls.

①

11-19-03

Doug,
 Got your letter. I was about to write again. I didn't know if the letter I wrote got through. Anyway, I'm at work. Things are a little different. I'm done with that one job that they had me do. Now there's another job of putting stacks of papers in numerical order. How fun! But there's tons of papers, so at least I know I'll have a job for a while. And somebody else already came up to me and said when I'm done with these papers, they have stuff for me to do. Yippee!

I forgot to bring your letter with me to work, so I could write from it. But I remember it pretty much. So do they have fences or walls? Or is it just "the honor system"? How long during the day do you stay in your cube?

I've worked all day today non-stop. I got here at 7:45AM and it's now 12:00PM. It's time to do some day-dreaming. We've got colored paper-clips. That's something to stare at.

Hey that reminds me. I saw a really cool rainbow the other day. Not just a little one or part of one. A full rainbow, a full arch.

(3)

from one end to the other. Not faded either. But as you get closer to it, it disappeared. No gold there! Damn, we shoulda won the lottery that time. We were just starting out too. Things would have been much different. Orange peel.

The papers that I'm putting in numerical order are P.A.F.'s (Patient Authorization Forms). Patients have to sign these when the rescue teams go out and take them to the hospitals etc. But sometimes the patient won't or can't sign it. So they have to give a reason. My favorite reason they give is "fecal matter on hands" then there's "Mentally altered" or "in handcuffs" or "patient is contaminatid" "Patient refused" "Patient is combatative"

Oh boy! I've got to tell you! I have a Bibby on my hands! no! It's worse than Bibby! Everytime I walk into the Kitchen Charlie (the kitten) runs in and is underfoot. Meowing and meowing and jumping on the counter and running into the white box when it opens. Everytime we go in there there he is! And when we arent there, he goes in there and cries.
says I did it. He says I shouldn't be giving him any human food. Now he knows where it comes from.

⑤

I can't help it. I'm weak. He's so cute, and he cries. ☹

Oh, about the PAF'S; it says to be specific when saying why the patient couldn't sign. So my favorite "specific" one is "pt. couldn't sign due to medical condition". Well, duh!

It's 1:00PM. I think I'll stay until 1:30. I can't take anymore than that.

You know my parents moved here to Florida, right? Well, if you didn't, now you know. They want us to go to their house for Thanksgiving. To tell you the truth

I don't feel much like celebrating anymore. But then they'll get all concerned that I'll kill myself or something. Which to tell you the truth has been on my mind. I'm just tired of living. He and ___ never seem to get out of debt no matter what we do. I told ___ to let me know when he wants to kill himself cuz then we could do it together. The only thing that scares me about doing it, is failing to do it. If somehow somebody finds me or whatever, I lose my job and go to the hospital and go back to therapy. Oh ypee. Nope, if I was to

(7)

do it, I'd have to make damn sure I'd succeed this time. But I'm not doing it yet. I'd write you a goodbye note. Don't worry. I'm too scared of failing right now, to do it.

It's 1:15! Almost time to go home. Yea. a sinkful of dishes and a disheveled bed awaits my attention. Then make something for lunch. Then take a shower.

I'm hoping my paycheck will be direct deposited tomorrow. If not. If I have to travel all the way to Boca Raton on Friday to pick it up. That's almost an hour there, then I have to wait an hour (the bus ride makes you spend an hour at your destination) then an hour back, just to get my fucking check. I've done it the last 3 or 4 weeks waiting for the direct deposit to come through. I hope it does tomorrow.

11/20/03

I had to go quickly yesterday. 1:30 came quick. My ride was right on time. I keep checking the bank to see if my paycheck was deposited, but it hasn't yet. It's not yet 8 AM. So I'm hoping it will be later. Please please! I don't wanna go, I don't wanna go.

Orange peel. I just got off the phone with them. The direct deposit isn't set up yet. What the fuck is taking them so long? So now I have to go from work to Headway (to get the check) then to Winn Dixie (grocery store) to cash the check 🙂 and get stuff and then go home. I'll leave work around 1 PM and not get home until around 7:30 or 8 PM. What a hassle.

"Okay, I'm gonna 'wrap it up.'"
"I doubt you'll find anything in there, but I appreciate the attempt!"

Mara

P.S. "We can laugh about it now. We're alright now."

But I didn't have time. I got a card from Mara about two days later, which included a page of a letter as well; she and her husband had decided to go to Thanksgiving at her parents after all, just to keep the peace. She said she'd write me all about how it went when they got back home.

But I never heard from Mara again. I must have received the card around December 1st, the anniversary of when we started dating, and the anniversary of her suicide attempt. After that, silence.

A few weeks later I asked Heather to start checking the internet for any sort of news report or obituary notice in Florida, in case the worst had happened. I wasn't **certain** there would be terrible news. Mara had her own life and it was getting busier. But in my gut, I felt something was wrong. Maybe she'd been hospitalized again, or it could have been worse.

Heather sent out holiday cards that year, including mailing one to Mara. Within a week or two, Heather found Mara's card returned unopened in her mail box, with the word "Deceased" written across the address. We spoke on the phone a day or two later, and while I felt guilty and terrible, it also felt like a bad dream because it was happening in the outside world, while I was stuck in prison. I couldn't investigate or call anybody, so in a way that forced me to be detached from what must have happened and made it a little easier to deal with.

Just after New Year's Heather finally found an obituary notice online, which confirmed what we already knew. Mara and her husband had died on December 11th "from complications of life." It was clear from the detail in the notice that her husband's family had done the obituary, as Mara was listed as simply survived by a "large loving family." Mara had only made it about two weeks after her last letter to me before she gave up. Her death was almost exactly five years from her previous suicide attempt. But this time, she had succeeded.

I provided Heather with some information on Mara's sister and her parents. Eventually she managed to find a phone number for Mara's sister, and the two of them spoke on the phone. Mara's sister said she only learned I was in prison when she found a letter of mine in the apartment, and saw where it had been sent from. She asked Heather to look around our place in case there were photos or other things that we might be willing to send her, as she had very little of Mara's personal stuff to remember her by. She also asked about getting copies of the letters Mara had written me.

She promised to call Heather back in a few weeks to see what Heather had located, and to give her a good shipping address. But Heather never heard from her again. No phone calls and no letters. That was the last contact either of us had with anyone in Mara's family.

It took me many years to get over the guilt I carried about our relationship, and to stop thinking of all the things I should have done differently or said or not said. The mess we found ourselves in was a lot bigger than either of us could handle, and unfortunately, we were living in a time when there weren't a lot of resources available to help us get through them.

But for all of that, and for all the times I went to sleep not caring if I woke up the next morning, we still had a lot of laughs over the years. And we shared a lot of love, of each other and of our cats. Sometimes, it was enough, or more than enough. And I truly did the best I could with what I knew at the time. I guess that may be the biggest regret: that I didn't know then all the things I know now. But how much can a fifteen-year-old kid know? It's difficult to remember that I was only fifteen when things had all started. It feels like three lifetimes ago, and if feels like a month ago at the same time.

I still think of Mara nearly every day. Sometimes it makes me sad and depressed, and sometimes I laugh to myself, or even out loud. But there's not really any way I can share what I remember with anyone. So, I just keep it to myself, or I talk to Mara about it. I doubt she can hear me, but maybe she can?

I do know one thing. If there is such a thing as reincarnation, Mara came back as a cat, or not at all. Even if that was against the rules, she would have made a big enough stink that she probably got her way.

Epilogue

It has been over fifteen years since Mara died. It took me a long time to even consider writing this memoir, and then years to get started. It wasn't magically cathartic, but it hasn't been a terrible experience either. There were only a few things I've been reminded of that hadn't stayed in my memory anyway.

To the best of my knowledge, Mara's Dad passed away a few years ago, while her brother and mother are still with us. I have no idea what happened to her sister, and I can't find any hints about her fate online, good or bad.

I've realized in the last year that I still, in my own way, mourn the failure of our marriage and the death of the dreams we had. Even though by the time we were legally married I knew a happy ending wasn't the likely path, that didn't mean I had given up the hope of somehow finding our way there. All it takes is a good day or two and you can begin to see a possibility of overcoming the odds. So that's what you fight for and work towards. Maybe it was as unlikely as Don Quixote's "Impossible Dream" in Man of La Mancha, but as he sings about, perhaps the world is a better place just for the trying, win or lose.

And, of course, I still miss Mara. Her life held such unfulfilled promise, it hurts to know how much was lost. Even today I say or do or think of things and realize that if she were here, she'd appreciate them. I think she'd appreciate this book too. All she ever really wanted was to be understood.

Printed in Poland
by Amazon Fulfillment
Poland Sp. z o.o., Wrocław